Jaguar Books on Lati

D0392878

Series Editors

WILLIAM H. BEEZLEY, Neville G. Penrose Chair of Latin
American Studies, Texas Christian University
COLIN M. MACLACHLAN, Professor and Chair, Department
of History, Tulane University

Volumes Published

John E. Kicza, ed., *The Indian in Latin American History: Resistance, Resilience, and Acculturation* (1993). Cloth ISBN 0-8420-2421-2
Paper ISBN 0-8420-2425-5

Susan E. Place, ed., *Tropical Rainforests: Latin American Nature and Society in Transition* (1993). Cloth ISBN 0-8420-2423-9 Paper ISBN 0-8420-2427-1

Paul W. Drake, ed., *Money Doctors, Foreign Debts, and Economic Reforms in Latin America from the 1890s to the Present* (1994).
Cloth ISBN 0-8420-2434-4 Paper ISBN 0-8420-2435-2

John A. Britton, ed., *Molding the Hearts and Minds: Education, Communications, and Social Change in Latin America* (1994).
Cloth ISBN 0-8420-2489-1 Paper ISBN 0-8420-2490-5

Darién J. Davis, ed., *Slavery and Beyond: The African Impact on Latin America and the Caribbean* (1994). Cloth ISBN 0-8420-2484-0
Paper ISBN 0-8420-2485-9

David J. Weber and Jane M. Rausch, eds., *Where Cultures Meet: Frontiers in Latin American History* (1994). Cloth ISBN 0-8420-2477-8
Paper ISBN 0-8420-2478-6

Gertrude M. Yeager, ed., *Confronting Change, Challenging Tradition: Women in Latin American History* (1994). Cloth ISBN 0-8420-2479-4
Paper ISBN 0-8420-2480-8

Linda Alexander Rodríguez, ed., *Rank and Privilege: The Military and Society in Latin America* (1994). Cloth ISBN 0-8420-2432-8
Paper ISBN 0-8420-2433-6

Where
Cultures
Meet

Where Cultures Meet

Frontiers in Latin American History

David J. Weber and Jane M. Rausch
Editors

Jaguar Books on Latin America
Number 6

A Scholarly Resources Inc. Imprint
Wilmington, Delaware

Scholarly Resources Inc.
104 Greenhill Avenue
Wilmington, DE 19805-1897

The epigraphs are from Harold Molineu, *U.S. Policy toward Latin America* (Boulder, CO: Westview, 1986), 20, and Sergio Villalobos R., "Tres siglos y medio de vida fronteriza Chilena," in *Estudios (nuevos y viejos) sobre la frontera*, ed. Francisco de Solano and Salvador Bernabeu (Madrid: Consejo Superior de Investigaciones Científicas, 1991), 294.

Library of Congress Cataloging-in-Publication Data

Where cultures meet : frontiers in Latin American history / David J.
  Weber and Jane M. Rausch, editors.
     p.   cm. — (Jaguar books on Latin America ; no. 6)
    Includes bibliographical references (p.   ).
    ISBN 0-8420-2477-8 (cloth). — ISBN 0-8420-2478-6 (pbk.)
    1. Latin America—Civilization—Philosophy. 2. Frontier thesis.
3. Pluralism (Social sciences)—Latin America. 4. Acculturation—Latin
America. I. Weber, David J. II. Rausch, Jane M., 1940–   . III. Series.
F1408.3.W47   1994
980'.001—dc20   94-1788
                                    CIP

Acknowledgments

With the exceptions of the essays by Walter Nugent and David Sweet, all articles in this anthology have been published previously. In general, we have reproduced those articles as they originally appeared, correcting only typographical errors in the original works. We have, however, condensed some pieces, noting our deletions with elipses. On occasions where we have clarified language by making additions to the text, we have done so in square brackets.

We are grateful to the authors and publishers who permitted us to reprint these important essays and to the editors of the Jaguar Series, William Beezley and Colin MacLachlan, who invited us to prepare this volume. Special thanks to William B. Taylor, who read an earlier version of the introduction, and to our students at the University of Massachusetts and at Southern Methodist University, who have forced us to sharpen our thinking about the nature of frontiers in Latin America.

Contents

Our continents are bound together by a common history—the endless exploration of new frontiers.

John F. Kennedy, 1961

The history of Latin America has been, in great measure, a frontier history, and it continues to be in many places.

Sergio Villalobos R., 1991

Introduction

David J. Weber
Jane M. Rausch

For the last century the idea that the frontier experience shaped the character of North Americans and their institutions has constituted the most influential explanation of the distinctive character of the United States and its citizens. Many parts of Latin America also experienced processes of conquest and settlement by Europeans that seem, at least on the surface, analogous to Anglo-Americans' frontier experiences. Nonetheless, with the exceptions of Brazilians and Argentines, Latin American intellectuals have seldom considered their own frontiers central to the formation of national identities or of national institutions.[1]

The difference between North American and Latin American perceptions of the importance of their respective frontiers can be explained in many ways. The question has engaged scholars from several disciplines, and the answer has varied from country to country and from time to time within Latin America. Indeed, in parts of Argentina and Brazil the similarities to the North American experience seem as remarkable as the differences.

As used popularly the word *frontier* holds different meanings for Latin Americans and Anglo Americans. In this anthology we are not using the frontier in the restricted sense of a border or boundary, as it is commonly used in Latin America (and in Europe). Nor do we define a frontier as a simple line between settled and "unsettled" areas or the narrow edge of "civilization" where it advances on "savagery" or wilderness, as it has been imagined in the United States.[2] Geographic areas may have a low man-land ratio, but they are rarely "unsettled," and areas that urbanites see as "wilderness" have nearly always contained their own distinctive indigenous civilizations. Moreover, native societies usually have regarded themselves as at the center rather than on the frontier. As used by the invading culture, the word *frontier* has had a decidedly ideological quality.

We would prefer to regard frontiers more broadly and neutrally, defining them as geographic zones of interaction between two or more distinctive cultures. Those frontier zones might be conflict-ridden places where invading Europeans move onto Indian lands of low population density—an image widely held in Anglo-American culture. But frontiers might also be densely populated urban places where different cultures compete peacefully—as we explain later in this introduction.

Frontiers, in short, are places where cultures contend with one another and with their physical environment to produce a dynamic that is unique to time and place. As such, frontiers represent both place and process, linked inextricably. Various writers represented in this anthology do not, of course, use the word the same way. Any term elastic enough to do interpretive tasks as disparate as explaining a small region, a country, or the entire Western Hemisphere defies simple definition—and unavoidably runs the risk of losing meaning.[3]

Historically, from pre-Columbian times to the present, all of Latin America has gone through a frontier stage or stages of kaleidoscopic variety, each shaped by a particular combination of physical and human environments. Some regions within Latin America, for example, have experienced several types of frontier economies: tributary frontiers, cattle frontiers, mining frontiers, agricultural frontiers, and commercial frontiers—sometimes in succession and sometimes simultaneously. Distinctive types have inhabited those frontiers, including Indians, gauchos, *llaneros* (plainsmen of Colombia and Venezuela), miners, farmers, ranchers, rubber tappers, *bandeirantes* (Brazilian expeditionaries who sought slaves and gold), *cimarrones* (runaway African-American slaves), and merchants. These economic activities have occurred on geopolitical frontiers, where different modes of organizing societies have competed with one another. On a more abstract level, one might also think of spiritual frontiers, where different religious systems have contended with one another.

Initially, Europeans understood all of Latin America as a frontier occupied by Indians, but the nature and population density of particular indigenous societies usually shaped the way in which non-Indians exploited that new frontier. For example, those zones where Indian nomads used warfare or guerrilla tactics to maintain their autonomy elicited different responses from non-Indians than did places where Indian agriculturalists could be incorporated into a sophisticated labor force by non-Indian intruders. As cultures fused into one in the latter zones, they ceased to be frontiers. Where Indians continued to resist incorporation and assimilation, they remained in areas usually regarded as frontiers.

Distinctive physical environments also supported different types of frontiers, ranging from the pampas of Argentina and Brazil to the forests of Chile, and from the tropical lands of the Amazon to the deserts of northern Mexico. Even today, much of tropical Latin America might still be considered a frontier—perhaps even a "permanent frontier," as geographer Isaiah Bowman has suggested. The eastern fringes of Bolivia, Colombia, Ecuador, and Peru, in Bowman's view, represent "permanent" frontiers, where inhospitable jungles have checked Spanish advances and yielded only slightly to improved health conditions and technology in modern times. Bowman defined the twentieth-century inhabitants of those tropical lands as "pioneers," although they might live on farms or in villages occupied by their families for generations.[4] But for scholars, such as Valerie Fifer, who see frontiers as processes that occur in rural places, "there are no permanent frontiers of settlement." Settlement either succeeds or fails. If modern-day frontiers of settlement succeed, she argues, then they cease to exist as frontiers. "The community matures politically by making the transition into some larger non-frontier society and becoming absorbed into the latter's more stable political and economic networks."[5]

It is the power of frontiers to transform cultures as well as themselves that gives them special interest. "Human populations," as anthropologist Eric Wolf has argued, "construct their cultures in interaction with one another, and not in isolation."[6] In some places the actions of frontier peoples have transformed political and economic institutions well beyond the frontier itself, contributing to national cultures and shaping a people's understanding of their identity. In turn, larger historical processes have shaped the lives of frontier peoples, often as a result of decisions made by policymakers in distant centers of political, economic, or cultural power. Transformations associated with frontiers, then, occur on the local and global levels and can be fully understood only when we "capture the interplay of local and global interests."[7]

A subject so large and complex cannot be contained easily between the covers of a single volume.[8] We have chosen the selections in this book to be suggestive rather than exhaustive, to raise questions rather than answer them. Each essay illuminates the transformative or reciprocal forces that operate on frontiers rather than simply recounting events that happened to occur in frontier settings.

The Significance of the Frontier

The idea that the frontier played a significant role in shaping the United States and its peoples gained scholarly currency largely as a result of its eloquent articulation one hundred years ago by Frederick Jackson Turner, a professor of history at the University of Wisconsin. Speaking in Chicago in 1893 as part of a general celebration of the four-hundredth anniversary of Columbus's landfall, Turner asserted that the availability of "free land" on the North American frontier, by which he meant land free of rents and not of people, provided opportunity for upward social mobility not enjoyed by Europeans. Second, the struggle for survival on the frontier, which required that newcomers simplify their lives—what he termed "a return to primitive conditions"—gave westering peoples a chance to rebuild their societies afresh.[9] Those twin social processes of settling and surviving on free frontier lands shaped American character and institutions, Turner argued, quickening the assimilation of immigrants of different ethnic groups, "consolidating" and "nationalizing" young America, and promoting social and political democracy. Moreover, Turner wrote, "to the frontier the American intellect owes its striking characteristics": inventiveness, practicality, inquisitiveness, restlessness, optimism, and individualism.[10]

For much of this century scholars have regarded the Turner thesis as the single most useful concept for understanding the distinctive features of North American civilization. The thesis has enjoyed widespread public acceptance, informed the making of American foreign policy, influenced disciplines other than history, and continues to be debated and tested.[11] Thus Turner's influential address, "The Significance of the Frontier in American History" (Selection 1), remains the starting point for any inquiry into frontier phenomena.

Although the study of the frontier was "invented" by a North American historian as an explanation for American exceptionalism and has been a preoccupation principally but not exclusively of North American scholars, Turner's argument that the frontier shaped national character would seem to apply to other places in the hemisphere where Europeans settled and survived on Native American lands. Another of America's foremost historians, Herbert Eugene Bolton of the University of California at Berkeley, suggested the existence of parallel frontier processes as part of his broader argument that the Americas had a common history. The colonial systems and experiences of England, Portugal, and Spain were more similar than different, Bolton asserted in a speech in December 1932, just before Franklin Roosevelt launched the Good Neighbor policy: "Everywhere, contact with frontier environment and native peoples tended to modify the Europeans and their institutions. This was quite as true in the Latin as in the Saxon colonies."[12]

As early as 1917, Bolton had written of the need to study "the Spanish-American frontier" with "Turner's insight," and in later years

Bolton continued to urge his students to apply Turner's thesis to the whole of the Americas as well as to its parts.[13] Among Bolton's many doctoral students only Arthur S. Aiton accepted the challenge of sketching out an overview. In a brief but suggestive essay published in 1940, Aiton outlined the process of settling frontiers in Latin America and offered several interesting generalizations (Selection 2). He stressed differences as well as similarities between the Latin and Anglo worlds, but his essay has a triumphalist tone in the Turnerian tradition. The frontiers of Latin America, Aiton concluded, engendered many virtues in its peoples: "individualism, self-reliance, democracy, initiative, and a willingness to experiment."[14]

Contemporary Latin American intellectuals might agree with Bolton and Aiton that frontier experiences modified Europeans and their institutions. A case in point is Argentine historian Hebe Clementi, who regards frontiers as the "interpretive key" to understanding Latin America.[15] But few Latin American intellectuals would suppose that their frontiers modified Iberians in Turnerian ways, either real or imagined.[16]

In contrast to Turner's positive formulation, Latin American frontiers have engendered powerful negative myths, both in scholarly literature and in popular culture. As one specialist recently observed, "The frontier in Latin America is conceived of as a brutal place where the weak are devoured by the strong, and where justice must be imposed (and re-imposed) through forceful action by representatives of legal and traditional authority from far-off centers of power."[17] Nowhere are negative associations clearer than in novels depicting frontier life. In classics such as those by Brazil's Euclides da Cunha, *Os sertões* (1902); Venezuela's Rómulo Gallegos, *Doña Bárbara* (1929); Colombia's José Eustacio Rivera, *La vorágine* (1924); and Jorge Amado's *Terras do sem fim* (1943), most encounters between man and wilderness end in failure rather than in triumph. Latin American frontier myths tend to be tragic, and the environment is most often perceived as overwhelming and dangerous rather than gardenlike and brimming with promise. The menacing image presented in the Peruvian feature film *The Green Wall* (1970), written and directed by Armando Robles Godoy, stands in stark contrast to Anglo-Americans' view of wilderness after Turner "recast its role from that of an enemy which civilization had to conquer to a beneficent influence on men and institutions."[18]

Well before Turner articulated his famous thesis, North Americans and Latin Americans had already developed opposing images of their frontiers. Turner, as Theodore Roosevelt once noted, had put "into shape a good deal of thought that has been floating around rather loosely."[19] That partly explains the alacrity with which Anglo Americans adopted his thesis. Similar ideas were rare in nineteenth-century Latin America. Those Anglo Americans who journeyed to Argentina, Brazil, and Chile in the late nineteenth century expecting to discover a "new West" in the temperate zones of South America were quickly disabused.[20] Instead of finding opportunity on undeveloped lands, most North American entrepreneurs only confirmed their prejudices toward Hispanic peoples. Latin Americans, said one Anglo-American visitor to the Brazilian Amazon in the 1840s, were "an imbecile and indolent people" who lacked "energy and enterprise equal to subject the forest and develop and bring forth the vast resources that lay hidden there."[21] Instead of free land "that would prolong [their] spiritual and economic regeneration," North Americans found in Latin America a people who seemed irredeemable, whether on frontiers or in cities.[22]

Few influential Latin Americans regarded their frontiers as places of regeneration that went through a temporary "return to primitive conditions" as they gave birth to individual liberty. Instead, most nineteenth-century Latin American urbanites and intellectuals saw their frontiers as violent, brutal places that engendered despotism rather than democracy. Rather than celebrate the decline of European influences and the birth of a vital, new national type on their frontiers, Latin American intellectuals generally looked to Europe as the source of virtue, fashion, and progress.[23]

The classic nineteenth-century articulation of that viewpoint had come from the pen of the Argentine intellectual, statesman, and president (1868–1874), Domingo Faustino Sarmiento, whose book *Civilización y barbarie: vida de Juan Facundo de Quiroga*, first published in 1845, contrasted Europeanized urban "civilization," as represented by the Argentine capital city of Buenos Aires, and the "barbaric" gauchos, or cowboys, who hunted cattle on the pampas of Argentina's pastoral provinces (Selection 3). In his disdain for frontier peoples, Sarmiento typified nineteenth-century Latin American intellectuals, most of whom came from the urban elite and equated cities with progress and frontiers with ignorance and primitivism. The viewpoints of *pensadores*, or thinkers, such as João Capistrano de Abreu, who celebrated the exploration and settlement of the Brazilian interior in his *Os caminhos antigos* (1889), remained the exception.[24]

Even in the twentieth century, after Turner's thesis became fashionable for historians in the United States, native-born Latin American historians responded to it tepidly, if at all. Turner's essay, so influential in the historiography of the United States, apparently remained untranslated and unpublished in Spanish until it appeared in Madrid in 1960 and in Argentina in 1968.[25] Reflecting a widespread view, one of Mexico's foremost historians, Edmundo O'Gorman, wrote in 1961: "Latin America was never a frontier land in the sense of dynamic transformation that has been given to that term by American historians ever since Frederick Jackson Turner; it was rather the passive object of transplantation and grafting."[26] Guillermo Céspedes, the distinguished Spanish historian of Latin America, criticized Turner for his "excessive attention to the geographic and relative neglect of the cultural." Human beings respond differently to frontiers, Céspedes noted, and "people penetrate the frontier only when they are culturally and technically prepared."[27]

Differences seemed to outweigh the similarities between the North American frontier that Turner described and the frontiers that Latin American historians knew. The differences began at the fundamental level of geography. As the Peruvian *pensador* Victor Andrés Belaúnde explained in an essay published in English in 1923 (Selection 4), "free land," the essential ingredient on the American frontier according to Turner, was less important than the potential utility of the land. Only accessible land, capable of productivity, could be useful, Belaúnde argued. Since much of Latin America was tropical rain forest, marginal sierra, or highlands (*altiplano*), he believed that it possessed little of what he called "human value." Belaúnde concluded that the expanding frontier in the Turnerian sense appeared only rarely in Latin America because so much of its lands could not be exploited effectively—a judgment echoed by some historians, who have since probed Latin American frontiers more deeply.[28]

Turner, who claimed that the American frontier was unique, might not have disagreed. Although he never reduced complex explanations to simple environmental determinism, he would hardly have expected the Amazon jungle or the arid frontiers of northern Mexico to make an equally strong impact on society as did the more hospitable woodlands of the midwestern United States—the frontier he knew best.

Mexican historian Silvio Zavala, who along with Belaúnde stands among the few native-born Latin American historians to test Turner's thesis for Latin America, also found few similarities between the frontiers of the United States and Latin America. In a more descriptive and wide-ranging essay than Belaúnde's, published in 1965, Zavala surveyed the succession of Hispanic frontiers, from Iberia to America, and noted their characteristics (Selection 5). Only in a few sparsely populated regions—northern Mexico, southern Chile, and the pampas of Argentina, where Hispanics faced potentially hostile Indians long after the colonial era ended—did Zavala imagine that one might find traces of the individualism, social equality, and enterprise of a Turnerian frontier.

As Zavala's essay suggests, it was not simply the physical environment that determined the impact of frontiers on a people, but the values that people brought to the physical environment.[29] Similarly, it was the nature not only of Latin American indigenous cultures but of Spaniards' interest in incorporating those cultures into their own society that further explains why Latin American frontiers differed from those in North America. On Latin American frontiers, as Chilean historian Sergio Villalobos wrote in 1991,

> the existence of native peoples has played a role of primary importance depending on their numbers and, in some cases, on the high level of their culture, which permitted them to survive and participate—even though it be through coercion. The greatest consequences of that reality was *mestizaje* [racial mixture] and transculturation, which gave distinctive characteristics to the Latin American peoples.[30]

In the useful formulation of geographer Marvin W. Mikesell, the Latin Americans' "frontier of inclusion" contrasted sharply with Anglo Americans' "frontier of exclusion."[31] These two types of frontier are exemplified by the culture of the cowboy—the most celebrated frontier type. In Argentina and Venezuela, Hispanic cowboys—gauchos and *llaneros*— borrowed language from Native Americans and incorporated indigenous terms into their vocabularies; gauchos adopted their characteristic weapon, the *bolas*, and favorite beverage, *mate*, from native cultures. Yet with the exception of Oklahoma, historian Richard Slatta finds that "no indigenous element is detectable in Anglo-American cowboy life."[32]

Latin America as a Frontier of Europe

If Turner's thesis failed to excite intellectuals in Latin America or historians of Latin America, it continued to hold interest for a few North American scholars who placed it in a global context.[33] None of these was more influential than Walter Prescott Webb, a professor of history at the University of Texas. Rather than examine frontier zones within Latin America, Webb saw all of Latin America as part of an immense frontier of a western European metropolis. Webb's articulation of this argument in *The Great Frontier*, published in 1951, represented an extension of Turner's suggestion that the American frontier "affected profoundly . . . even the Old World."[34] But whereas Turner focused on the way in which frontiers fostered democracy, individualism, and dynamism in the United States, Webb widened the lens to look at how the "great frontier"—which included the entire Western Hemisphere—made Europe more democratic, capitalistic, and dynamic (Selection 6). Like Turner, but on a larger scale, Webb was decidedly Eurocentric. Places that he regarded as frontiers of Europe, such as Cuzco and Tenochtitlan, would have represented a metropolis from the vantage point of an Inca or an Aztec.[35]

In probing the relationships between American frontiers and the European metropolis, Webb enlarged our understanding and anticipated a school of thought that would see all of Latin America as a "periphery," if not a frontier, of Europe.[36] Where Webb emphasized the positive transformations brought about by the Great Frontier, the "dependency" theorists and "world systems" analysts who followed him tended to look at ways in which the metropolis retarded development in the periphery, keeping Latin America in a state of economic dependency. If frontier historians seemed overly deterministic in attributing too much to the influence of the frontier, dependency and world systems theorists have been criticized for granting capitalism too much explanatory power and ignoring other historical, cultural, and environmental forces.[37]

Webb's provocative thesis has won many admirers, among them William McNeill of the University of Chicago, who has also sought out larger historical patterns in many distinguished books. McNeill applauded Webb's idea of the Great Frontier as "an appropriate framework for reappraising the history of this country by recognizing that our past was part of a global process of civilizational expansion."[38] Like many other scholars, McNeill views frontiers as especially dynamic places, for they often bring peoples of different levels of skill together and force one or both parties to make adjustments. The resulting transformations, he concludes, "seem to me to be the principal drive wheel of historic change."[39]

For McNeill, however, the "process of civilizational expansion" had a darker side than Webb or Turner acknowledged. "Progress and liberty, so dear to our forebears, played a part in the process," McNeill wrote in 1983, "but so did their opposites—slavery and the destruction of all those non-European cultures and societies that got in the way."[40] As Europeans traveled to other continents, they brought deadly diseases that decimated natives and created "free land" but left those areas with a critical shortage of labor. In much of North and South America, however, McNeill reminds us, Europeans met labor shortages by enslaving or indenturing others (Selection 7).[41] McNeill's view contrasts with Turner's idealized frontier, where Europeans responded to scarcity of labor by working with their hands and creating more egalitarian societies. And McNeill's view differs from Webb's, who emphasized how the Great Frontier offered an opportunity for some Europeans to flee to freedom, thus weakening institutions of social control in Europe and expanding the scope of individual freedom.[42]

If Webb failed to take into account the ways in which the Great Frontier contributed to hierarchy as well as freedom, he also failed to build his case from examples drawn from Latin America. Instead, as noted by one of his Brazilian critics, historian José Honório Rodrigues, Webb depended excessively on examples from the United States. "Webb's thesis," Rodrigues wrote in 1963, "sometimes appears to be a Texan conception of modern world history because of his insistence on universalizing facts that are peculiar to or characteristic of the North American frontier."[43] There was not one single "Great Frontier," Rodrigues argued, nor was western Europe a single "metropolis." Just as England differed from Spain and Spain from Portugal, so did frontiers differ:

> The frontier has not always produced the same results. None of the characteristics of love of work, desire for efficiency, belief in *laissez faire*, in profit, in competition, in the machines, and in corporations was characteristic of Brazil, or, I think, of Spanish America; they did not belong to the creed of the Metropolis and the frontier did not suggest or impose them.[44]

Webb may have anticipated such criticism, for he pointed to the need for more studies of the frontier in Latin America, observing that "the Latin-American frontier was, in comparison with the Anglo-Saxon, very confused and quite different in character from that of the United States."[45]

In suggesting that Webb had failed to account adequately for the impact that the values of the "metropolis" had on its frontiers, Rodrigues echoed charges that historians had also leveled at Frederick Jackson Turner. Whereas Turner emphasized the impact of the frontier on man, his critics and even his staunchest defender, Ray Allen Billington, noted that the culture and institutions that peoples brought from the metropolis to the frontier were more significant in shaping their new societies than the frontier setting itself. "Let no one . . . be misled," Billington urged, "into believing that the frontier could affect major changes in either the personalities or the behavioral patterns of frontiersmen. As in human behavior today, the bulk of the customs and beliefs of the pioneers were transmitted, and were only slightly modified by the changing culture in which they lived."[46]

Granted that assumption, then, it makes little sense to presume that the frontier experience would affect Latin American settlers in the same way that it affected Anglo Americans, even if physical circumstances were identical. As Billington put it, "individuals of different backgrounds will respond in different ways to identical physical environments."[47] For example, Domingo Sarmiento did not look to the frontier to transform Argentina. Instead, he hoped that nineteenth-century European civilization would transform the Argentine frontier—eradicating the characteristics of the frontier implanted by Spain, with its "evil traditions" and "ideas and concerns of other times."[48]

Long after Spain lost control of its New World empire, Latin America remained a frontier for individual Europeans who continued to cross the Atlantic in search of fresh opportunities. The extent to which those Europeans found opportunity on the frontiers of the Americas depended in large part on the ways in which the public policies of individual nations made public and private lands accessible to newcomers. Would nations find ways to integrate their developing frontiers into their national economies, or follow programs aimed primarily at enriching the existing landowners?[49] Historian Walter Nugent explores such questions in a remarkably wide-ranging essay, which focuses on the period 1870 to World War I and examines the four countries that received the largest numbers of European immigrants: Argentina, Brazil, Canada, and the United States (Selection 8). Nugent's analysis of statistics yields special insights because he has used them comparatively, identifying similarities and differences.

Frontier Peoples and Institutions

Frontiers, where peoples of different cultures interact with one another as well as with physical space, contain so many cultural and environmental variables—including moments in time—that they are always unique.[50] Thus understanding the dynamics of frontiers in Latin America must include considerations of frontier peoples and institutions at specific times and places. In Part III we offer a sampling of case studies from the colonial era, with essays on five institutions that Iberians used to extend their empire onto New World frontiers—the mission, the encomienda, the military, the town, and the family (Selections 9, 10, 11, 12, and 13). As several of the essays remind us, life on the frontier forced Iberians to modify these institutions. Moreover, other frontier peoples—Indians and blacks—often used them to further their own interests.

Our starting point, on Indo-Spanish frontiers in the sixteenth century, is arbitrary. Before there were Spaniards in America there were frontiers—places where Indian societies edged up against one another. Like the Euro-Indian frontiers that followed them, Native American frontiers could be places of conflict and accommodation, characterized by many levels of interaction in the political, military, commercial, religious, and cultural spheres. Certainly the processes of conquest and settlement of new lands *by* state societies, such as the Incas, antedated the arrival of Europeans. So, too, did the conquest *of* state societies by frontier peoples, as in the case of those Chichimecs, known to us as Aztecs, who came to dominate the sophisticated peoples of the central plateau of Mexico. Aztec culture itself, as elaborated in the great city of Tenochtitlan, continued to be shaped by the frontiers of empire until the meeting of Moctezuma and Hernán Cortés.[51] And after the arrival of Spaniards, some Indians moved onto new frontiers as allies of Spaniards and aided in the conquest or control of other native peoples.[52]

Before Spaniards arrived in America, their own frontier experience— seven centuries of reconquering Iberia from the Moors—had shaped the institutions and attitudes they would bring across the Atlantic. The long *reconquista*, which began in the eighth century and did not end until 1492, when the combined forces of Isabel of Castile and Fernando of Aragón entered the Alhambra in triumph, had nurtured political liberty and provided unusual opportunities for upward social mobility for brave, audacious, or fortunate Spanish warriors. Out of centuries of struggle along the southward-moving Christian-Muslim frontier, Castilians cultivated what Spanish historian Claudio Sánchez-Albornoz has called "a frontier soul."[53] Spaniards dreamed of the material rewards that might be had from conquering rich Muslim lands of Andalusia, and of spiritual benefits that would accrue from extending the religion of Christ into lands served by the followers of Muhammad.

In the Americas, Spaniards entered new frontiers inhabited by Indians instead of Muslims, and institutions forged in Iberia continued to be honed and modified in response to new peoples and new circumstances. To convert Indians, the Spanish Crown relied particularly on missionaries—Dominicans, Franciscans, Jesuits, and members of other religious orders. Missionaries did more, however, than convert and minister to natives. As Herbert Bolton explained in a highly influential essay first published in 1917, missions functioned "as frontier agencies of Spain" and were so recognized and supported by the Crown. "Designedly or incidentally," Bolton argued, in the course of spreading Christianity, missionaries explored, promoted, defended, and ultimately settled new frontiers by Hispanicizing Indians.[54]

Bolton's positive view of the mission as a beneficial frontier institution has dominated American scholarship, but some historians have also seen a darker side.[55] In a previously unpublished essay, "Reflections on the Ibero-American Frontier Mission as an Institution in Native American History" (Selection 9), David Sweet examines the impact of missionization on the missionized. He finds substantial costs as well as benefits for Indian peoples on the frontiers of Latin America. Where state-supported and state-directed missionaries and soldiers combined to pacify Indians in the colonial era, however, the settlement of frontiers had "the flavor of an operation of conquest rather than the character of a colonizing venture," as one Colombian historian has observed.[56] Nonetheless, well into the twentieth century in Colombia, and perhaps in some other countries as well, the state continued to use missionaries as "powerful instruments" to deliver "civilization and culture" to frontier regions.[57]

To exploit the labor of Indians while also Christianizing them, Spaniards established the encomienda, another institution with antecedents on Iberian frontiers.[58] In theory if not consistently in practice, officials granted some of the fruits of Indian labor (but not Indian lands) to individual Spanish trustees, or encomenderos. They, in turn, were to protect the Indians they held in encomiendas, instruct them in the ways of Christians, and bear arms for the Crown. As in Spain, rewards of encomiendas usually went to the earliest settlers of a dangerous region—those who risked their lives in frontier warfare to extend the realm. For those individuals, tribute and services collected from encomienda Indians might bring wealth and rapid upward mobility. Encomiendas—a phenomenon mainly of the sixteenth and seventeenth centuries—also facilitated the replication of social hierarchy on frontiers, for they were commonly granted to encomenderos and their heirs for two generations. Encomiendas created an elite class from the earliest days of settlement and limited opportunities for later arrivals—as did the existence of forced labor itself.[59]

Like other institutions originating on Iberian frontiers, however, the encomienda in the New World was never an exact copy of its Spanish antecedent. Across successive frontiers of the Americas, encomenderos modified the institution as they adapted it to local conditions. Anthropologist Elman R. Service, for example, explained in a classic essay, "The Encomienda in Paraguay" (Selection 10), how poverty, distance from markets, and the nature of Indian society itself altered the functioning of the institution in Paraguay. There, encomenderos not only proved unusually lax at supervising the conversion of Guaraní Indians to Christianity but also adopted some native customs (Turner's "return to primitive conditions"?). As historian Steve Stern succinctly put it: "The Paraguayan conquistadors discarded the fusion of formal monogamy and informal concubinage tolerated by the Church, and turned toward the Guaraní practice of open polygamy."[60]

If relatively peaceful accommodation and mutual acculturation characterized Spanish-Indian relations on the Paraguayan frontier, a state of ongoing, low-intensity warfare typified other frontiers. One of those war zones was along the Araucanian-Spanish frontier in Chile—a military one until the late nineteenth century. In "Frontier Warfare in Colonial Chile," Louis de Armond explains that Araucanians resisted Spanish encroachment so successfully because the Indians adapted imaginatively to the fighting techniques of their adversaries (Selection 11). If frontier conditions promoted inventiveness, as Turner believed, then the case of the Araucanians shows that frontiers could engender inventiveness among peoples encroached upon as well as the encroachers. Unable to defeat Araucanian Indians by means of offensive punitive expeditions, Spaniards in Chile adopted an essentially defensive posture. The Spanish military met similar, highly effective resistance from natives on the pampas of Argentina and the plains of western America. As a result, Spanish officials reoriented their frontier institutions and strategies in the eighteenth century. Fixed garrisons won a measure of security across the frontiers, but peace came only in the late 1700s, when Spaniards bought Indian friendship by distributing gifts—a technique that they used with Pehuenches and Tehuelches in Argentina as well as with Comanches and Apaches on their North American frontiers.[61]

Indians were not the only peoples to resist the expansion of European frontiers in colonial Latin America. Over the centuries thousands of black slaves transported from Africa to labor on New World plantations fled the horrors of cruel bondage to seek refuge in the wilderness. Known as *cimarrones* (or "maroons" as the word came to be corrupted in English), they formed free communities, called *palenques* in Spanish America and *quilombos* in Brazil, in which they sought to replicate the institutions they had known in Africa while adapting to their new environment.[62] The Spanish and Portuguese authorities regarded these communities as a threat to their slavocracies. They mounted punitive expeditions against them, often recapturing the fugitives within a few months. Other *palenques* proved more durable. In Ecuador, for example, a cargo of West African slaves en route from Panama to Peru was shipwrecked in 1570 off the northern coast at Esmeraldas. The newly freed slaves seized possession of the territory from the local Indians, killing men and taking the women as wives. Isolated by high mountains from the Spanish capital of Quito, the *zambo palenque* flourished, blending Indian and African traits into a unique culture and attaining a population of five thousand by the end of the sixteenth century. Unable to conquer Esmeraldas militarily, the Quito Audiencia negotiated a treaty with its leaders in 1599 agreeing not to collect tribute or demand labor so long as the *zambos* would swear allegiance to the Spanish king and permit Catholic missionaries to enter their region.[63] Such treaties were not uncommon, but as Franklin W. Knight points out in his survey of maroons in the Caribbean, if *cimarrones* managed to gain legal or quasi-legal recognition, "their structure, internal organization, methods of recruitment, and political attitudes underwent significant changes" (Selection 12). A peace treaty signed by maroons in Jamaica in 1795 obligated them to return runaway slaves to their owners, a concession "that incurred a lot of ill will among the slaves." Knight concludes that in accepting a form of collective security, the maroons inadvertently reinforced the very system of slavery they had defied by "removing, reducing, or otherwise restricting one option of personal escape from slavery to freedom."

In places such as Argentina or Paraguay, where distinctive cultures contended with one another well into the eighteenth century, frontier institutions such as the encomienda, the mission, and the presidio lasted much longer than they did in "core" areas of the Spanish empire.[64] After those frontier institutions faded away, however, villages and towns remained. From the outset, urban centers had also served to advance Spanish and Portuguese frontiers—modifying some and, in turn, being modified by them.[65] Some frontier towns, such as Querétaro in northern Mexico, grew into cities; other towns stagnated and disappeared; still other towns, such as nineteenth-century Manaus on the Amazon, went through the boom-and-bust cycles characteristic of many mining towns in the American West.[66]

In towns, forts, missions, and ranches, wherever Spanish men had gone, so had women and children.[67] Across the frontiers of Latin America, Hispanic families built new communities in which they tried to replicate the village and town life of Iberia.[68] They succeeded all too well, as Alida Metcalf illustrated in a case study of a Brazilian community, Santana de Parnaíba, located just to the west of São Paulo (Selection 13). Like other writers, Metcalf found that Brazilians replicated a stratified class system on their frontier, preventing it from becoming the land of opportunity that Turner imagined the American frontier had been. In Brazil, elite white families manipulated institutions to ensure that they would derive maximum wealth from the frontier's human and material resources and then pass that wealth on to their sons and daughters. Although the Brazilian frontier provided some opportunities for persons from the lower strata of society to achieve independence and self-sufficiency, the elite hindered upward mobility for others. Metcalf explains in her recent book how elite families turned the frontier into "one of the roots of inequality in Brazilian society"—an argument that might be advanced for Spanish America as well as Portuguese America.[69]

Frontier Peoples and National Identity

Latin American frontiers apparently did not transform frontier peoples or institutions in the manner that Turner supposed happened in North America. Nonetheless, some Latin Americans have argued that frontiers forged important features of their national identities. Nowhere is this clearer than in Brazil and Argentina, where two frontier types—the *bandeirante* and the gaucho—came to epitomize national virtues, much as the westward-moving pioneer did in the United States. In her essay

"National Identity and the Frontier," Argentine historian Hebe Clementi outlines the distinguishing features of three national archetypes: Anglo-American pioneers, Brazilian *bandeirantes*, and Argentine gauchos (Selection 14). "Each," she argues, "helps to define his nation's character."

Sarmiento and other nineteenth-century Argentine elites usually viewed gauchos as barbarians. But as historian E. Bradford Burns has noted, their writings also revealed "a general schizophrenia"; they had romanticized as well as demonized frontier peoples.[70] Thus after the gaucho had largely disappeared, writers in the twentieth century did not have to stretch their imaginations much to recast the gaucho as a national symbol. In "The Gaucho in Argentina's Quest for National Identity" (Selection 15), historian Richard Slatta explains how later Argentine intellectuals generally abandoned the image of the gaucho as a deplorable rustic and celebrated him as the emblem of Argentina's most authentic values and traditions. This transformation had little to do with gauchos. Rather, as Slatta suggests, circumstances unique to Argentina at the turn of the century, including a heavy stream of foreign immigrants who threatened to erode traditional culture, led some *pensadores* to search within Argentina itself for the sources of national identity. Thus urban elites who once looked abroad to Europe for their models and reviled native-born gauchos came to romanticize the gaucho as an enduring if problematic symbol for the nation.[71]

The exaltation of the gaucho in Argentina had its counterpart in twentieth-century Brazil, where *bandeirantes* became the symbol of national identity. The word *bandeirantes* defies translation because it means more than its literal definition, "flag-bearers." Rather, it refers to those expeditionaries who set out from communities along the Brazilian coast, principally São Paulo, to exploit the resources of the interior. Comprising a variety of people, such as priests, officials, chroniclers, soldiers, and workers, and led by a flag bearer, these prolonged raiding expeditions came to be called *bandeiras*, and their members *bandeirantes*. Pathfinders, prospectors, and slavers, who established permanent settlements only as a by-product of their search for quick wealth, the *bandeirantes* extended and consolidated the Brazilian frontier. In the process they won a place in the country's folklore as a national archetype but did not, Clodomir Vianna Moog argues in a provocative book, lay a solid foundation for a modern Brazil (Selection 16). Vianna Moog's interpretation of the *bandeirantes* contrasts sharply with more celebratory views of some of his countrymen.[72]

In looking to frontier types as national symbols, Brazil and Argentina seem exceptional among Latin American countries. Mexico and Chile, where the presence of important frontiers did not lead to the romanticization of frontier types, represent the norm.[73]

Contemporary Frontiers

"The majority of Latin American nations today," Alistair Hennessy wrote in 1978, "are still in the frontier stage of development."[74] Or, he might have said, underdevelopment. Vast tropical frontiers, in particular—places that one historian has called "detained societies"—seem to cry out for further economic development.[75] The wisdom and consequences of developing Latin America's remaining tropical frontiers has been a subject of bitter debate. Do tropical frontiers serve as places of opportunity? If so, for whom? And at what cost to the environment? At what cost to native peoples? Or is opportunity in the late twentieth century to be found only on urban frontiers rather than on new lands?

North Americans had long believed that open lands not only offered opportunity but served as a "safety valve" to release pressures building up in more settled areas. The unemployed could simply pack up and move out to the frontier to rebuild their lives, thus alleviating stresses that an impoverished underclass might put on urban areas. The idea that the frontier served as a safety valve in the United States enjoyed widespread acceptance in Turner's day, then fell into disfavor as scholars realized that it required capital to move to frontiers and develop them. The poor could not afford the journey. Then, in modified form, the idea came into acceptance once again.[76]

If we judge from the large number of peasants who have fled the countryside for the cities since World War II, contemporary Latin American rural frontiers appear to function badly as safety valves. But the postwar era has also seen numerous peasants try their luck on new lands— exemplified by the thousands who have left the Andean highlands for the Amazon and Orinoco frontierlands of Bolivia, Colombia, Ecuador, Peru, and Venezuela.[77] Some of these frontiers in contemporary Latin America seem to work as safety valves, if the conclusions of a case study of Pejibaye, a remote province in southwestern Costa Rica, have broader applicability (Selection 17). Economist James Sewastynowicz argues that critics who dismissed Turner's idea of the "safety valve" overstated their case and that upward mobility is often achieved in "steps," as settlers acquire capital in one frontier location and then move on to a newer one. Sewastynowicz suggests that upward mobility, achieved through what he calls "two-step" migration, occurred commonly on Brazilian and North American frontiers as well as those of Costa Rica.

In contrast to Sewastynowicz, British economist Joe Foweraker takes a dim view of peasants' prospects on Brazilian frontiers. In a close study of Brazil's contemporary frontiers, from 1930 to the present (Selection 18), Foweraker finds deep social tensions that often erupted in violence, instead of tension-relieving safety valves. State-sanctioned violence, he concludes, succeeded in terrorizing peasants and driving them off lands that they had farmed for years. Peasants, too, resorted to violence as they attempted to defend lands they had worked but did not clearly own and as they resisted a chaotic land-tenure system that favored (and still favors) influential large landowners. Conditions on the Brazilian frontier, then, do not provide opportunity for hard-working individuals in Foweraker's view. Rather, those conditions perpetuate inequality, and the struggle for new lands represents "less a question of the brutal battle with nature than of 'man's inhumanity to man.' "[78]

The violent exchanges between peasants asserting rights to land and bureaucrats, soldiers, or hired thugs arrayed against them have been endemic in other times and places throughout Latin America. On frontiers where the state has used violence to control the poor and deny them access to land, it has fostered a culture of violent lawlessness and retarded the development of the very democratic institutions that Turner believed the American frontier engendered. Two scholars, for example, have explained how cowboys in Latin America "probably considered cattle rustling an act of justice, a reparation which was their due; and rebellion against political authority was rebellion against oppression."[79] Similarly, historian Catherine LeGrande sees the dispossession of peasants by the expansion of great estates onto the frontiers of Colombia as the root of bitter landlord-tenant conflicts in that country during its infamous decade of civil war—La Violencia of 1948–1959—and "an explanation for the success of guerrilla groups in building a support base in frontier regions today."[80] The same might be said of the bitter insurgencies of the 1980s in El Salvador, Guatemala, and Nicaragua.

If the Hispanic occupiers of frontier lands—the rich and the poor—have fought bitterly among themselves, so too have they used violence to despoil Indians of their lands. This story, which began in 1492, remains far from ended. In an overview of Brazilian expansion into the Amazon—often called "the last great" frontier—Brazilian anthropologist Alcida R. Ramos looks at the toll on native peoples of economic development in the Amazonian frontier (Selection 19). Although Ramos wrote in the early 1980s, her argument applies equally well to the 1990s, for Brazil's Indian frontier continues to recede at remarkable rates. Meanwhile, the push of non-Indians into the Brazilian Amazon continues. Notwithstanding the success of a government-sponsored "Decade of Colonization" in the 1970s, when "practically all the land that is good for small farming became private property," according to a recent study by Brazilian scholar Anna Luiza Ozorio, "the myth of plentiful free land is persistent."[81]

Although we continue to think of the push into new lands as the usual form of frontier expansion, cities in Latin America have become new frontiers. In "Social Change on the Latin American Frontier" (Selection 20), anthropologist Emilio Willems argues that impoverished rural people who move into the great squatter settlements that surround Latin American cities experience many of the adjustments required of new arrivals to traditional back-country frontiers. Taking great risks, squatters occupy land that does not belong to them in order to exploit opportunities offered by the urban labor market. They encounter hostile natives. They adapt their institutions and culture to the new environment. Some achieve upward social mobility.

Conclusion

Throughout Latin America, frontiers had different impacts than those imagined by Turner for the United States. Nonetheless, Latin American frontiers played significant roles in shaping the new Iberoamerican societies. They became places of more intense racial and cultural blending than occurred in more homogenous areas, and they provided opportunities for upwardly mobile non-Indians—especially the earliest arrivals on new frontiers. At the same time, the nature of Latin American economic and political institutions and the influence of powerful family networks limited opportunities and fostered inequality. But, in contrast to the United States, most frontiers in the region have not captured the popular imagination. Nor, in general, have Latin American intellectuals regarded their frontiers as central to explaining their national cultures or institutions as have North American scholars.

Why do frontiers hold different meanings for the Latin and Anglo Americans, and even within Latin America itself? Why do processes that appear similar on the surface differ so profoundly on closer inspection? Or do they? The selections in this book provide only tentative and partial answers to those questions, for much research remains to be done in Latin America and the meaning of that research seems likely to elude definitive interpretations.

The same may be said about the United States, where scholars have continued to reexamine the meaning and significance of their own frontiers since the publication of Turner's arresting address in 1893. Lone but firm voices of dissent, which began to be heard in the 1920s, swelled to a chorus after Turner's death in 1932. The ideas of a closing frontier, of "free land," or of the frontier as a safety valve or cradle of democracy or individualism all came under attack. Instead of regarding the Anglo-American frontier as a font of American virtues, some of Turner's critics saw it as a source of anti-intellectualism, ethnic division, class conflict, and pessimism—as a place where the "environment crushed the human spirit."[82] This darker view, which resembled that held by many Latin American intellectuals about their own frontiers, continued to have strong and eloquent adherents who offered competing interpretations of the meaning of North American frontiers even as Turner's paradigm dominated popular and pedagogical literature.

In the 1980s the darker view of the American West prevailed as it came to be associated with the highly publicized group of historians popularly identified with the "New Western History." Much of what is new about the New Western History has been overstated in the popular press and by some of its most ardent proponents.[83] Nonetheless, the New Western Historians have built effectively on the work of their predecessors. Some have not only moved beyond Turner but also have abandoned the idea of the "frontier" itself as a useful category of analysis. They consider the frontier as an ethnocentric construct, too time-bound to accommodate the postfrontier twentieth-century West, and they prefer to emphasize place over process.[84] Regarding the place that has become the North American West, they have concerned themselves less with the impact of the region on westering Anglo-American males, as did Turner, than with the impact of Anglo-American males on the region—on women, Native Americans, Hispanics, and other minorities, and on the environment itself. Instead of seeing the West as a source of American egalitarianism, they find class conflict and inequality, reenforced through violence and unequal relations of power.[85] Instead of seeing Anglo Americans moving westward along the "edge" of Turner's line that separated "savagery and civilization," New Western Historians concern themselves with zones of transculturation—multiethnic and multiracial worlds.[86] Rather than suggest the impact of the American frontier on Europe, they focus on how the influence of European markets contributed to the dependency of Native Americans, and how an economy based largely on the extraction of raw materials and short of capital rendered the West dependent on the East.[87] In short, as New Western Historians have moved further away from Turner's model, with its emphasis on American virtue and exceptionalism, they have moved closer to issues that have engaged historians of Latin American frontiers (and, indeed, historians in general).

Evidently, neither Latin American nor North American frontiers operated along Turnerian lines. Turner's thesis, historian John Mack Faragher recently noted, "long ago found its way onto the trash heap of historical interpretations."[88] But reports of the trash heap may be premature. Turner's thesis continues to attract those who find it useful in modified forms, and the "frontier" remains a compelling heuristic device, used even by Turner's detractors.[89] "Anti-Turnerians are strangely haunted by his silent scholarly ghost," historian Martin Ridge argues, "for they deny the usefulness of his historical vision but often unwittingly work within it."[90] Another prominent historian, William Cronon, claims that Turner "gave American history its central and most persistent story. However much we may modify the details and outline of that story, we are unlikely ever to break entirely free of it."[91]

Questing after new frontiers, Americans have imagined outer space as a frontier; John F. Kennedy saw the beginnings of his administration in 1960 as a New Frontier; Ronald Reagan, riding tall, frequently invoked frontier values during his presidency; one historian has even described the recent flight from the cities to the suburbs as the opening up of a "crabgrass frontier."[92] A century after Turner made his famous address Americans continue to search for new frontiers, with one of the most ingenious solutions offered by foreign policy expert Walter Russell Mead. In 1992, Mead proposed that the United States purchase Siberia from Russia. This, he argued, would both strengthen Russia's economy and make the United States "once again . . . a frontier society, with all the attendant opportunities and freedoms."[93] North Americans, in sum, remain as captivated by frontiers as Latin Americans remain indifferent to them.

Whatever their views of frontiers, as historians of North America and Latin America try to construct more fully realized portraits of their respective societies, their questions will be sharpened and their answers more interesting if they continue to learn about one another. The deepest self-knowledge may perhaps be best obtained by looking from the outside in, rather than from the inside out. And the differences that we discover among us may contribute more understanding than the similarities, for differences suggest alternative scenarios that inevitably shake teleological assumptions. We hope that North American readers, to whom we have addressed this volume, may learn about themselves even as they come to understand more about Latin America.

Notes

1. By "North America" we mean the area that is today Canada and the United States; "Latin America" generally includes Mexico, Central America, the Caribbean, and South America.

2. The classic formulation of this position is by Frederick Jackson Turner, whose essay appears herein (Selection 1).

3. For a compelling discussion of the term and guidance to some of the literature, see Howard Lamar and Leonard Thompson, eds., *The Frontier in History:
North America and Southern Africa Compared* (New Haven: Yale University Press,
1981), 7–13. One of the most frequent criticisms of scholars who have written
about the frontier, from Frederick Jackson Turner to Alistair Hennessy, is their
failure to formulate an adequate definition. We doubtless leave ourselves open to
the same criticism.

4. Isaiah Bowman, *The Pioneer Fringe* (New York: American Geographical
Society Special Publication no. 12, 1931), 296–99. See also Raymond E. Crist,
"Fixed Physical Boundaries and Dynamic Cultural Frontiers: A Contrast," *American Journal of Economics and Sociology* 12 (April 1953): 230; Raye Platt, "Opportunities for Agricultural Colonization in the Eastern Border Valleys of the
Andes," in *Pioneer Settlement* (New York: American Geographical Society Special Publication no. 14, 1932), 84; Jane M. Rausch, *The Llanos Frontier in Colombian History, 1830–1930* (Albuquerque: University of New Mexico Press,
1993), ix.

5. J. Valerie Fifer, "The Search for a Series of Small Successes: Frontiers of
Settlement in Eastern Bolivia," *Journal of Latin American Studies* 14, no. 2 (1982):
407–8. For a recent overview of frontiers in colonial Latin American history,
see James Lockhart and Stuart B. Schwartz, *Early Latin America: A History of
Colonial Spanish America and Brazil* (Cambridge: Cambridge University
Press, 1983), 287–302, who see frontiers as areas beyond the "fringes" of Latin
America.

6. Eric R. Wolf, *Europe and the People without History* (Berkeley: University
of California Press, 1982), ix.

7. Jay Gitlin, "On the Borders of Empire: Connecting the West to Its Imperial
Past," in *Under an Open Sky: Rethinking America's Western Past,* ed. William
Cronin, George Miles, and Gitlin (New York: Norton, 1962), 74. See also
William B. Taylor, "Between Global Process and Local Knowledge: An Inquiry
into Early Latin American Social History, 1500–1900," in *The Worlds of Social
History*, ed. Oliver Zunz (Chapel Hill: University of North Carolina Press, 1985),
115–89, and Thomas D. Hall, *Social Change in the Southwest, 1350–1880*
(Lawrence: University of Kansas Press, 1989).

8. The only attempt at a one-volume treatment of this subject is Alistair
Hennessy, *The Frontier in Latin American History* (Albuquerque: University of
New Mexico Press, 1978).

9. Frederick Jackson Turner, "The Significance of the Frontier in American
History," *Annual Report of the American Historical Association . . . 1893* (Washington: Government Printing Office, 1894), 200.

10. For the most thorough examination of Turner's life, and the formation and
impact of the speech he gave at the World's Columbian Exposition, see Ray Allen
Billington's biography, *Frederick Jackson Turner: Historian, Scholar, Teacher*
(New York: Oxford University Press, 1973).

11. In addition to Billington's *Frederick Jackson Turner*, 449, see Richard
Slotkin, *Gunslinger Nation: The Myth of the Frontier in Twentieth-Century
America* (New York: Atheneum, 1992).

12. "The Epic of Greater America," *American Historical Review* 38 (April
1933), in *Bolton and the Spanish Borderlands*, ed. John Francis Bannon (Norman:
University of Oklahoma Press, 1974), 308. For considerations of Bolton's argu-

ment, see Lewis Hanke, ed., *Do the Americas Have a Common History? A Critique of the Bolton Theory* (New York: Knopf, 1964).

13. David J. Weber, "Turner, the Boltonians, and the Borderlands," *American Historical Review* 91 (February 1986): 68.

14. Arthur S. Aiton, "Latin-American Frontiers," Canadian Historical Association *Reports* (1940): 104.

15. Hebe Clementi, *La frontera en América*, 4 vols. (Editorial Leviatan, 1986–88), 1:19–20. See also Cuban philosopher Jorge Mañach, *Frontiers in the Americas: A Global Perspective*, trans. Philip H. Phenix (New York: Teachers College Press, 1975), 13.

16. Latin American historians who write about frontiers rarely make reference to Turner or frame questions in Turnerian terms. See, for example, the essays in Alvaro Jara, ed., *Tierras Nuevas. Expansión territorial y ocupación del suelo en América (siglos XVI–XIX)* (Mexico: Colegio de Mexico, 1969), and Elsy Marulanda Alvarez, *Colonización y conflicto: las lecciones del Sumapaz* (Bogotá: Tercer Mundo, 1991).

17. Tom R. Sullivan, *Cowboys and Caudillos: Frontier Ideology of the Americas* (Bowling Green, OH: Bowling Green State University Popular Press, 1990), 31.

18. Roderick Nash, *Wilderness and the American Mind* (3d ed., New Haven: Yale University Press, 1982), 146. See also Frederick B. Pike, *The United States and Latin America: Myths and Stereotypes of Civilization and Nature* (Austin: University of Texas Press, 1992). In a statement that seems to overlook Brazil and Argentina, at least, and to suppose that all national myths are myths of national identity, Hennessy argued that in Latin America "there was no frontier experience which could provide the basis for a nationalist myth. The frontier had either crushed those who had ventured to it, or in those cases where it had expanded successfully it had done so under the aegis of foreign capital. . . . This was not material from which national myths could be spun." Hennessy, *The Frontier in Latin American History*, 21.

19. Quoted in Billington, *Frederick Jackson Turner*, 130.

20. See J. Valerie Fifer, *United States Perceptions of Latin America, 1850–1930: A "New West" South of Capricorn?* (Manchester: Manchester University Press, 1991).

21. Matthew F. Maury, quoted in Pike, *The United States and Latin America*, 125.

22. Pike, *The United States and Latin America*, 19. See also 19–25, 70–75, 86–89.

23. E. Bradford Burns, *The Poverty of Progress: Latin America in the Nineteenth Century* (Berkeley: University of California Press, 1980), and Silvio R. Duncan Baretta and John Markoff, "Civilization and Barbarism: Cattle Frontiers in Latin America," *Comparative Studies in Society and History* 20 (October 1978): 587–620.

24. For an especially cogent analysis, see Burns, *The Poverty of Progress*, 22–29, 70.

25. In a book of essays by Turner, *The Frontier in American History* (1920), translated as Frederick Jackson Turner, *La frontera en la historia de América*, trans. Rafael Cremades Cepa (Madrid: Ediciones Castilla, S.A., 1960), 21–47, and in Hebe Clementi, *F. J. Turner* (Buenos Aires: Centro Editor de América

Latina, 1968), 44–76. Turner's essay was published again in *Estudios (nuevos y viejos) sobre la frontera*, ed. Francisco de Solano and Salvador Bernabeu (Madrid: Consejo Superior de Investigaciones Cientifícas, Centro de Estudios Históricos, 1991), 9–44.

26. Edmundo O'Gorman, *The Invention of America: An Inquiry into the Historical Nature of the New World and the Meaning of Its History* (Bloomington: Indiana University Press, 1961), 142. O'Gorman continues with a dubious assertion: "Notwithstanding the many changes that took place, the Spaniards, unlike their English brothers in the northern part of America, never engaged in any widespread and tenacious effort to transform forests and deserts into cultivable areas; they confined their settlement to regions that seemed to be naturally destined by Providence for man's benefit."

27. "Prólogo" to Turner, *La frontera en la historia de América*, 14.

28. Two Colombian examples: William Frederick Sharp, *Slavery on the Spanish Frontier: The Colombian Chocó, 1610–1810* (Norman: University of Oklahoma Press, 1976), 3, and Jane M. Rausch, *A Tropical Plains Frontier: The Llanos of Colombia, 1531–1831* (Albuquerque: University of New Mexico Press, 1984), 230, 245.

29. See also the observation of geographer Preston E. James, "Expanding Frontiers of Settlement in Latin America: A Project for Future Study," *Hispanic American Historical Review* 21 (May 1941): 184.

30. Sergio Villalobos R., "Tres siglos y medio de vida fronteriza Chilena," in Solano and Bernabeu, eds., *Estudios (nuevos y viejos) sobre la frontera*, 294.

31. "Comparative Studies in Frontier History," *Annals of the Association of American Geographers* 50 (March 1960): 65. See also Gitlin, "On the Borders of Empire," in Cronon, Miles, and Gitlin, eds., *Under an Open Sky*, 74–75.

32. Richard W. Slatta, *Cowboys of the Americas* (New Haven: Yale University Press, 1990), 220. In this respect, the cowboy stands in sharp contrast to Anglo-American trappers in the Rocky Mountain West, who did adopt elements of Indian material culture.

33. See Thomas M. Bader, "A 'Second Field' for Historians of Latin America: An Application of the Theories of Bolton, Turner, and Webb," *Journal of Inter-American Studies and World Affairs* 12 (1970): 47–54.

34. Turner, "The Significance of the Frontier," 221.

35. See the suggestive remarks of Florencia E. Mallon, "Indian Communities, Political Cultures, and the State in Latin America, 1780–1990," *Journal of Latin American Studies* 24 (Quincentenary Supplement 1992): 42. Brought to our attention by Edward Countryman.

36. Different writers have employed various definitions of terms like *periphery*, *borderlands*, and *hinterland*. See, for example, Richard Von Glahn, *The Country of Streams and Grottoes: Expansion, Settlement, and the Civilizing of the Sichuan Frontier in Song Times* (Cambridge: Council on East Asian Studies and Harvard University Press, 1987), 215–20. Brought to our attention by David Ownby.

37. We refer to the work of Fernando Henrique Cardoso and Andre Gunder Frank, who in the 1960s elaborated what came to be called dependency theory, and Immanuel Wallerstein, whose studies of what he termed the "modern world system" began to appear in the 1970s. For recent guides to, and critiques of, that literature, see Steve J. Stern, "Feudalism, Capitalism, and the World-System in the Perspective of Latin America and the Caribbean," *American Historical Re-*

view 93 (October 1988): 829–72, and Louis A. Pérez, Jr., "Dependency," *Journal of American History* 77 (June 1990): 133–42.

38. *The Great Frontier: Freedom and Hierarchy in Modern Times* (Princeton: Princeton University Press, 1983), 8. For another appreciative view of Webb, see Villalobos R., "Tres siglos y medio de vida fronteriza Chilena," in Solano and Bernabeu, eds., *Estudios (nuevos y viejos) sobre la frontera*, 294.

39. McNeill, *The Great Frontier*, 10. See also Wolf, *Europe and the People without History*, quoted above in n. 6.

40. McNeill, *The Great Frontier*, 8–9.

41. If the frontier is a place of freedom according to the conventional wisdom in the United States, recent scholarship, informed by world systems theory, has gone in the opposite direction by portraying peripheries as places of coerced labor. For an elaboration on these ideas and guidance to the extensive scholarly literature behind them, see Howard Lamar, "From Bondage to Contract: Ethnic Labor in the American West, 1600–1890," in *The Countryside in the Age of Capitalist Transformation: Essays in the Social History of Rural America*, ed. Steven Hahn and Jonathan Prude (Chapel Hill: University of North Carolina Press, 1985), and Susan M. Deeds, "Rural Work in Nueva Vizcaya: Forms of Labor Coercion on the Periphery," *Hispanic American Historical Review* 69 (August 1989): 425–49.

42. Webb, *The Great Frontier* (Austin: University of Texas Press, 1952), 106.

43. José Honório Rodrigues, "Webb's Great Frontier and the Interpretation of Modern History," in *The New World Looks at Its History*, ed. Archibald R. Lewis and Thomas McGann (Austin: University of Texas Press, 1963), 158.

44. Ibid.

45. Webb, *The Great Frontier*, 441.

46. Ray Allen Billington, *America's Frontier Heritage* (New York: Holt, Rinehart and Winston, 1966), 54.

47. Ibid.

48. Letters of May 29 and December 15, 1871, in Alice Houston Luiggi, ed., "Some Letters of Sarmiento and Mary Mann, 1865–1876, Part II," *Hispanic American Historical Review* 32 (August 1952): 362, 366.

49. For considerations of this question, see Fifer, *United States Perceptions of Latin America*, who compares the American West with southern South America; Paul W. Gates, *Land and Law in California: Essays on Land Policies* (Ames: Iowa State University Press, 1991), who contrasts Mexican and Anglo-American land policies; and Marianne Schmink and Charles Howard Wood, *Contested Frontiers in Amazonia* (New York: Columbia University Press, 1992), who reveal the complexities of legislating wise public policy in recent times.

50. As José Honório Rodrigues put it, "The Great Frontier is divided into little frontiers, which had different destinies and exercised different influences." Rodrigues, "Webb's Great Frontier," 163.

51. Mary W. Helms, *Middle America: A Culture History of Heartland and Frontiers* (Englewood Cliffs, NJ: Prentice-Hall, 1975), 111–23, and Davíd Carrasco, "Myth, Cosmic Terror, and the Templo Mayor," in *The Great Temple of Tenochtitlan: Center and Periphery in the Aztec World*, ed. Johanna Broda, Davíd Carrasco, and Eduardo Matos Moctezuma (Berkeley: University of California Press, 1987), 150–54, who argues that Aztecs carried human sacrifice to great extremes in order to awe, intimidate, and maintain control over the frontiers of their empire. See also ibid., 148–49.

52. See, for example, Marc Simmons, "Tlascalans in the Spanish Borderlands," *New Mexico Historical Review* 39 (April 1964): 101–10, and Oakah L. Jones, Jr., *Pueblo Warriors and Spanish Conquest* (Norman: University of Oklahoma Press, 1966).

53. Claudio Sánchez-Albornoz, *Spain: A Historical Enigma*, trans. Colette Joly Dees and David Sven Reher (1st ed., 1956; 2 vols.; Madrid: Fundación Universitaria Española, 1975), 2:656. Among the many good discussions of the effect of the *reconquista* on the Spanish ethos and institutions is J. H. Elliott, *Imperial Spain, 1469–1716* (1st ed., 1963; Harmondsworth, England: Penguin Books, 1970), 56–76. For a sampling of some of the literature, see H. B. Johnson, Jr., ed., *Reconquest to Empire: The Iberian Background to Latin American History* (New York: Knopf, 1970).

54. "The Mission as a Frontier Institution in the Spanish American Colonies," reprinted many times, as in Bannon, ed., *Bolton and the Spanish Borderlands*. The quotes are on pp. 210–11.

55. See, for example, James Schofield Saeger, "Another View of the Mission as a Frontier Institution: The Guaycuruan Reductions of Santa Fe, 1743–1810," *Hispanic American Historical Review* 65 (August 1985): 493–517; Erick D. Langer, "Franciscan Missions and Chiriguano Workers: Colonization, Acculturation, and Indian Labor in Southeastern Bolivia," *The Americas* 43 (January 1987): 305–22; David J. Weber, "Blood of Martyrs, Blood of Indians: Toward a More Balanced View of Spanish Missions in Seventeenth-Century North America," in *Columbian Consequences*, ed. David Hurst Thomas, 3 vols. (Washington, DC: Smithsonian Institution Press, 1990), 2:429–48.

56. Jaime Jaramillo Uribe, "El significado de la colonización Antioqueña del Occidente Colombiano en el marco de la historia nacional," in *La colonización Antioqueña* (Manizales: Imprenta Departamental Gobernación de Caldas, 1989), 27.

57. Colombian president Pedro Nel Ospina, 1926, quoted in Jane M. Rausch, "Church-State Relations on the Colombian Frontier: The National Intendency of Meta, 1909–1930," *The Americas* 49 (July 1992): 68.

58. James Lockhart and Stuart B. Schwartz, *Early Latin America: A History of Colonial Spanish America and Brazil* (Cambridge, England: Cambridge University Press, 1993), 21, 92–96.

59. See, for example, Juan Carlos Garavaglia and Juan Carlos Grosso, "Mexican Elites of a Provincial Town: The Landowners of Tepeaca (1700–1870)," *Hispanic American Historical Review* 70 (May 1990): 255–93. This is not to say that rural elite families remained entrenched. Many failed and had to sell their lands, but those who replaced them usually made their fortunes in commerce. Susan E. Ramírez, "Large Landowners," in *Cities & Society in Colonial Latin America*, ed. Louisa Schell Hoberman and Susan Migden Socolow (Albuquerque: University of New Mexico Press, 1986), 35, 38–40.

60. Steve Stern, "Paradigms of Conquest: History, Historiography, and Politics," *Journal of Latin American Studies* 24 (Quincentenary Supplement 1992): 13–14.

61. Alfred J. Tapson, "Indian Warfare on the Pampa During the Colonial Period," *Hispanic American Historical Review* 42 (February 1962): 1–28; David J. Weber, *The Spanish Frontier in North America* (New Haven: Yale University Press, 1992), chapter 8.

62. Many of the essays in Richard Price, ed., *Maroon Societies: Rebel Slave Communities in the Americas* (1973: 2d ed., Baltimore: Johns Hopkins University Press, 1979), describe replication of African systems. For adaptation to the environment, see ibid., 11.

63. John L. Phelan, *The Kingdom of Quito* (Madison: University of Wisconsin Press, 1967), 8–10.

64. James S. Saeger, "Survival and Abolition: The Eighteenth Century Paraguayan Encomienda," *The Americas* 38 (July 1981): 59–86; Lockhart and Schwartz, *Early Latin America*, 303.

65. As in the case of towns along the Chichimec frontier of northern Mexico, where defensive considerations shaped layout and architecture; Phillip Wayne Powell, *Soldiers, Indians, & Silver: North Americans First Frontier War* (Berkeley: University of California Press, 1952), 151–57.

66. For the disappearance of many frontier towns, see Rausch, *The Llanos Frontier in Colombian History*, 330. For Manaus, see E. Bradford Burns, "Manaus, 1910: Portrait of a Boom Town," *Journal of Inter-American Studies* 7 (July 1965): 400–421. Perhaps the most extensive argument for considering civilian communities as institutions on the Spanish frontiers of the Americas is Oakah L. Jones, Jr., *Los Paisanos: Spanish Settlers on the Northern Frontier of New Spain* (Norman: University of Oklahoma Press, 1979).

67. The role of women and children on Latin American frontiers has yet to be explored adequately. For pioneering studies, see Richard W. Slatta, *Gauchos and the Vanishing Frontier* (Lincoln: University of Nebraska Press, 1983), 57–88; Antonia I. Castañeda, "Gender, Race and Culture: Spanish-Mexican Women in the Historiography of Frontier California," *Frontiers: A Journal of Women's Studies* 11 (1990): 8–20; John Charles Chasteen, "María Antonia Muniz: Frontier Matriarch," in *The Human Tradition in Latin America: The Nineteenth Century*, ed. Judith Ewell and William H. Beezley (Wilmington, DE: Scholarly Resources, 1989); and the work of Alida Metcalf cited in Selection 13.

68. See Hoberman and Socolow, eds., *Cities & Society*.

69. See Garavaglia, cited above in n. 59.

70. Burns, *The Poverty of Progress*, 23.

71. Nonetheless, "none of the effects imputed to the frontier by Turner . . . functioned on the Argentina pampa [plains]" where gauchos roamed. Richard W. Slatta, *Gauchos and the Vanishing Frontier* (Lincoln: University of Nebraska Press, 1983), 22.

72. Richard B. Morse, ed., *The Bandeirantes: The Historical Role of the Brazilian Pathfinders* (New York: Knopf, 1965), remains the best introduction to the variety of viewpoints on this subject. The essay by Cassaino Ricardo, "Westward March," 191–211, represents a counterpoint to Vianna Moog's darker view.

73. See Philip Wayne Powell, "Of Mexican Northerns and Anglo Westerns," in *Mexico's Miguel Cadera: The Taming of America's First Frontier, 1548–1597* (Tucson: University of Arizona Press, 1977), 262–66. For the importance of the Chilean frontier, see Villalobos R., "Tres siglos y medio de vida fronteriza Chilena," in Solano and Bernabeu, eds., *Estudios (nuevos y viejos) sobre la frontera*, 289–359.

74. Hennessy, *The Frontier in Latin American History*, 3.

75. Jaramillo Uribe, "El significado de la colonización Antioqueña," 26, introduced us to the term *sociedades detenidas*.

76. For a review of the arguments, see Billington, *America's Frontier Heritage*, 29–38.

77. For an overview, see Raymond E. Crist and Charles N. Nissly, *East from the Andes: Pioneer Settlements in the South American Heartlands* (Gainesville: University of Florida Press, 1973). James J. Parsons offers a comparative survey of recent colonization in the Colombian and Venezuelan llanos in "Europeanization of the Savanna Lands of Northern South America," in *Human Ecology in Savanna Environments*, ed. David H. Harris (London: Academic Press, 1980), 267–89.

78. P. ix. See also Judith Lisansky, *Migrants to Amazonia: Spontaneous Colonization in the Brazilian Frontier* (Boulder, CO: Westview, 1990), which contains vivid first-person accounts of unofficial attempts at colonization and a useful summary of theories of frontier expansion (pp. 11–15).

79. Silvio R. Duncan Baretta and John Markoff, "Civilization and Barbarism: Cattle Frontiers in Latin America," *Studies in Comparative Society and History* 20 (October 1978): 606. See also Miguel Izard, "Ni cuatreros ni montoneros: llaneros," *Boletín Americanista* 31 (1981): 83–142, who makes this case strongly for the Venezuelan llaneros.

80. Catherine LeGrand, "Labor Acquisition and Social Conflict on the Colombian Frontier, 1850–1936," *Journal of Latin American Studies* 16 (May 1984): 47.

81. Anna Luiza Ozorio de Almeida, *The Colonization of the Amazon* (1st ed., in Portuguese, 1984; Austin: University of Texas Press, 1992), 8, 332, who analyzes the settlement of small farmers on formerly public land by official or private projects in the 1970s. See also Mac Margolis, *The Last New World: The Conquest of the Amazon Frontier* (New York: Norton, 1992), and John Hemming, *Amazon Frontier: The Defeat of the Brazilian Indians* (Cambridge: Harvard University Press, 1987), who looks at an earlier era, chronicling the decline of Brazilian natives from some two million in 1760 to one million in 1910.

Augusto Gómez G. describes the ongoing struggles between Indians and *colonos* in the Colombian llanos in *Indios, colonos y conflictos: una historia regional de los llanos orientales, 1870–1970* (Bogotá: Pontificia Universidad Javeriana, 1991).

82. Gerald D. Nash, *Creating the West: Historical Interpretations, 1890–1990* (Albuquerque: University of New Mexico Press, 1991), 26, summarizes this early criticism.

83. For cogent, even-handed analyses, see Allan G. Bogue, "The Significance of the History of the American West: Postscripts and Prospects," *Western Historical Quarterly* 24 (February 1993): 45–68, and John Mack Faragher, "The Frontier Trail: Rethinking Turner and Reimagining the American West," *American Historical Review* 98 (February 1993): 106–17.

84. For general surveys written in this vein, as well as guides to the literature, see Patricia Nelson Limerick, *The Legacy of Conquest: The Unbroken Past of the American West* (New York: Norton, 1987), and Richard White, *"It's Your Misfortune and None of My Own": A New History of the American West* (Norman: University of Oklahoma Press, 1991). For historiographical discussions, see especially Patricia Nelson Limerick, Clyde A. Milner II, and Charles E. Rankin, eds., *Trails: Toward a New Western History* (Lawrence: University Press of Kansas, 1991), which includes the critical comments of Michael Malone and Gerald Thompson as well as viewpoints of the New Western Historians.

85. See, especially, Slotkin, *Gunslinger Nation*, and his earlier work, *Regeneration Through Violence: The Mythology of the American Frontier, 1600–1860* (Middletown, CT: Wesleyan University Press, 1973), and *The Fatal Environment: The Myth of the Frontier in the Age of Industrialization, 1800–1900* (New York: Atheneum, 1985).

86. Turner, "The Significance of the Frontier," 200; Richard White, *The Middle Ground: Indians, Empires, and Republics in the Great Lakes Region, 1650–1815* (New York: Cambridge University Press, 1991). See also Daniel H. Usner, Jr., *Indians, Settlers, and Slaves in a Frontier Exchange Economy: The Lower Mississippi Valley Before 1783* (Chapel Hill: University of North Carolina Press, 1992).

87. Richard White, who was introduced to dependency theory through early study of Latin American history, makes especially sophisticated use of it in *The Roots of Dependency: Subsistence, Environment, and Social Change among the Choctaws, Pawnees, and Navajos* (Lincoln: University of Nebraska Press, 1983).

88. "Gunslingers and Bureaucrats: Some Unexpected Truths about the American West," *The New Republic* (December 14, 1992): 30.

89. See, for example, Andrew R. L. Cayton and Peter S. Onuf, *The Midwest and the Nation: Rethinking the History of an American Region* (Bloomington: Indiana University, 1990).

90. Ridge, "Frederick Jackson Turner and His Ghost," in *Writing the History of the American West*, ed. George Miles (Worcester: American Antiquarian Society, 1991), 76.

91. "Revisiting the Vanishing Frontier: The Legacy of Frederick Jackson Turner," *Western Historical Quarterly* 18 (April 1987): 176. See also Cronon, "Turner's First Stand: The Significance of Significance in American History," in *Writing Western History: Essays on Major Western Historians*, ed. Richard W. Etulain (Albuquerque: University of New Mexico Press, 1991), 93–94; Cronon, George Miles, and Jay Gitlin, "Becoming West: Toward a New Meaning for Western History," in Cronon, Miles, and Gitlin, eds., *Under An Open Sky*, 6; Donald K. Pickens, "The Turner Thesis and Republicanism: A Historiographical Commentary," *Pacific Historical Review* 61 (August 1991): 319–40.

92. Kenneth T. Jackson, *Crabgrass Frontier: The Suburbanization of the United States* (New York: Oxford University Press, 1985).

93. Walter Russell Mead, "More Stars in Our Flag: A Modest Proposal for U.S. Policy after the Cold War," *World Policy Journal* 9 (Fall–Winter 1992): 587.

I

The Significance of the Frontier

1 Frederick Jackson Turner ◆ The Significance of the Frontier in American History

Greeted initially with indifference, Frederick Turner's address on "The Significance of the Frontier in American History" became the key paradigm in our century for explaining American history.* The popularity of Turner's thesis rested in part on its incorporation of popular ideas about the frontier and its importance. "Americans," as historian Ray Allen Billington noted, "had been aware of the significance of that frontier for generations."† It was the genius of the young professor from the University of Wisconsin, however, to bring several of those ideas together in a unified, compelling argument and so "postulate a completely new interpretation of American history."‡

Turner's thesis enjoyed widespread acceptance because it appealed to conventional wisdom, explained American virtues, and found the source of those virtues in America itself. In this respect, Turner's argument ran counter to the teachings of one of his graduate school mentors at Johns

From "The Significance of the Frontier in American History," *Annual Report of the American Historical Association . . . 1893* (Washington, DC: Government Printing Office, 1894): 199–227.

*We have abridged the essay and omitted Turner's notes entirely. His citations to the work of other scholars are dated, and researchers have easy access to the full essay, as in *History, Frontier, and Section: Three Essays by Frederick Jackson Turner*, ed. Martin Ridge (Albuquerque: University of New Mexico Press, 1993).

†Ray Allen Billington, *The Genesis of the Frontier Thesis: A Study in Historical Creativity* (San Marino, CA: Huntington Library, 1971), 71.

‡Ibid., 61.

Hopkins University, the Europeanist Herbert Baxter Adams, who sub-
scribed to what Turner refers to as the "germ theory of politics"—the
idea that traced the "germs" of American institutions to ancient Teutonic
tribes. Nineteenth-century Latin American intellectuals tended to be closer
to Adams's position than to Turner's, in the sense that they too saw
Europe as the wellspring of their civilization.

Born in Portage, Wisconsin, at a time that valued frontier virtues,
Frederick Jackson Turner (1861–1932) earned his B.A. and M.A. in his-
tory at the University of Wisconsin before pursuing the Ph.D. at Johns
Hopkins University (1888–1891). He returned to the University of Wis-
consin to teach until moving to Harvard University in 1910. In 1927, three
years after retiring from Harvard, he accepted a position as a research
scholar at the Huntington Library, San Marino, California. Turner's dis-
ciples remember him not only for his highly influential essay on the fron-
tier but also for the breadth and originality of his mind and for his early
espousal of multicausal, interdisciplinary approaches to the past that
*emphasized deep social and economic explanations.**

In a recent bulletin of the Superintendent of the Census for 1890 appear
these significant words: "Up to and including 1880 the country had a
frontier of settlement, but at present the unsettled area has been so broken
into by isolated bodies of settlement that there can hardly be said to be a
frontier line. In the discussion of its extent, its westward movement, etc.,
it can not, therefore, any longer have a place in the census reports." This
brief official statement marks the closing of a great historic movement.
Up to our own day American history has been in a large degree the history of the colonization of the Great West. The existence of an area of
free land, its continuous recession, and the advance of American settlement westward, explain American development.

Behind institutions, behind constitutional forms and modifications,
lie the vital forces that call these organs into life and shape them to meet
changing conditions. The peculiarity of American institutions is, the fact
that they have been compelled to adapt themselves to the changes of an
expanding people—to the changes involved in crossing a continent, in
winning a wilderness, and in developing at each area of this progress out
of the primitive economic and political conditions of the frontier into the
complexity of city life. Said [John C.] Calhoun in 1817, "We are great,
and rapidly—I was about to say fearfully—growing!" So saying, he
touched the distinguishing feature of American life. All peoples show
development; the germ theory of politics has been sufficiently emphasized. In the case of most nations, however, the development has occurred

*Ray Allen Billington's biography, *Frederick Jackson Turner: Historian,*
Scholar, Teacher (New York: Oxford University Press, 1973), 472–97.

in a limited area; and if the nation has expanded, it has met other growing peoples whom it has conquered. But in the case of the United States we have a different phenomenon. Limiting our attention to the Atlantic coast, we have the familiar phenomenon of the evolution of institutions in a limited area, such as the rise of representative government; the differentiation of simple colonial governments into complex organs; the progress from primitive industrial society, without division of labor, up to manufacturing civilization. But we have in addition to this a recurrence of the process of evolution in each western area reached in the process of expansion. Thus American development has exhibited not merely advance along a single line, but a return to primitive conditions on a continually advancing frontier line, and a new development for that area. American social development has been continually beginning over again on the frontier. This perennial rebirth, this fluidity of American life, this expansion westward with its new opportunities, its continuous touch with the simplicity of primitive society, furnish the forces dominating American character. The true point of view in the history of this nation is not the Atlantic coast, it is the great West. Even the slavery struggle, which is made so exclusive an object of attention by writers like Prof. [Hermann Eduard] von Holst, occupies its important place in American history because of its relation to westward expansion.

In this advance, the frontier is the outer edge of the wave—the meeting point between savagery and civilization. Much has been written about the frontier from the point of view of border warfare and the chase, but as a field for the serious study of the economist and the historian it has been neglected.

The American frontier is sharply distinguished from the European frontier—a fortified boundary line running through dense populations. The most significant thing about the American frontier is that it lies at the hither edge of free land. In the census reports it is treated as the margin of that settlement which has a density of two or more to the square mile. The term is an elastic one, and for our purposes does not need sharp definition. We shall consider the whole frontier belt, including the Indian country and the outer margin of the "settled area" of the census reports. This paper will make no attempt to treat the subject exhaustively; its aim is simply to call attention to the frontier as a fertile field for investigation, and to suggest some of the problems which arise in connection with it.

In the settlement of America we have to observe how European life entered the continent, and how America modified and developed that life and reacted on Europe. Our early history is the study of European germs developing in an American environment. Too exclusive attention has been paid by institutional students to the Germanic origins, too little to the

American factors. The frontier is the line of most rapid and effective Americanization. The wilderness masters the colonist. It finds him a European in dress, industries, tools, modes of travel, and thought. It takes him from the railroad car and puts him in the birch canoe. It strips off the garments of civilization and arrays him in the hunting shirt and the moccasin. It puts him in the log cabin of the Cherokee and Iroquois and runs an Indian palisade around him. Before long he has gone to planting Indian corn and plowing with a sharp stick; he shouts the war cry and takes the scalp in orthodox Indian fashion. In short, at the frontier the environment is at first too strong for the man. He must accept the conditions which it furnishes, or perish, and so he fits himself into the Indian clearings and follows the Indian trails. Little by little he transforms the wilderness, but the outcome is not the old Europe, not simply the development of Germanic germs, any more than the first phenomenon was a case of reversion to the Germanic mark. The fact is that here is a new product that is American. At first, the frontier was the Atlantic coast. It was the frontier of Europe in a very real sense. Moving westward, the frontier became more and more American. As successive terminal moraines result from successive glaciations, so each frontier leaves its traces behind it, and when it becomes a settled area the region still partakes of the frontier characteristics. Thus the advance of the frontier has meant a steady movement away from the influence of Europe, a steady growth of independence on American lines. And to study this advance, the men who grew up under these conditions, and the political, economic, and social results of it is to study the really American part of our history. . . .

The Frontier Furnishes a Field for Comparative Study of Social Development

At the Atlantic frontier one can study the germs of processes repeated at each successive frontier. We have the complex European life sharply precipitated by the wilderness into the simplicity of primitive conditions. The first frontier had to meet its Indian question, its question of the disposition of the public domain, of the means of intercourse with older settlements, of the extension of political organization, of religious and educational activity. And the settlement of these and similar questions for one frontier served as a guide for the next. The American student needs not to go to the "prim little townships of Sleswick" for illustrations of the law of continuity and development. For example, he may study the origin of our land policies in the colonial land policy; he may see how the system grew by adapting the statutes to the customs of the successive frontiers. He may see how the mining experience in the lead regions of Wisconsin, Illinois, and Iowa was applied to the mining laws of the Rockies, and how our Indian policy has been a series of experimentations on successive frontiers. Each tier of new States has found in the older ones material for its constitutions. Each frontier has made similar contributions to American character, as will be discussed farther on.

But with all these similarities there are essential differences, due to the place element and the time element. It is evident that the farming frontier of the Mississippi Valley presents different conditions from the mining frontier of the Rocky Mountains. The frontier reached by the Pacific Railroad, surveyed into rectangles, guarded by the United States Army, and recruited by the daily immigrant ship, moves forward at a swifter pace and in a different way than the frontier reached by the birch canoe or the pack horse. The geologist traces patiently the shores of ancient seas, maps their areas, and compares the older and the newer. It would be a work worth the historian's labors to mark these various frontiers and in detail compare one with another. Not only would there result a more adequate conception of American development and characteristics, but invaluable additions would be made to the history of society.

Loria, the Italian economist, has urged the study of colonial life as an aid in understanding the stages of European development, affirming that colonial settlement is for economic science what the mountain is for geology, bringing to light primitive stratifications. "America," he says, "has the key to the historical enigma which Europe has sought for centuries in vain, and the land which has no history reveals luminously the course of universal history." There is much truth in this. The United States lies like a huge page in the history of society. Line by line as we read this continental page from west to east we find the record of social evolution. It begins with the Indian and the hunter; it goes on to tell of the disintegration of savagery by the entrance of the trader, the pathfinder of civilization; we read the annals of the pastoral stage in ranch life; the exploitation of the soil by the raising of unrotated crops of corn and wheat in sparsely settled farming communities; the intensive culture of the denser farm settlement; and finally the manufacturing organization with city and factory system. This page is familiar to the student of census statistics, but how little of it has been used by our historians. Particularly in eastern States this page is a palimpsest. What is now a manufacturing State was in an earlier decade an area of intensive farming. Earlier yet it had been a wheat area, and still earlier the "range" had attracted the cattleherder. Thus Wisconsin, now developing manufacture, is a State with varied agricultural interests. But earlier it was given over to almost exclusive grain-raising, like North Dakota at the present time.

Each of these areas has had an influence in our economic and political history; the evolution of each into a higher stage has worked political transformations. But what constitutional historian has made any adequate attempt to interpret political facts by the light of these social areas and changes?

The Atlantic frontier was compounded of fisherman, fur-trader, miner, cattle-raiser, and farmer. Excepting the fisherman, each type of industry was on the march toward the West, impelled by an irresistible attraction. Each passed in successive waves across the continent. Stand at Cumberland Gap and watch the procession of civilization, marching single file—the buffalo following the trail to the salt springs, the Indian, the fur-trader and hunter, the cattle-raiser, the pioneer farmer—and the frontier has passed by. Stand at South Pass in the Rockies a century later and see the same procession with wider intervals between. The unequal rate of advance compels us to distinguish the frontier into the trader's frontier, the rancher's frontier, or the miner's frontier, and the farmer's frontier. When the mines and the cow pens were still near the fall line the traders' pack trains were tinkling across the Alleghenies, and the French on the Great Lakes were fortifying their posts, alarmed by the British trader's birch canoe. When the trappers scaled the Rockies, the farmer was still near the mouth of the Missouri.

The Indian Trader's Frontier

Why was it that the Indian trader passed so rapidly across the continent? What effects followed from the trader's frontier? The trade was coeval with American discovery. The Norsemen, Vespuccius [Amerigo Vespucci], [Giovanni da] Verrazano, [Henry] Hudson, John Smith, all trafficked for furs. The Plymouth pilgrims settled in Indian cornfields, and their first return cargo was of beaver and lumber. The records of the various New England colonies show how steadily exploration was carried into the wilderness by this trade. What is true for New England is, as would be expected, even plainer for the rest of the colonies. All along the coast from Maine to Georgia the Indian trade opened up the river courses. Steadily the trader passed westward, utilizing the older lines of French trade. The Ohio, the Great Lakes, the Mississippi, the Missouri, and the Platte, the lines of western advance, were ascended by traders. They found the passes in the Rocky Mountains and guided Lewis and Clark, [John C.] Fremont, and [John] Bidwell. The explanation of the rapidity of this advance is connected with the effects of the trader on the Indian. The trading post left the unarmed tribes at the mercy of those that had purchased fire-arms—a truth which the Iroquois Indians wrote in blood, and so the remote and unvisited tribes gave eager welcome to the trader. "The savages," wrote La Salle, "take better care of us French than of their own children; from us only can they get guns and goods." This accounts for the trader's power and the rapidity of his advance. Thus the disintegrating forces of civilization entered the wilderness. Every river valley and Indian trail became a fissure in Indian society, and so that society became honeycombed. Long before the pioneer farmer appeared on the scene, primitive Indian life had passed away. The farmers met Indians armed with guns. The trading frontier, while steadily undermining Indian power by making the tribes ultimately dependent on the whites, yet, through its sale of guns, gave to the Indians increased power of resistance to the farming frontier. French colonization was dominated by its trading frontier; English colonization by its farming frontier. There was an antagonism between the two frontiers as between the two nations. Said Duquesne to the Iroquois,

> Are you ignorant of the difference between the king of England and the king of France? Go see the forts that our king has established and you will see that you can still hunt under their very walls. They have been placed for your advantage in places which you frequent. The English, on the contrary, are no sooner in possession of a place than the game is driven away. The forest falls before them as they advance, and the soil is laid bare so that you can scarce find the wherewithal to erect a shelter for the night.

And yet, in spite of this opposition of the interests of the trader and the farmer, the Indian trade pioneered the way for civilization. The buffalo trail became the Indian trail, and this because the trader's "trace;" the trails widened into roads, and the roads into turnpikes, and these in turn were transformed into railroads. The same origin can be shown for the railroads of the South, the far West, and the Dominion of Canada. The trading posts reached by these trails were on the sites of Indian villages which had been placed in positions suggested by nature; and these trading posts, situated so as to command the water systems of the country, have grown into such cities as Albany, Pittsburg, Detroit, Chicago, St. Louis, Council Bluffs, and Kansas City. Thus civilization in America has followed the arteries made by geology, pouring an ever richer tide through them, until at last the slender paths of aboriginal intercourse have been broadened and interwoven into the complex mazes of modern commercial lines; the wilderness has been interpenetrated by lines of civilization growing ever more numerous. It is like the steady growth of a complex nervous system for the originally simple, inert continent. If one would understand why we are to-day one nation, rather than a collection of isolated states, he must study this economic and social consolidation of the country. In this progress from savage conditions lie topics for the evolutionist.

The effect of the Indian frontier as a consolidating agent in our history is important. From the close of the seventeenth century various intercolonial congresses have been called to treat with Indians and establish common measures of defense. Particularism was strongest in colonies with no Indian frontier. This frontier stretched along the western border like a cord of union. The Indian was a common danger, demanding united action. Most celebrated of these conferences was the Albany congress of 1754, called to treat with the Six Nations, and to consider plans of union. Even a cursory reading of the plan proposed by the congress reveals the importance of the frontier. The powers of the general council and the officers were, chiefly, the determination of peace and war with the Indians, the regulation of Indian trade, the purchase of Indian lands, and the creation and government of new settlements as a security against the Indians. It is evident that the unifying tendencies of the Revolutionary period were facilitated by the previous cooperation in the regulation of the frontier. In this connection may be mentioned the importance of the frontier, from that day to this, as a military training school, keeping alive the power of resistance to aggression, and developing the stalwart and rugged qualities of the frontiersman. . . .

Composite Nationality

First, we note that the frontier promoted the formation of a composite nationality for the American people. The coast was preponderantly English, but the later tides of continental immigration flowed across to the free lands. This was the case from the early colonial days. The Scotch Irish and the Palatine Germans, or "Pennsylvania Dutch," furnished the dominant element in the stock of the colonial frontier. With these peoples were also the freed indentured servants, or redemptioners, who at the expiration of their time of service passed to the frontier. Governor Spottswood [Alexander Spotswood] of Virginia writes in 1717, "The inhabitants of our frontiers are composed generally of such as have been transported hither as servants, and, being out of their time, settle themselves where land is to be taken up and that will produce the necessarys of life with little labour." Very generally these redemptioners were of non-English stock. In the crucible of the frontier the immigrants were Americanized, liberated, and fused into a mixed race, English in neither nationality or characteristics. The process has gone on from the early days to our own. [Edmund] Burke and other writers in the middle of the eighteenth century believed that Pennsylvania was "threatened with the danger of being wholly foreign in language, manners, and perhaps even inclinations." The German and Scotch-Irish elements in the frontier of the South were only less great. In the middle of the present century the German element in Wisconsin was already so considerable that leading publicists looked to the creation of a German state out of the common-wealth by concentrating their colonization. Such examples teach us to beware of misinterpreting the fact that there is a common English speech in America into a belief that the stock is also English.

Industrial Independence

In another way the advance of the frontier decreased our dependence on England. The coast, particularly of the South, lacked diversified indus-tries, and was dependent on England for the bulk of its supplies. In the South there was even a dependence on the Northern colonies for articles of food. Governor [James] Glenn, of South Carolina, writes in the middle of the eighteenth century:

> Our trade with New York and Philadelphia was of this sort, draining us of all the little money and bills we could gather from other places for their bread, flour, beer, hams, bacon, and other things of their produce, all which, except beer, our new townships begin to supply us with, which are settled with very industrious and thriving Germans. This no doubt diminishes the number of shipping and the appearance of our trade, but it is far from being a detriment to us.

Before long the frontier created a demand for merchants. As it re-treated from the coast it became less and less possible for England to bring her supplies directly to the consumer's wharfs, and carry away staple crops, and staple crops began to give way to diversified agriculture for a time. The effect of this phase of the frontier action upon the northern section is perceived when we realize how the advance of the frontier aroused seaboard cities like Boston, New York, and Baltimore, to engage in rivalry for what [George] Washington called "the extensive and valu-able trade of a rising empire."

Effects on National Legislation

The legislation which most developed the powers of the National Gov-ernment, and played the largest part in its activity, was conditioned on the frontier. Writers have discussed the subjects of tariff, land, and internal improvement, as subsidiary to the slavery question. But when American history comes to be rightly viewed it will be seen that the slavery ques-tion is an incident. In the period from the end of the first half of the present century to the close of the civil war slavery rose to primary, but far from exclusive, importance. But this does not justify Dr. von Holst (to take an example) in treating our constitutional history in its formative period down to 1828 in a single volume, giving six volumes chiefly to the history of slavery from 1828 to 1861, under the title *Constitutional History of the United States*. The growth of nationalism and the evolution of American political institutions were dependent on the advance of the frontier. Even so recent a writer as [James Ford] Rhodes, in his *History of the United States since the Compromise of 1850*, has treated the legislation called out by the western advance as incidental to the slavery struggle.

This is a wrong perspective. The pioneer needed the goods of the coast, and so the grand series of internal improvement and railroad legislation began, with potent nationalizing effects. Over internal improvements occurred great debates, in which grave constitutional questions were discussed. Sectional groupings appear in the votes, profoundly significant for the historian. Loose construction increased as the nation marched westward. But the West was not content with bringing the farm to the factory. Under the lead of [Henry] Clay—"Harry of the West"—protective tariffs were passed, with the cry of bringing the factory to the farm. The disposition of the public lands was a third important subject of national legislation influenced by the frontier.

The Public Domain

The public domain has been a force of profound importance in the nationalization and development of the government. The effects of the struggle of the landed and the landless States, and of the ordinance of 1787, need no discussion. Administratively the frontier called out some of the highest and most vitalizing activities of the general government. The purchase of Louisiana was perhaps the constitutional turning point in the history of the Republic, inasmuch as it afforded both a new area for national legislation and the occasion of the downfall of the policy of strict construction. But the purchase of Louisiana was called out by frontier needs and demands. As frontier States accrued to the Union the national power grew. In a speech on the dedication of the Calhoun monument Mr. [Lucius Quintus Cincinnatus] Lamar explained: "In 1789 the States were the creators of the Federal Government; in 1861 the Federal Government was the creator of a large majority of the States."

When we consider the public domain from the point of view of the sale and disposal of the public lands we are again brought face to face with the frontier. The policy of the United States in dealing with its lands is in sharp contrast with the European system of scientific administration. Efforts to make this domain a source of revenue, and to withhold it from emigrants in order that settlement might be compact, were in vain. The jealousy and the fears of the East were powerless in the face of the demands of the frontiersmen. John Quincy Adams was obliged to confess: "My own system of administration, which was to make the national domain the inexhaustible fund for progressive and unceasing internal improvement, has failed." The reason is obvious; a system of administration was not what the West demanded; it wanted land. Adams states the situation as follows: "The slaveholders of the South have bought the cooperation of the western country by the bribe of the western lands, abandoning to the new Western States their own proportion of the public property and aiding them in the design of grasping all the lands into their own hands." Thomas H. Benton was the author of this system, which he brought forward as a substitute for the American system of Mr. Clay, and to supplant him as the leading statesman of the West. Mr. Clay, by his tariff compromise with Mr. Calhoun, abandoned his own American system. At the same time he brought forward a plan for distributing among all the States of the Union the proceeds of the sales of the public lands. His bill for that purpose passed both Houses of Congress, but was vetoed by President [Andrew] Jackson, who, in his annual message of December, 1832, formally recommended that all public lands should be gratuitously given away to individual adventurers and to the States in which the lands are situated.

"No subject," said Henry Clay, "which has presented itself to the present, or perhaps any preceding, Congress, is of greater magnitude than that of the public lands." When we consider the far-reaching effects of the Government's land policy upon political, economic, and social aspects of American life, we are disposed to agree with him. But this legislation was framed under frontier influences, and under the lead of Western statesmen like Benton and Jackson. Said Senator Scott of Indiana in 1841: "I consider the preemption law merely declaratory of the custom or common law of the settlers."

National Tendencies of the Frontier

It is safe to say that the legislation with regard to land, tariff, and internal improvements—the American system of the nationalizing Whig party— was conditioned on frontier ideas and needs. But it was not merely in legislative action that the frontier worked against the sectionalism of the coast. The economic and social characteristics of the frontier worked against sectionalism. The men of the frontier had closer resemblances to the Middle region than to either of the other sections. Pennsylvania had been the seed-plot of frontier emigration, and, although she passed on her settlers along the Great Valley into the west of Virginia and the Carolinas, yet the industrial society of these Southern frontiersmen was always more like that of the Middle region than like that of the tide-water portion of the South, which later came to spread its industrial type throughout the South.

The Middle region, entered by New York harbor, was an open door to all Europe. The tide-water part of the South represented typical Englishmen, modified by a warm climate and servile labor, and living in baronial fashion on great plantations; New England stood for a special English movement—Puritanism. The Middle region was less English than the other sections. It had a wide mixture of nationalities, a varied society, the mixed town and county system of local government, a varied economic life, many religious sects. In short, it was a region mediating between New England and the South, and the East and the West. It represented that composite nationality which the contemporary United States exhibits, that juxtaposition of non-English groups, occupying a valley or a little settlement, and presenting reflections of the map of Europe in their variety. It was democratic and nonsectional, if not national; "easy, tolerant, and contented;" rooted strongly in material prosperity. It was typical of the modern United States. It was least sectional, not only because it lay between North and South, but also because with no barriers to shut out its frontiers from its settled region, and with a system of connecting waterways, the Middle region mediated between East and West as well as between North and South. Thus it became the typically American region. Even the New Englander, who was shut out from the frontier by the Middle region, tarrying in New York or Pennsylvania on his westward march, lost the acuteness of his sectionalism on the way.

The spread of cotton culture into the interior of the South finally broke down the contrast between the "tide-water" region and the rest of the State, and based Southern interests on slavery. Before this process revealed its results the western portion of the South, which was akin to Pennsylvania in stock, society, and industry, showed tendencies to fall away from the faith of the fathers into internal improvement legislation and nationalism. In the Virginia convention of 1829–'30, called to revise the constitution, Mr. [Benjamin Watkins] Leigh, of Chesterfield, one of the tide-water counties, declared:

> One of the main causes of discontent which led to this convention, that which had the strongest influence in overcoming our veneration for the work of our fathers, which taught us to contemn the sentiments of Henry

and Mason and Pendleton, which weaned us from our reverence for the constituted authorities of the State, was an overweening passion for internal improvement. I say this with perfect knowledge, for it has been avowed to me by gentlemen from the West over and over again. And let me tell the gentleman from Albemarle (Mr. Gordon) that it has been another principal object of those who set this ball of revolution in motion, to overturn the doctrine of State rights, of which Virginia has been the very pillar, and to remove the barrier she has interposed to the interference of the Federal Government in that same work of internal improvement, by so reorganizing the legislature that Virginia, too, may be hitched to the Federal car.

It was this nationalizing tendency of the West that transformed the democracy of [Thomas] Jefferson into the national republicanism of [James] Monroe and the democracy of Andrew Jackson. The West of the war of 1812, the West of Clay, and Benton, and [William Henry] Harrison, and Andrew Jackson, shut off by the Middle States and the mountains from the coast sections, had a solidarity of its own with national tendencies. On the tide of the Father of Waters, North and South met and mingled into a nation. Interstate migration went steadily on—a process of cross-fertilization of ideas and institutions. The fierce struggle of the sections over slavery on the western frontier does not diminish the truth of this statement; it proves the truth of it. Slavery was a sectional trait that would not down, but in the West it could not remain sectional. It was the greatest of frontiersmen who declared: "I believe this Government can not endure permanently half slave and half free. It will become all of one thing or all of the other." Nothing works for nationalism like intercourse within the nation. Mobility of population is death to localism, and the western frontier worked irresistibly in unsettling population. The effects reached back from the frontier and affected profoundly the Atlantic coast and even the Old World.

Growth of Democracy

But the most important effect of the frontier has been in the promotion of democracy here and in Europe. As has been indicated, the frontier is productive of individualism. Complex society is precipitated by the wilderness into a kind of primitive organization based on the family. The tendency is anti-social. It produces antipathy to control, and particularly to any direct control. The tax-gatherer is viewed as a representative of oppression. Prof. Osgood, in an able article, has pointed out that the frontier conditions prevalent in the colonies are important factors in the explanation of the American Revolution, where individual liberty was sometimes confused with absence of all effective government. The same conditions aid in explaining the difficulty of instituting a strong government in the period of the confederacy. The frontier individualism has from the beginning promoted democracy.

The frontier States that came into the Union in the first quarter of a century of its existence came in with democratic suffrage provisions, and had reactive effects of the highest importance upon the older States whose peoples were being attracted there. An extension of the franchise became essential. It was *western* New York that forced an extension of suffrage in the constitutional convention of that State in 1821; and it was *western* Virginia that compelled the tide-water region to put a more liberal suffrage provision in the constitution framed in 1830, and to give to the frontier region a more nearly proportionate representation with the tide-water aristocracy. The rise of democracy as an effective force in the nation came in with western preponderance under Jackson and William Henry Harrison, and it meant the triumph of the frontier—with all of its good and with all of its evil elements. An interesting illustration of the tone of frontier democracy in 1830 comes from the same debates in the Virginia convention already referred to. A representative from western Virginia declared:

> But, sir, it is not the increase of population in the West which this gentleman ought to fear. It is the energy which the mountain breeze and western habits impart to those emigrants. They are regenerated, politically I mean, sir. They soon become *working politicians*; and the difference, sir, between a *talking* and a *working* politician is immense. The Old Dominion has long been celebrated for producing great orators; the ablest metaphysicians in policy; men that can split hairs in all abstruse questions of political economy. But at home, or when they return from Congress, they have negroes to fan them asleep. But a Pennsylvania, a New York, an Ohio, or a western Virginia statesman, though far inferior in logic, metaphysics, and rhetoric to an old Virginia statesman, has this advantage, that when he returns home he takes off his coat and takes hold of the plow. This gives him bone and muscle, sir, and preserves his republican principles pure and uncontaminated.

So long as free land exists, the opportunity for a competency exists, and economic power secures political power. But the democracy born of free land, strong in selfishness and individualism, intolerant of administrative experience and education, and pressing individual liberty beyond its proper bounds, has its dangers as well as its benefits. Individualism in America has allowed a laxity in regard to governmental affairs which has rendered possible the spoils system and all the manifest evils that follow from the lack of a highly developed civic spirit. In this connection may be noted also the influence of frontier conditions in permitting lax business honor, inflated paper currency and wild-cat banking. The colonial and revolutionary frontier was the region whence emanated many of the worst forms of an evil currency. The West in the war of 1812 repeated the phenomenon on the frontier of that day, while the speculation and wild-cat banking of the period of the crisis of 1837 occurred on the new frontier belt of the next tier of States. Thus each one of the periods of lax financial integrity coincides with periods when a new set of frontier communities had arisen, and coincides in area with these successive frontiers, for the most part. The recent Populist agitation is a case in point. Many a State that now declines any connection with the tenets of the Populists, itself adhered to such ideas in an earlier stage of the development of the State. A primitive society can hardly be expected to show the intelligent appreciation of the complexity of business interests in a developed society. The continual recurrence of these areas of paper-money agitation is another evidence that the frontier can be isolated and studied as a factor in American history of the highest importance.

Attempts to Check and Regulate the Frontier

The East has always feared the result of an unregulated advance of the frontier, and has tried to check and guide it. The English authorities would have checked settlement at the headwaters of the Atlantic tributaries and allowed the "savages to enjoy their deserts in quiet lest the peltry trade should decrease." This called out Burke's splendid protest:

> If you stopped your grants, what would be the consequence? The people would occupy without grants. They have already so occupied in many places. You can not station garrisons in every part of these deserts. If you drive the people from one place, they will carry on their annual tillage and remove with their flocks and herds to another. Many of the people in the back settlements are already little attached to particular situations. Already they have topped the Appalachian mountains. From thence they behold before them an immense plain, one vast, rich, level meadow; a square of five hundred miles. Over this they would wander without a possibility of restraint; they would change their manners with their habits of life; would soon forget a government by which they were disowned; would become hordes of English Tartars; and, pouring down upon your unfortified frontiers a fierce and irresistible cavalry, become masters of your governors and your counselors, your collectors and comptrollers, and of all the slaves that adhered to them. Such would, and in no long time must, be the effect of attempting to forbid as a crime and to suppress as an evil the command and blessing of Providence, "Increase and multiply." Such would be the happy result of an endeavor to keep as a lair of wild beasts that earth which God, by an express charter, has given to the children of men.

But the English Government was not alone in its desire to limit the advance of the frontier and guide its destinies. Tide-water Virginia and

South Carolina gerrymandered those colonies to insure the dominance of the coast in their legislatures. Washington desired to settle a State at a time in the Northwest; Jefferson would reserve from settlement the territory of his Louisiana purchase north of the thirty-second parallel, in order to offer it to the Indians in exchange for their settlements east of the Mississippi. "When we shall be full on this side," he writes, "we may lay off a range of States on the western bank from the head to the mouth, and so range after range, advancing compactly as we multiply." [James] Madison went so far as to argue to the French minister that the United States had no interest in seeing population extend itself on the right bank of the Mississippi, but should rather fear it. When the Oregon question was under debate, in 1824, [Alexander] Smyth, of Virginia, would draw an unchangeable line for the limits of the United States at the outer limit of two tiers of States beyond the Mississippi, complaining that the seaboard States were being drained of the flower of their population by the bringing of too much land into market. Even Thomas Benton, the man of widest views of the destiny of the West, at this stage of his career declared that along the ridge of the Rocky mountains "the western limits of the Republic should be drawn, and the statue of the fabled god Terminus should be raised upon its highest peak, never to be thrown down." But the attempts to limit the boundaries, to restrict land sales and settlement, and to deprive the West of its share of political power were all in vain. Steadily the frontier of settlement advanced and carried with it individualism, democracy, and nationalism, and powerfully affected the East and the Old World.

Missionary Activity

The most effective efforts of the East to regulate the frontier came through its educational and religious activity, exerted by interstate migration and by organized societies. Speaking in 1835, Dr. Lyman Beecher declared: "It is equally plain that the religious and political destiny of our nation is to be decided in the West," and he pointed out that the population of the West

> is assembled from all the States of the Union and from all the nations of Europe, and is rushing in like the waters of the flood, demanding for its moral preservation the immediate and universal action of those institutions which discipline the mind and arm the conscience and the heart. And so various are the opinions and habits, and so recent and imperfect is the acquaintance, and so sparse are the settlements of the West, that no homogeneous public sentiment can be formed to legislate immediately into being the requisite institutions. And yet they are all needed immediately in their utmost perfection and power. A nation is being "born in a day." . . . But what will become of the West if her prosperity

rushes up to such a majesty of power, while those great institutions linger which are necessary to form the mind and the conscience and the heart of that vast world. It must not be permitted. . . . Let no man at the East quiet himself and dream of liberty, whatever may become of the West. . . . Her destiny is our destiny.

With the appeal to the conscience of New England, he adds appeals to her fears lest other religious sects anticipate her own. The New England preacher and school-teacher left their mark on the West. The dread of Western emancipation from New England's political and economic control was paralleled by her fears lest the West cut loose from her religion. Commenting in 1850 on reports that settlement was rapidly extending northward in Wisconsin, the editor of the *Home Missionary* writes: "We scarcely know whether to rejoice or mourn over this extension of our settlements. While we sympathize in whatever tends to increase the physical resources and prosperity of our country, we can not forget that with all these dispersions into remote and still remoter corners of the land the supply of the means of grace is becoming relatively less and less." Acting in accordance with such ideas, home missions were established and Western colleges were erected. As seaboard cities like Philadelphia, New York, and Baltimore strove for the mastery of Western trade, so the various denominations strove for the possession of the West. Thus an intellectual stream from New England sources fertilized the West. Other sections sent their missionaries; but the real struggle was between sects. The contest for power and the expansive tendency furnished to the various sects by the existence of a moving frontier must have had important results on the character of religious organization in the United States. The multiplication of rival churches in the little frontier towns had deep and lasting social effects. The religious aspects of the frontier make a chapter in our history which needs study.

Intellectual Traits

From the conditions of frontier life came intellectual traits of profound importance. The works of travelers along each frontier from colonial days onward describe certain common traits, and these traits have, while softening down, still persisted as survivals in the place of their origin, even when a higher social organization succeeded. The result is that to the frontier the American intellect owes its striking characteristics. That coarseness and strength combined with acuteness and inquisitiveness; that practical, inventive turn of mind, quick to find expedients; that masterful grasp of material things, lacking in the artistic but powerful to effect great ends; that restless, nervous energy; that dominant individualism, working for good and for evil, and withal that buoyancy and exuberance which comes with freedom—these are traits of the frontier, or traits called out elsewhere because of the existence of the frontier. Since the days when the fleet of Columbus sailed into the waters of the New World, America has been another name for opportunity, and the people of the United States have taken their tone from the incessant expansion which has not only been open but has even been forced upon them. He would be a rash prophet who should assert that the expansive character of American life has now entirely ceased. Movement has been its dominant fact, and, unless this training has no effect upon a people, the American energy will continually demand a wider field for its exercise. But never again will such gifts of free land offer themselves. For a moment, at the frontier, the bonds of custom are broken and unrestraint is triumphant. There is not *tabula rasa*. The stubborn American environment is there with its imperious summons to accept its conditions; the inherited ways of doing things are also there; and yet, in spite of environment, and in spite of custom, each frontier did indeed furnish a new field of opportunity, a gate of escape from the bondage of the past; and freshness, and confidence, and scorn of older society, impatience of its restraints and its ideas, and indifference to its lessons, have accompanied the frontier. What the Mediterranean Sea was to the Greeks, breaking the bond of custom, offering new experiences, calling out new institutions and activities, that, and more, the ever retreating frontier has been to the United States directly, and to the nations of Europe more remotely. And now, four centuries from the discovery of America, at the end of a hundred years of life under the Constitution, the frontier has gone, and with its going has closed the first period of American history.

2 Arthur S. Aiton ◆ Latin-American Frontiers

Arthur S. Aiton (b. 1893) was one of the first North American historians to assess the role of frontiers in Latin America along Turnerian lines. He earned his doctorate at the University of California at Berkeley, where he studied under the direction of Herbert Eugene Bolton. A professor of history at the University of Michigan for many years, Aiton was best known for his outstanding biography of Antonio de Mendoza, the first viceroy of Mexico. In this paper, delivered at the 1940 annual meeting of the Canadian Historical Association, he provided a brief overview of Hispanic advance into the Western Hemisphere and offered eight general conclusions concerning "the nature and influence of the frontier on the evolution of societies to the south of us."

Undeterred by lack of research on his subject, Aiton argued that the main stages of frontier development were clear. During the colonial era, when Spanish and Portuguese officials promoted the steady movement of pioneers into relatively unoccupied lands, frontiers in Latin America most closely approximated the expanding Anglo-American West. With the winning of independence and the emergence of separate states, however, the unity imposed by imperial rule disappeared. Some movement continued along the frontiers of colonial times but without central direction and regulation. By the late nineteenth century, foreign capital and immigration renewed frontier expansion in Argentina, Chile, and Uruguay. In the twentieth century, Aiton observed that throughout Latin America arable land still beckoned the frontiersmen, but excessive urbanization was producing a countermovement away from the marginal areas of earlier settlement. These so-called hollow frontiers were especially evident in Brazil, where, for example, the withdrawal of pioneers from marginal coffee lands to the more profitable regions of cotton growth had left deserted strips behind the new frontier.* While more recent scholarship has confirmed some of Aiton's sweeping generalizations, little evidence

From *Canadian Historical Association Report, 1940* (Ottawa: Canadian Historical Association, 1940): 100–104. Reprinted by permission of the Canadian Historical Association/Société Historique du Canada.

*Geographer Preston E. James was the first to coin the term "hollow frontier." In *Latin America* (New York: Odyssey Press, 1942), he wrote:

> Today the urban nucleus of a Latin American area of settlement exerts such a strong attraction that the tendency is for people to move in toward the center rather than to expand the frontier into a new pioneer zone. There are many expanding frontiers in Latin America, but most of them are hollow ones, that is, they represent waves of exploitation moving across a country, followed by abandonment and population decline. (p. 5)

*had emerged to support his assertion that "frontier conditions in Latin
America, as elsewhere, developed individualism, self-reliance, democracy
initiative, and a willingness to experiment despite closer control" (see
Zavala, Selection 5).*

S pain and her little neighbour Portugal were the first European nations
to establish frontiers of settlement in the Americas. The study of these
frontiers is rich in parallels and contrasts for the student of the movement
of colonization in the regions of North America—where French and English frontiers expanded to produce present-day Canada and the United
States, with their characteristic institutions, sectional differences, and
cultural complexes. While no Turner has as yet appeared to interpret the
larger implications of the far-flung pioneer areas of European settlement
in "Greater America," contributions toward such an all-inclusive thesis
can be made on the basis of the evidence now available. Professor Bolton
has already made important contributions towards such a synthesis. The
present paper is an attempt to present a general outline of the Hispanic
advance into the continents, together with some general conclusions as to
the nature and influence of the frontier on the evolution of societies to the
south of us. The main stages are clear. Further detail will only serve to
confirm or correct our reading of the record now in hand, as the archives
continue to yield their contents to systematic and persistent search. The
key to a better understanding in the Americas lies in this direction. If we
can find the motivating forces and the historical influences which have
shaped the present pattern of peoples and relations, and properly appreciate the common experience of the conquest of the wilderness, we shall, I
believe, be in a better position to bridge the gaps of linguistic, geographical, cultural, and nationalistic variations, in that, despite rivalries and
differences, we have a common heritage, namely, the great American
adventure—the settlement of the New World.

Spain embarked on the conquest and settlement of new lands in the
"Ocean-Sea" of the West with centuries of experience in the long reconquest of the Iberian Peninsula behind her effort. Her entry into America
coincided with the capture of Granada in Spain and released the trained
forces of that frontier to the tremendous task of American exploration
and settlement. Expert officials, completely developed frontier institutions, military methods, and a whole policy and polity, developed in the
Moslem wars, were ready when that frontier was projected overseas in
the astounding conquest of the Indies. The first stages, under the direction of "the Admiral" and his successors in the Greater Antilles, were
characterized by violence, and destruction. Nevertheless, tropical colonies were successfully established and the whole range of useful Euro-

pean plant and animal life was introduced. It was a self-critical age in
Spain and the mistakes made were studied and remedies applied. African
slaves had to be introduced to take the place of the vanishing native in the
West Indies, so a great programme to conserve the native element was
initiated, which bore fruit on the continental frontiers in a high percentage of Indian survival.

From these West Indian bases the Spaniards explored in every direction, and the realities of American geography caused the dream of a short
route to India to fade as the opportunity at hand became apparent. The
existence of groups of sedentary Indians who had achieved superior cultural levels gave both direction and character to frontiers of Spain on the
continents. The semi-civilized Nahuas of the central valley of Mexico,
with clustering lesser cultures; the Mayans of Yucatán and Central
America; the Chibchas of Upland Colombia; the Incas of Peru; and the
Pueblo Indians of Arizona and New Mexico inevitably attracted the Spanish conquistadores toward their centres of culture and accumulated wealth.
In a series of lightning strokes, aided by surprise and the tremendous superiority accorded by steel weapons and armour, horses, artillery, and the
thundering harquebus, the intruders were amazingly successful. Relatively
small numbers of Spaniards under audacious leaders moved swiftly inland from coastal bases, making adroit use of "fifth columns" of dissatis-
fied or rival Indian groups. It should be stressed that the Indians of America
played an important role in their own conquest as allies of the invading
Europeans. It was common procedure, after Cortés seized Montezuma in
Mexico, to capture the head of the government and paralyse resistance at
the centre. From these capitals the conquest spread out under lesser leaders throughout the surrounding areas. The Spaniards, once masters, superimposed their rule and institutions from the top on the existing native
social, economic, and political structures which were, in the main, undisturbed save in the field of religion where the Cross, moving in side by
side with the sword, helped in a vigorous substitution of Christianity for
a multiplicity of older faiths. The church may be said to have exerted a
restraining and moderating influence on the conquest. Due to its influence the Indian found a definite place in the new society; Indian slavery
was prohibited; and the harsh personal service features of the *repartimiento*
gave way to the *encomienda*, as a mere right to collect tribute, under close
supervision aimed to obviate abuses. Nuclei of Spaniards as a ruling class
were floated on the great mass of the Indian population, with definite
castes gradually emerging in between the two, as racial intermixture produced the *mestizo*, *mulato*, the *Zambo*, and other lesser combinations of
the racial strains. Spanish life in all its richness was transplanted to these
regions from university, hospital, and printing press to pure food laws,

sale taxes, and cart roads. Out beyond lay the wide borderlands of roving tribes and exposed frontiers. After the first great exploring rush through eighty degrees of American latitude, which revealed no further Indian societies comparable to Mexico and Peru, the Spanish advance in the Americas settled down to the slower pace of the natural movement of the cattle, mining, and missionary frontiers. This process in the late sixteenth, the seventeenth, and eighteenth centuries exhibits features of frontier movement into pioneer zones of relatively unoccupied lands which offer the best comparisons with our more familiar Anglo-American frontier.

This phase of the history of Latin-American frontiers saw great captains, *Adelantados*, like proprietary governors, assume the expense of conquest and settlement in return for special privileges. The occupation of northern Mexico (Nueva Vizcaya, Nuevo Leon, Nuevo México) offers especially good examples of this frontier device. The *rancho*, mission, *presidio*, and *pueblo* are characteristic institutions used on these frontiers. Mining towns (*reales de minas*) and mining rushes to areas of new strikes are frequent phenomena observed throughout. A high degree of government direction, in an elaborately developed system of centralized administrative control, gives these frontiers a unity lacking in comparable English or French frontiers. Each new province is entered with government permission, all expeditions are licensed, and even missionaries only undertake the conversion of Indian groups with the permission of the Crown. Frontier towns (*pueblos*) are laid out in conformance with general law, and, rather difficult to credit, frontier military posts (*presidios*) are laid out and equipped in accordance with printed specifications. In the eighteenth century the government assumed the expense of founding and maintaining defensive frontiers like California and Texas. The work of the great religious orders, such as the Franciscan and Jesuit orders, cannot be over-emphasized in the frontier mission field. Brown robes and black robes not only converted and instructed the Indian but they also served as potent agents of frontier expansion and their influence on the social and economic life of the outpost areas is pre-eminent. In their schools and churches they extended the sway and influence of Spain and left behind them lasting monuments in the persistence of the way of life they taught. Men like Father Salvatierra in Lower California, Father Kino in Arizona, and Father Serra in Upper California, were more valuable to Spain than regiments of troops. The imprint of Spain is clearly visible today in the lands they conquered—while law, language, religion, folklore, customs, and the livestock, even to methods of handling them, reflect the potency of Spain's thrust in the American south-west over which other frontiers have swept and over which another flag floats today.

Portugal, farther removed from the Moorish reconquest than Spain, also entered her field of colonizing activity in Brazil over three decades after her rival had initiated the settlement of Española. Moreover, Portugal brought to bear on her problem the knowledge gained by prior occupation of the Atlantic Islands and the building of her great trade empire around Africa to the Far East. Portugal founded coastal colonies from the Amazon to Rio Grande do Sul under a system of proprietory grants with a gradual process of royalization creating a line of crown colonies under loose central control which can be compared to that in the English colonies. In Brazil, tropical colonies, producing sugar with slave labour, clung tenaciously to the coast, save in the south, where hardy Paulista pioneers, of mixed Portuguese and Indian blood, blazed trails into the vast interior of the continent. Only the belated discovery of gold and diamonds in the provinces of Minas Geraes [Gerais] and Diamantina led to any great movement of frontiers into the hinterland, in the eighteenth century, following the footsteps of Jesuit and slave-hunting predecessors. Official government explorers pushed far beyond the areas of settlement and the work of these brilliant flag-bearers—the *bandeirantes* won half a continent for little Portugal before the close of the colonial period.

The wars of independence in Latin America in the second and third decades of the nineteenth century witnessed the separation of the colonies of Spain and Portugal from the mother countries with the exception of Cuba and Puerto Rico. About twenty million people were involved in the change and, while Brazil remained a unit, Spanish America split into the score of nations of today, along the lines of old administrative areas of colonial days. With this change the unity of the frontier ends and, while old movements continued along the frontiers of colonial days, the central direction and regulation disappeared. National growth was substituted for imperial policy in the new nations. Disregarding the details, one notes, in the subsequent period, a remarkable advance in the former backward agricultural areas of the Spanish Empire now released from an excessive preoccupation with mineral production. Argentina with its broad *pampa*, Uruguay with its rolling plains, and Chile with its rich interior valley and northern nitrate beds forge ahead rapidly along the same road as the Anglo-American nations to the north. The same general factors are at work here. Foreign capital and foreign immigration have been determining factors. Invention and improvement of agricultural implements, the wind-mill, dry-farming methods, cheap fencing material, and above all, improvement in transportation facilities—roads and railroads making markets available—have permitted the conquest of the *pampa* and similar areas. New capital and the exploitation of hitherto unused resources such as oil, open wider horizons into the future. Already Latin America has passed the hundred million mark in population while Brazil, with a greater area than continental United States, bids fair to enter on a new and brilliant phase of its history as it poises on the edge of modern industrialization. Only the lack of coal and the dangers of external conquest, which now encompass all American nations, stand between them and realization. Great modern cities like Santiago, Rio de Janeiro, Buenos Aires, São Paulo, and Mexico City testify to the material progress which has been made.

Despite this the frontiers still exist and wide stretches of unoccupied but remote arable land beckon the frontiersman. Indeed, it might be said that while improved transportation and increased numbers of people have accelerated the pace of land occupancy they have also complicated the picture. While the pioneer fringes are shrinking in Latin America as the area of free land grows less, excessive urbanization has produced a countermovement away from the marginal areas of earlier settlement. In addition, the opening of new frontiers has drained population away from older areas in such fashion that, together with the attraction of the great cities, the curious phenomenon of "hollow frontiers" has been produced. This is especially noteworthy in Brazil where withdrawal from the marginal coffee lands to the more profitable regions of cotton growth has left deserted strips behind the new frontier. In the tropics, especially in and around the shores of the Caribbean, progress has been less spectacular and, in general, the areas of greatest colonial development are the relatively retarded regions of today. Oil and fruit, notably the banana, have provided recent frontiers of expansion in old and backward tropical nations.

When at some future date the historian, disregarding national boundaries and with the happy possession of the full documentation, is able to write the synthesis of the frontiers of European spread into the Americas, he will be able to trace the distribution of animals, of plants, of ideas, and techniques, in addition to the advance of mere humans, free from narrowly national considerations and unworried by the roll call of old wars and colonial and imperial rivalries. A summary statement of the four centuries and a half of Latin-American frontiers must necessarily be incomplete today—but certain conclusions about them are possible in the light of available information. These are, in brief, that, unlike the Anglo-American frontiers in certain aspects and like them in others:

(1) They were established, at the outset, by men already skilled in frontier methods.
(2) A series of vast settled areas of Indian political units were quickly overrun and strong imperial governments were set up which func-

tioned effectively over the greater portion of the land within fifty years of the discovery.

(3) There were no sea to sea movements of definite frontier lines passing through a series of physiographic regions.

(4) Only in cases like the movement into the Argentine *pampa*, the interior of Brazil, or the northward thrust from Mexico were large areas of a thinly populated character encountered.

(5) The native populations were not pushed back or destroyed but were generally subdued and incorporated into the expanding colonial society.

(6) The Latin-American frontiers were subjected to a higher degree of governmental control and supervision than comparable Anglo-American frontiers. It was, after the first stages, a planned rather than a haphazard advance.

(7) Better records were kept and when they are made available we shall have a more complete story of these southern frontiers than we shall ever possess for our own.

(8) Frontier conditions in Latin America, as elsewhere, developed individualism, self-reliance, democracy, initiative, and a willingness to experiment despite closer controls.

3 Domingo Faustino Sarmiento ◆ Frontier Barbarism

Domingo Faustino Sarmiento (1811–1888), writer, educator, and president of Argentina from 1868 to 1888, was one of the most influential leaders of his country. Born in the remote province of San Juan, he was working as a self-taught schoolteacher and journalist when Juan Manuel de Rosas seized power in Buenos Aires in 1829 in the name of the Federalist party. Identified with the opponents of Rosas—the Unitarians—and an eloquent critic of the ruthless dictator, Sarmiento spent most of the years until his overthrow in 1852 in exile agitating against him. Thus it was in Chile that he published his most famous work, Civilization and Barbarism: Life of Juan Facundo Quiroga *(1845), ostensibly a biography of one of Rosas's most vicious associates but, more significantly, an attack on Rosas himself.*

Sarmiento's volume, translated into English in 1868 as Life in the Argentine Republic in the Days of the Tyrants *is worth reading in its entirety because it combines a vivid description of Argentine geography and people with an insightful analysis of the causes of dictatorship. Literary critics celebrate the book for its vivid style and because Sarmiento, by borrowing from French romantic writers, broke free of allegiance to Spain's obsolete academic rules.* But the fame of* Facundo *rests primarily on the author's interpretation of the Rosas era as an epic struggle between civilization and barbarism—civilization represented by the city of Buenos Aires and the Unitarians and barbarism personified by Rosas and his gaucho supporters from the pampas. Sarmiento states this thesis clearly in the section that follows, taken from his introduction. Buenos Aires, he proclaims, is destined to be "the most gigantic city of either America." Its inhabitants "wear European dress, live in a civilized manner, and possess laws, ideas of progress, means of instruction, some municipal organization, regular forms of government, etc." Beyond the city, however, in the great pampas, everything "civilized" vanishes. The gauchos live without laws, schools, or religion, and this lack of life's amenities "induces all the externals of barbarism" until "society has altogether disappeared." In short, Sarmiento writes, before 1810 "two different kinds of civilization existed in the Argentine Republic; one being Spanish, European, and cultivated, the other barbarous, American, and almost wholly of native growth." Rosas, by seizing power in 1829, "applied the*

From *Life in the Argentine Republic in the Days of the Tyrants; or Civilization and Barbarism, from the Spanish of Domingo F. Sarmiento*, trans., with a biographic sketch, by Mrs. Horace Mann (New York, 1868), 5–55 passim.

*Emir Rodríguez Monegal, ed., *The Borzoi Anthology of Latin American Literature* (2 vols.; New York: Knopf, 1977), 1:224.

26

*knife of the gaucho to the culture of Buenos Aires, and destroyed the work
of centuries—of civilization, law and liberty."*

*This vision of the pernicious nature of the frontier in Argentina could
hardly be more different from Turner's view of its redeeming qualities in
the United States. Twentieth-century scholars have charged that as a
member of the urban elite, Sarmiento was too quick to reject the authentic folk traditions nurtured on the pampas, and that men such as Facundo
and Rosas were natural, charismatic leaders who inculcated local and
regional values.* These criticisms notwithstanding, Sarmiento's thesis
found wide acceptance among nineteenth-century Latin American intellectuals and still reverberates in contemporary writings.*

B uenos Ayres [*sic*] is destined to be some day the most gigantic city of
either America. Under a benignant climate, mistress of the naviga-
tion of a hundred rivers flowing past her feet, covering a vast area, and
surrounded by inland provinces which know no other outlet for their products, she would ere now have become the Babylon of America, if the
spirit of the Pampa had not breathed upon her, and left undeveloped the
rich offerings which the rivers and provinces should unceasingly bring.
She is the only city in the vast Argentine territory which is in communication with European nations; she alone can avail herself of the advantages of foreign commerce; she alone has power and revenue. Vainly have
the provinces asked to receive through her, civilization, industry, and
European population; a senseless colonial policy made her deaf to these
cries. But the provinces had their revenge when they sent to her in Rosas
the climax of their own barbarism.

The cities of Buenos Ayres and Cordova have succeeded better than
the others in establishing about them subordinate towns to serve as new
foci of civilization and municipal interests; a fact which deserves notice.
The inhabitants of the city wear the European dress, live in a civilized
manner, and possess laws, ideas of progress, means of instruction, some
municipal organization, regular forms of government, etc. Beyond the
precincts of the city everything assumes a new aspect; the country people
wear a different dress, which I will call South American, as it is common
to all districts; their habits of life are different, their wants peculiar and
limited. The people composing these two distinct forms of society, do not
seem to belong to the same nation. Moreover, the countryman, far from
attempting to imitate the customs of the city, rejects with disdain its luxury
and refinement; and it is unsafe for the costume of the city people, their
coats, their cloaks, their saddles, or anything European, to show themselves in the country. Everything civilized which the city contains is block-

*E. Bradford Burns, *Poverty of Progress* (Berkeley: University of California
Press, 1980), 90–93.

aded there, proscribed beyond its limits; and any one who should dare
to appear in the rural districts in a frock-coat, for example, or mounted
on an English saddle, would bring ridicule and brutal assaults upon
himself.

The whole remaining population inhabit the open country, which,
whether wooded or destitute of the larger plants, is generally level, and
almost everywhere occupied by pastures, in some places of such abundance and excellence, that the grass of an artificial meadow would not
surpass them. . . .

Nomad tribes do not exist in the Argentine plains; the stock-raiser is
a proprietor, living upon his own land; but this condition renders association impossible, and tends to scatter separate families over an immense
extent of surface. Imagine an expanse of two thousand square leagues,
inhabited throughout, but where the dwellings are usually four or even
eight leagues apart, and two leagues, at least, separate the nearest neighbors. The production of movable property is not impossible, the enjoy-
ments of luxury are not wholly incompatible with this isolation; wealth
can raise a superb edifice in the desert. But the incentive is wanting; no
example is near; the inducements for making a great display which exist
in a city, are not known in that isolation and solitude. Inevitable privations justify natural indolence; a dearth of all the amenities of life induces all the externals of barbarism. Society has altogether disappeared.
There is but the isolated self-concentrated feudal family. Since there is
no collected society, no government is possible; there is neither municipal nor executive power, and civil justice has no means of reaching criminals. I doubt if the modern world presents any other form of association
so monstrous as this. . . .

Moral progress, and the cultivation of the intellect, are here not only
neglected, as in the Arab or Tartar tribe, but impossible. Where can a
school be placed for the instruction of children living ten leagues apart in
all directions? Thus, consequently, civilization can in no way be brought
about. Barbarism is the normal condition, and it is fortunate if domestic
customs preserve a small germ of morality. Religion feels the consequences
of this want of social organization. The offices of the pastor are nominal,
the pulpit has no audience, the priest flees from the deserted chapel, or
allows his character to deteriorate in inactivity and solitude. Vice, simony,
and the prevalent barbarism penetrate his cell, and change his moral
superiority into the means of gratifying his avarice or ambition, and he
ends by becoming a party leader. . . .

In the absence of all the means of civilization and progress, which
can only be developed among men collected into societies of many individuals, the education of the country people is as follows: The women

look after the house, get the meals ready, shear the sheep, milk the cows, make the cheese, and weave the coarse cloth used for garments. All domestic occupations are performed by women; on them rests the burden of all the labor, and it is an exceptional favor when some of the men undertake the cultivation of a little maize, bread not being in use as an ordinary article of diet. The boys exercise their strength and amuse themselves by gaining skill in the use of the lasso and the bolas, with which they constantly harass and pursue the calves and goats. When they can ride, which is as soon as they have learned to walk, they perform some small services on horseback. When they become stronger, they race over the country, falling off their horses and getting up again, tumbling on purpose into rabbit burrows, scrambling over precipices, and practicing feats of horsemanship. On reaching puberty, they take to breaking wild colts, and death is the least penalty that awaits them if their strength or courage fails them for a moment. With early manhood comes complete independence and idleness.

Now begins the public life of the gaucho, as I may say, since his education is by this time at an end. These men, Spaniards only in their language and in the confused religious notions preserved among them, must be seen, before a right estimate can be made of the indomitable and haughty character which grows out of this struggle of isolated man with untamed nature, of the rational being with the brute. It is necessary to see their visages bristling with beards, their countenances as grave and serious as those of the Arabs of Asia, to appreciate the pitying scorn with which they look upon the sedentary denizen of the city, who may have read many books, but who cannot overthrow and slay a fierce bull, who could not provide himself with a horse from the pampas, who has never met a tiger alone, and received him with a dagger in one hand and a poncho rolled up in the other, to be thrust into the animal's mouth, while he transfixes his heart with his dagger.

This habit of triumphing over resistance, of constantly showing a superiority to Nature, of defying and subduing her, prodigiously develops the consciousness of individual consequence and superior prowess. The Argentine people of every class, civilized and ignorant alike, have a high opinion of their national importance. All the other people of South America throw this vanity of theirs in their teeth, and take offense at their presumption and arrogance. I believe the charge not to be wholly unfounded, but I do not object to the trait. Alas, for the nation without faith in itself! Great things were not made for such a people. To what extent may not the independence of that part of America be due to the arrogance of these Argentine gauchos, who have never seen anything beneath the sun superior to themselves in wisdom or in power? The European is in their eyes the most contemptible of all men, for a horse gets the better of him in a couple of plunges. . . .

Country life, then, has developed all the physical but none of the intellectual powers of the gaucho. His moral character is of the quality to be expected from his habit of triumphing over the obstacles and the forces of nature; it is strong, haughty, and energetic. Without instruction, and indeed without need of any, without means of support as without wants, he is happy in the midst of his poverty and privations, which are not such to one who never knew nor wished for greater pleasures than are his already. Thus if the disorganization of society among the gauchos deeply implants barbarism in their natures, through the impossibility and use-lessness of moral and intellectual education, it has, too, its attractive side to him. The gaucho does not labor; he finds his food and raiment ready to his hand. If he is a proprietor, his own flocks yield him both; if he pos-sesses nothing himself, he finds them in the house of a patron or a rela-tion. The necessary care of the herds is reduced to excursions and pleasure parties; the branding, which is like the harvesting of farmers, is a festival, the arrival of which is received with transports of joy, being the occasion of the assembling of all the men for twenty leagues around, and the opportunity for displaying incredible skill with the lasso. . . .

The horse is an integral part of the Argentine rustic; it is for him what the cravat is to an inhabitant of the city. In 1841, El Chacho, a chieftain of the Llanos, emigrated to Chili [*sic*]. "How are you getting on, friend?" somebody asked him. "How should I be getting on?" returned he, in tones of distress and melancholy. "Bound to Chili, and on foot!" Only an Argentine gaucho can appreciate all the misfortune and distress which these two phrases express.

Here again we have the life of the Arab or Tartar. The following words of Victor Hugo might have been written in the pampas: "He cannot fight on foot; he and his horse are but one person. He lives on horseback; he trades, buys, and sells on horseback; drinks, eats, sleeps, and dreams on horseback" (*Le Rhin*).

The men then set forth without exactly knowing where they are go-ing. A turn around the herds, a visit to a breeding-pen or to the haunt of a favorite horse, takes up a small part of the day; the rest is consumed in a rendezvous at a tavern or grocery store. There assemble inhabitants of the neighboring parishes; there are given and received bits of information about animals that have gone astray; the traces of the cattle are described upon the ground; intelligence of the hunting ground of the tiger or of the place where the tiger's tracks have been seen, is communicated. There, in short, is the Cantor; there the men fraternize while the glass goes round at the expense of those who have the means as well as the disposition to pay for it.

In a life so void of emotion, gambling exercises the enervated mind, and liquor arouses the dormant imagination. This accidental reunion becomes by its daily repetition a society more contracted than that from which each of its individual members came; yet in this assembly, without public aim, without social interest, are first formed the elements of those characters which are to appear later on the political stage. We shall see how. The gaucho esteems skill in horsemanship and physical strength, and especially courage, above all other things, as we have said before. This meeting, this daily club, is a real Olympic circus where each man's merit is tested and assayed.

The gaucho is always armed with the knife inherited from the Spaniard. More fully even than in Spain is here realized that peninsular peculiarity, that cry, characteristic of Saragossa—*war to the knife*. The knife, besides being a weapon, is a tool used for all purposes; without it, life cannot go on. It is like the elephant's trunk, arm, hand, finger, and all. The gaucho boasts of his valor like a trooper, and every little while his knife glitters through the air in circles, upon the least provocation, or with none at all, for the simple purpose of comparing a stranger's prowess with his own; he plays at stabbing as he would play at dice. So deeply and intimately have these pugnacious habits entered the life of the Argentine gaucho that custom has created a code of honor and a fencing system which protect life. The rowdy of other lands takes to his knife for the purpose of killing, and he kills; the Argentine gaucho unsheathes his to fight, and he only wounds. To attempt the life of his adversary he must be very drunk, or his instincts must be really wicked, or his rancor very deep. His aim is only to *mark* his opponent, to give him a slash in the face, to leave an indelible token upon him. The numerous scars to be seen upon these gauchos, accordingly, are seldom deep. A fight is begun, then, for the sake of shining, for the glory of victory, for the love of fame. A close ring is made around the combatants, and excited and eager eyes follow the glitter of the knives which do not cease to move. When blood flows in torrents the spectators feel obliged to stop the fight. If a *misfortune* has resulted, the sympathies are with the survivor; the best horse is available for his escape to a distant place where he is received with respect or pity. If the law overtakes him he often shows fight, and if he rushes through soldiers and escapes, he has from that time a wide-spread renown. Time passes, the judge in place has been succeeded by another, and he may again show himself in the township without further molestation: he has a full discharge.

Homicide is but a misfortune, unless the deed has been so often repeated that the perpetrator has gained the reputation of an assassin. The landed proprietor, Don Juan Manuel Rosas, before being a public man, had made his residence a sort of asylum for homicides without ever extending his protection to robbers; a preference which would easily be explained by his character of gaucho proprietor, if his subsequent conduct had not disclosed affinities with evil which have filled the world with terror. . . .

Before 1810, two distinct, rival, and incompatible forms of society, two differing kinds of civilization existed in the Argentine Republic: one being Spanish, European, and cultivated, the other barbarous, American, and almost wholly of native growth. The revolution which occurred in the cities acted only as the cause, the impulse, which set these two distinct forms of national existence face to face, and gave occasion for a contest between them, to be ended, after lasting many years, by the absorption of one into the other.

I have pointed out the normal form of association, or want of association, of the country people, a form worse, a thousand times, than that of the nomad tribe. I have described the artificial associations formed in idleness, and the sources of fame among the gauchos—bravery, daring, violence, and opposition to regular law, to the civil law, that is, of the city. These phenomena of social organization existed in 1810, and still exist, modified in many points, slowly changing in others, and yet untouched in several more. These foci, about which were gathered the brave, ignorant, free, and unemployed peasantry, were found by thousands through the country. The revolution of 1810 carried everywhere commotion and the sound of arms. Public life, previously wanting in this Arabico-Roman society, made its appearance in all the taverns, and the revolutionary movement finally brought about provincial, warlike associations, called *montoneras*, legitimate offspring of the tavern and the field, hostile to the city and to the army of revolutionary patriots. As events succeed each other, we shall see the provincial montoneras headed by their chiefs; the final triumph, in Facundo Quiroga, of the country over the cities throughout the land; and by their subjugation in spirit, government, and civilization, the final formation of the central consolidated despotic government of the landed proprietor, Don Juan Manuel Rosas, who applied the knife of the gaucho to the culture of Buenos Ayres, and destroyed the work of centuries—of civilization, law, and liberty.

4 Victor Andrés Belaúnde ◆
The Frontier in Hispanic America

Accepting the major thrust of Turner's thesis, then at the height of its popularity, Peruvian historian Victor Andrés Belaúnde argued in 1923 that the thesis did not apply to Spanish America. Contrasting the Mississippi River with the Amazon, the Alleghenies with the Andes, and looking at the prevalence of tropical lowlands and tortuous mountains in Mexico and elsewhere, Belaúnde argued that the environment in much of Latin America prevented "the assimilation of new lands." If exploitation of lands "of human value" explains North America, he suggested, then the relative shortage of such lands in Latin America explains why it is different from the United States—why its colonial social structures remained intact in many places. "The absence of frontier," he noted, "has caused the rigidity of our structure and our lack of youth and vitality."

Like Turner, Belaúnde did not succumb to simple environmental determinism. Taking the examples of Mexico and Argentina, he points to institutions that impeded the equitable distribution of arable land. This suggests a question. What was the relative influence of colonial institutions in hindering the development of frontiers in Latin America, compared to the influence of the frontier environment itself?

In retrospect it seems ironic that Belaúnde's nephew, Fernando Belaúnde Terry, would make the opening of the trans-Andean frontier a key part of his presidential agenda (1963–1968), and so become "the first Peruvian president to incorporate the idea of an expanding frontier into the development programme of a political party."* One of Peru's leading historians and essayists, Victor Andrés Belaúnde (1883–1966) devoted much of his writing to questions of national character, as did Turner.

The differences between Anglo-Saxon America and Latin or Hispanic America pointed out by sociologists up to the present time are well known. They all refer to the following perfectly established factors: race, climate, religion and the system of government during the colonial régime. (The marked contrast which the two Americas have presented in the nineteenth century and actually present was more than sufficiently explained by the radical differences in those factors.) There are, however, other elements of differentiation as important, or perhaps more important, which

From *Rice Institute Pamphlets* 10 (Houston, October 1923): 202–13. Reprinted by permission of Rice University.

* Alistair Hennessy, *The Frontier in Latin American History* (Albuquerque: University of New Mexico Press, 1978), 12.

have been neither studied nor even, in some cases, insinuated: the process of the development of a country, its dynamic forces in operation have more importance than the static or permanent factors; it may be said that civilization is principally functional. The dynamic element par excellence in the development of Anglo-Saxon America has been the frontier. We owe this genial idea to Professor Turner; we know to-day, through his studies, that the frontier, that is, the progressive and assimilating advance on to new lands, has produced the perpetual renaissance and the greatest fluidity in American life and as essential consequences, in the psychological order, the American individualism, the spirit of enterprise and the creative activity; in the economic order, the necessarily solid physiocratic basis of society, and, in the political order, democracy, which is conceivable only when free land gives to all men equality of opportunity.

Does this same principle of progressive advance with its characteristics of individualism, solid economic development and democratic equality exist in Hispanic America? To answer this question is the object of this lecture.

A superficial examination may lead us to believe that in order for the frontier principle, such as Professor Turner understands it, to exist, the element of virgin and unknown lands suffices, regardless of their situation and of their being such as may be assimilated; and in that belief the influence of the frontier in Hispanic America, which even to-day has unknown and unexplored territory, might be asserted. But the frontier factor is not made up exclusively of the material element of territory, but principally of that slow process of assimilation of new lands to which civilizing action, which consolidates itself in them thanks to their situation in relation to the old nuclei of nationality and thanks also to their being available for agricultural production and human work, extends. In this sense we may affirm that the frontier appears only exceptionally in Hispanic America and that it is precisely on this that the essential difference between the United States and Canada and the other countries of the continent hinges. The frontier is not only quantitative but, principally, qualitative; it does not bear direct ratio to the gross extension of unknown territories but to their accessibility and their productivity, in one word, to their human value.

Latin America presents the frontier principle in the brilliant and almost miraculous beginning of the discovery and of the conquest but not in its slow and effective form of assimilating advance and progressive settlement.

Few contrasts shall history be able to offer more marked than that which exists between the English expansion and the Hispanic expansion on the continent. In the seventeenth century and in the first half of the eighteenth century, the Englishmen had hardly colonized the territory between the cordillera and the water line. It is true that the first concessions made by the King of England, like those made to the south by the King of Spain, extended from ocean to ocean; but it is no less true that that theoretical demarcation was not effected until the nineteenth century because events took another course and the English Monarchy, on the eve of the war of independence, not only did not foster enterprises of conquest and settlement towards the unknown lands of the west but expressly prohibited them.

On the other hand, see the process of Hispanic expansion. Spain, during the sixteenth century, had discovered and explored the territories stretching from California to the Strait of Magellan and had taken possession, by sudden expansion, of the greater part of the land available and of human value in that vast territorial extension. The plateaus of the Anahuac, the central American valleys, the plains of Cundinamarca, the narrow Andine canyons, the plain of Collao, the central valley of Chile and the highlands of the Plata were assimilated by the Spaniards; the famous pioneers of this race naturally disdained the nearest and most accessible lands, which were the low lands of warm climate in Mexico, Nueva Granada and Venezuela, and penetrating the very heart of the continent, they took possession of almost all the lands of agricultural value. If we were to compare the Spanish and Portuguese expansion of the beginning of the seventeenth century with that of the end of the eighteenth century, we would find the following difference only: the Portuguese advance in the valley of the Amazon, from the line of Tordecillas towards the head waters of the great river going beyond the line of San Ildefonso, to which advance Spain opposed its Missions of Mainas, Mojos and Guaranies. But the Portuguese advance was one of discoverers and not one of settlers, the Amazonic region not permitting the latter. The Spanish missions did no more than repeat the conquering effort of the soldiers of the sixteenth century and did not have an effective repercussion nor maintain a constant current of influences with that part of the Spanish colonies already definitely conquered. The Spanish frontier of the Amazon, in the heroic epoch of the military incursions in search of El Dorado or in the religious epoch of the missions, was not the progressive advance of the excess population of the old settlements towards free land nor did it establish the principle of fluidity and gradual expansion characteristic of the North American frontier of the Mississippi.

Synthesizing the foregoing it might be said that Spain, in the colonial period, took possession of the whole continent, settled the lands that could be assimilated and were of human value, scattering the centers or nuclei of culture and offering as regards the unknown lands only the work of pioneers but not that of definitive settlement. On the other hand, England, in the colonial period, colonized only the narrow strip between the Atlantic and the water line and did not advance on to the Alleghenies trying to enter the region of the future through the valleys of that chain, by the natural ways of the Ohio and the Cumberland until the end of the eighteenth century.

The contrast between the valley of the Mississippi and that of the Amazon is striking. The Mississippi, the theatre of the future American expansion, was, during the entire colonial period, completely foreign to the life of the English colonies. Discovered and possessed in its southern part by Spain, explored and run over in its northern part by the French pioneers, it was at that time, as was the Amazon, the theatre of incursions and of fantastic trips but not of gradual settlement. A historical destiny was reserving it for peoples different from those that discovered it and was to offer it as the theatre of future although slow advance of the new nationality that arose as a result of the American independence. The Amazon, discovered at its headwaters and run over by the Spaniards since the sixteenth century, is possessed in its lower part by the Portuguese. The centre of fantastic reigns, it attracted first the seekers for gold and later the missionaries. In the nineteenth century it still continues in almost the same condition in which it was at the end of the eighteenth century. The forest has not been dominated, there are no means of communication other than the rivers, the nation that possessed the mouth of the great river has affirmed its political sovereignty but has not assimilated it economically; the nations that possessed its headwaters have not done any more than the old colonies to which they succeeded. And the explanation lies in that there have been the two following essential differences between the valley of the Mississippi, theatre of the Saxon-American frontier, and the valley of the Amazon, theatre of the possible Hispanic-American frontier: the territories of the northern and central Mississippi were suitable for agriculture and easily accessible from the populated centres, whereas the territories of the valley of the Amazon consisting of tropical forests could not be converted into arable land and access to them from the region of the Andes was most difficult. As Nathaniel S. Shaler very well observed: "The valleys of the St. Lawrence, the Hudson, the Mississippi, in a fashion also, of the Susquehanna and the James, break through or pass around the low coast mountains, and afford free ways into the whole interior that is attractive to European peoples. No part of the Alleghenian system presents any insuperable obstacle to those who seek to penetrate the inner lands."

The same author sets out the easy application of the lands of the Mississippi to agricultural purposes when he says: "For the first time in human history, a highly skilled people have suddenly come into possession of a vast and fertile area which stands ready for tillage without the labor which is necessary to prepare forest lands for the plow."

And thus does one explain to one's self that the American pioneers of the eighteenth century, such as Daniel Boone and [George Rogers] Clark, should have been followed in the valley of the Mississippi by a stream which entered by the natural ways and which was later to turn into the colonizing torrent which was to assimilate those lands definitely to the new nationality. The Mississippi, or, rather, the West is since then a determining factor in the history of the United States in the nineteenth century.

On the other hand, the Andes, in contrast with the Alleghenies, have presented and continue to present insuperable obstacles to the access of the valley of the Amazon. The paths of the Incaic attempts were the same that were used by the captains of the conquest, and the same as those used by the missionaries and they continue to be the same entrances used by the few travellers of the nineteenth century. And the land continues to be "intractable" as the old chroniclers expressed it, that is, rebellious to human effort and work.

All that we have just said sets out the radical difference between the United States and the most typical of the countries of Hispanic America, which are Colombia, Ecuador, Peru and Bolivia. These nations are made up mainly of valleys and interior highlands. The lands easily accessible from the coast are either unhealthy tropical forests, such as those of Colombia and Ecuador, or deserts such as those of Peru and the former Bolivian coast. And the small part which they still have of the old Spanish patrimony in the valley of the Amazon has the inconveniences and insuperable disadvantages which we have just pointed out. The frontier such as we conceive it is the free land, the land within the reach of property and human effort; that free land does not exist in these countries. That has led Lord Bryce to state the disagreeable and perhaps exaggerated conclusion that the mountainous region of Ecuador, Peru and Bolivia does not deserve to have greater population than it actually has; and, as regards the valley of the Amazon, that settlement is hardly possible in it where man faces a nature so difficult to dominate.

It is thus explained why the Andine countries present to-day almost the same character that they presented in the colonial epoch; with motionless cities, with stagnant population and everywhere with evident signs of that lack of the characteristics of frontier countries: the youthful growth, the fluidity and the constant transformation in the social organism. It may be said that these Andine countries preserve the same colonial structure. The scarce area of land that is capable of assimilation, wrested from the indigenous natives, is in the hands of a few great owners. Immediately following comes a middle class which lives principally on the bureaucracy developed infinitely more than in colonial times; and last, forming the lowest social stratum, is the aboriginal class on which rests the work of the mines and of the land. And that structure has not changed, not for reasons of a psychic nature nor because of political factors but almost exclusively due to the absence of frontier, as the Andine pioneers of to-day, the men engaged in the rubber industry, are few in number and their work has not advanced further than that of their illustrious predecessors, the captain of the conquest and the missionary of the colony, in the direction of starting a current towards the virgin lands.

Chile shares the same character of the Andine regions. It is not a frontier country either; the land capable of assimilation is to-day, as in colonial times, in the hands of a small number of owners. Its middle class elements will not be able to find, as did the North Americans of the middle of the nineteenth century, the field of the free land. Its orientation will have to be for that reason essentially industrial.

In Venezuela it shall be possible to apply the frontier principle when the excess of population in the world and the modern means of progress determine the settlement in vast scale of the plains of the Orinoco which are to-day in a condition similar to that of the forests of the Amazon.

Mexico, although with different aspects, presents, as regards the frontier, the same characteristics as the Andine countries. In spite of the considerable extension of the Mexican territory, the tropical forests of the hot land on the coasts of the Pacific and of the Atlantic and the desert region of the central plain near the United States border must be deducted. Eliseo Reclus calculates that these regions which cannot be assimilated represent at least two-fifths of the Mexican territory. The rest of the lands capable of assimilation, unlike the new lands which presented themselves only gradually to the occupation and advance of the North Americans, was appropriated in its greater part either by the ecclesiastical institutions or by the great lords of colonial times, whence arose a régime of large estates, and, practically, the lack, or scarcity at least, of free land for the settler. Even the unoccupied lands belonging to the State were not in the same condition as were the frontier territories of the United States. So that Mexico's problem was not one of exploitation or assimilation of new lands but that of better distribution or allotment of those already known or exploited. The clergy possessed half the lands; it was natural that the new political factors created after the independence should wish to reach economic influence through the possession of the lands; this was the origin of the reform laws which vested in the State the property of the lands of the clergy. Then came the reaction; the dispossessed elements sought external influence in favor of an already impossible restoration and the Empire arose. The Empire having been destroyed, it was not possible for the land problem to have the natural solution of settlement by small land owners which the frontier countries have. New great lay land owners took the place of the clergy; the land, with different owners, continued to be in the hands of a few; the great popular mass continued in its condition of servitude, the middle class without any outlooks other than those of the bureaucracy. The dictatorship inaugurated on the downfall of the Empire distributed the lands of the State in the form of large and unlimited concessions. The land problem remained alive and, as time passed, it was to produce the formidable crisis of 1911, which has not yet ended. Had Mexico's free land been easy to assimilate and in the situation of frontier land, its history would have been very different. The frontier criterion applied to the history of Mexico throws new light on the problems that burden that country, and discards the interpretations of superficial sociologists who have done nothing other than to calumniate the aboriginal race, the qualities of which they have not known, or the Spanish education the fundamental principles of which they are unacquainted with.

The only countries in which the frontier can be considered as in North America are the lands of the River de la Plata and southern Brazil. In fact these countries are the most similar to the United States. Their being bounded by the Atlantic which makes them more accessible to European immigration, their temperate climate, the circumstance of having agricultural lands on the coast and that of having in it navigable rivers and, finally even the fact that the elevations of the land or Sierras do not present the inconvenient heights and unfavorable harshnesses of the Andes, contribute to accentuate the parallel. It cannot be denied that this region has been privileged with the gift of disposable land suitable for agriculture which brought as a result the considerable Italian, Portuguese, Spanish and German immigration. But a deeper observation of these countries reveals to us that the frontier principle appears in them in a form which is not precisely the same as the most advantageous form in which it appeared in the United States. To begin with, the area of the states of southern Brazil, São Paulo, Rio Grande do Sul, and Santa Catalina, to which we have referrred, is not very large. As regards Argentina, we may deduct the desert parts of Patagonia which cut the valleys of the Negro and Neuquen and the semi-tropical forests of the Chaco. As regards Paraguay, it is necessary to say that the land has, although not so accentuated, the same disadvantages of the Amazonic region. Uruguay comprises a relatively small territorial area. Let it be added to this that the situation of the Argentine Pampa and of the Brazilian plains is not similar from the topographical point of view nor from the point of view of its relation to the populated centres to that of the virgin lands of the Mississippi in relation to the originary nuclei of the United States. Above all, the Argentine Pampa was a spot of territory between the settled zone of the coast and the populated zone near the Andes of greatest importance in the colonial epoch. Although not settled and exploited, it may be said that the Pampa was in a certain way apprehended and in the course of time the romantic action of the gaucho was to make room for the governmental action which constructed railroads and made concessions of lands. Hence in Argentina the relation between the gaucho and the colonizer, who comes afterwards more due to official action than to the initiative of individuals, is different. The gaucho does not advance from populated centres, he is a product of the plain itself. The American pioneers are the advance guard of the settlers who immediately follow. These differences are not merely accidental and of scarce interest. The Argentine Pampa appears conquered by the railroads and distributed in the great lots of governmental concessions, the origin of the large estate; on the other hand, the American West is conquered principally by the individual advance of the settlers who establish there, as predominant and general, the régime of the small ownership. Thus, individualism and equality of opportunities, the two great derivations of the frontier principle, do not present in the countries of the River de la Plata the same intensity and relief as in the United States. They all recognize to-day, from Reclus to Lord Bryce and Reginald Enock, that the property régime in Brazil, Argentina and Uruguay is that of the large estate. In this sense these countries, in spite of the difference in their geographical and economical characteristics, resemble in their structure their brothers, the Andine countries. So that in Hispanic America the large estate continues to be the great obstacle in the way of democracy.

Professor Paul Reinsch on visiting the countries of South America observed in them the absence of certain freshness and energy, in one word, of youth, which is the characteristic of the North American democracy. "In a sense," Professor Reinsch says, "the South American societies were born old. . . . The dominance of European ideas in their intellectual life, the importance of the city as a seat of civilization never allowed the pioneer feeling to gain the importance which it has held and still holds in our life. This backwoodsman of South America has not achieved the national and estimable position of our frontiersman."

The observation is true but the explanation is inexact. It is not a psychological cause, the importance of the ideas of the city and the predominance of the European ideas that has caused the lack of youth in the life of Hispanic America and the different rôle of its pioneers. The effective causes of these facts lie rather in the land and in the process of our economic development. The absence of frontier, in the sense that Professor Turner gave the word, and of frontier currents, has caused the rigidity of our structure and our lack of youth and vitality. And in the very countries in which the frontier existed, the pioneer, because of the facts which we have just referred to, was more a character of legend and literature than a dynamic factor of progress and a vanguard of civilization. The frontier idea is a new point of view in the true interpretation of Hispanic-American life and is called upon to establish the sociology of the New Continent on new bases.

5 Silvio Zavala ◆ The Frontiers of Hispanic America

In a wide-ranging rumination that he began to write in the 1950s, the distinguished Mexican historian Silvio Zavala considered a variety of frontiers in Latin America. Zavala devoted part of his essay to describing the characteristics of the frontiers of Latin America, seeing them not as "safety valves" but rather as places of war and sources of Indian slaves. In the concluding section of his essay, "Evaluations," which appears here, Zavala raised several Turnerian questions about the frontiers of Argentina, southern Chile, and northern Mexico. Did they breed political freedom? Were they sources of egalitarianism? Did they influence national character? He seems to agree with Belaúnde that Turner's thesis explained little about most Latin American frontiers, but Zavala saw northern Mexico as a possible exception.

A much-honored historian of colonial Latin America, Zavala holds a doctorate in law and served as Mexico's ambassador to France. He founded and edited the Revista de historia de América *(1938–1966), directed the Museo Nacional de Historia del Palacio de Chapultepec (1946–1954), and served as president of El Colegio de México (1963–1966). Among his best known works are* La defensa de los derechos del hombre en América Latina, siglos XVI–XVIII *(Paris, 1963) and* El mundo americano en la época colonial *(México, 1968).*

E ven before the end of the Spanish settlement, it was realized that the society of northern Mexico was different from that of the central region, that the North had taken on a spirit in which the prevailing dangers and hardships could be confronted. Alexander von Humboldt observed in his *Political Essay on the Kingdom of New Spain* that the struggle against Indians and insecurity had stamped the character of the northern people with a certain energy and temper all their own. He noted the lack of docile Indians whom the whites might have exploited so they could live a life of idleness and indolence. The active life, lived for the most part on horseback, helped to develop physical strength, and in that country men had to be strong to deal with hostile Indians and herds of range cattle. Those men were strong in spirit, of unexcitable nature, and possessed of clean and robust bodies. To Humboldt this picture was—and this explains his benevolent point of view—"a state of nature, preserved amid the

From *The Frontier in Perspective*, ed. Walker D. Wyman and Clifton B. Kroeber (Madison: University of Wisconsin Press, 1965), 48–57. Reprinted by permission of the University of Wisconsin Press. A portion of the essay appeared earlier in *Cuadernos Americanos* 17 (1958): 374–84.

trappings of an ancient civilization."[1] In the same tone, a native son of Coahuila, Miguel Ramos de Arizpe, explained in his Memorial to the Cortes of Cádiz in 1811 that agriculture, source of the wealth of nations, was the common occupation of people in all the eastern inland provinces of Coahuila, Texas, Nuevo León, New Mexico, and Nuevo Santander. He said,

> it shapes their general character, and for this reason, busy night and day in honest work on the land, receiving their living from it rather than from any person, they are surely immune to intrigue, are virtuously upright in morals, and are enemies of arbitrary conduct and disorder. They are worshippers of true liberty and, naturally enough, are the best fitted for all the moral and political virtues. They are much devoted to the liberal and mechanical arts.[2]

Whether because of a naturalistic bent so typical of Enlightened philosophy or whether because of physiocratic leanings or localism, the fact is that the distinguishing natural and historical character of the northern provinces was understood by local people and foreigners alike, even though their conceptions and expressions of it were different. The local conditions, the relations with the Indians, and the kind of activities typical of the region, all had contributed to making the northern frontier and its people unique in New Spain. With the coming of independence when the conservatives and radicals, the federalists and centralists were struggling over the question of the nation's political organization, the northern provinces were seen by some republicans as bulwarks of liberal principles. These regions could more easily avoid involvement in the issues of theocracy, militarism, and the hierarchic lack of equality that was holding the Indian in subjection. When the central government was in the control of the conservatives, it could be resisted by those distant provinces. Seen in this light, the northern frontier seemed to be the guardian of liberty.

Some men of affairs who regarded the northern provinces in this way and who observed the thin population of these regions came to reflect on the possibility of foreign immigration. Thinking of the progress made by the first Anglo-American colonies in Texas, Lorenzo de Zavala wrote that within two or three generations that part of Mexico would be richer, more free, and more civilized than all the rest. Because of its immigrants, Mexican Texas would be an example to other states still in a semifeudal stage and ruled by military and clerical influences, fateful inheritances from Spanish rule.[3] Thus the northern frontier was seen not merely as a different society more favorable for the growth of democratic life but also as a hope for the regeneration of all Mexico. Precisely because these frontier regions had come through the colonial period so thinly populated did they seem particularly promising for new immigration projects in the nineteenth century.

The northern frontier had been ruled by military government, particularly after the Comandancia de Provincias Internas was organized in 1776. After several reorganizations, this command included the provinces of Nueva Viscaya, Sonora, Sinaloa, California, Coahuila, New Mexico, and Texas. Ramos de Arizpe petitioned the Cortes of Cádiz for the establishment of a civil government, arguing that a military commander, by his education and character, naturally seeks to execute the laws he knows and is accustomed to enforce, "demanding of the peaceful farmer, the quiet cattleman, the hard-working artisan, that blind obedience, that wordless compliance, that his soldiers must render at command—and this, sometimes, without meaning to do so. Finally, he makes himself a despot, with the worst results for the people, who would never suffer so under civil government which would hold more closely to civil and social law."[4] Thus regionalism did not signify an absolute guarantee of liberty since it could become the refuge of bossism (*caciquismo*) and local abuses.

The loyalty of Anglo-American immigrants to Mexico was not as strong as the ties that bound them to their own people, and they did not bring the hoped-for internal development of the northern provinces or the instructive example it was hoped they would offer the other states of the republic. Instead, there followed the revolt and independence of the Texans, their annexation to the United States, and the war between that nation and Mexico. These events were followed in turn by the loss of lands lying north of the Rio Grande.

For a brief moment during the revolution that began in Mexico in 1919, the northern provinces exercised great influence in national politics. The revolt gained impetus in Coahuila, Chihuahua, and Sonora. In this may be seen an extension of those historic liberal impulses already mentioned, but there were also such new factors as the help in arms and other resources obtained from north of the United States border. In any case, the cavalry and cattle of the North helped sustain the troops in their long marches and campaigns. Among these soldiers were creoles, mestizos, and even Yaqui and Mayo Indians, who went on to pitch their tents in the patios of the National Palace of Mexico City. During that long war, the northern fighter gained great fame for courage and endurance and his leaders were at the helm of a number of the revolutionary governments.

It remains to inquire, finally, whether the northern frontier may be considered a source of the Mexican national type. If a balanced mixture of ethnic stocks may be considered the symbol of what is Mexican, it is possible that the people of the old northern frontier meet this standard. On the other hand, there are scholars who hold that the great number of northerners are ethnically creole, i.e., descendants of whites. If Mexican nativism is based on the blending of the ancient civilization of the sedentary Indians and that of the Spaniards, then the central provinces rather than the northern must have originated the distinctive Mexican character. This is true if we accept a national character rather than a plurality of types that may be closer to reality. Certainly, the sedentary Indians were most numerous in the central region and presumably the greatest amalgamation of the races took place there. In accordance with this last interpretation, then, the North can be considered only a source of social peculiarities. It remains apart, however, from that nativism that stems from the pre-conquest culture of Middle America.

A diversity similar to what we have seen in Mexico—between the inland provinces (*tierra adentro*) and those of the central part (*tierra afuera*) of the viceroyalty—also appears in Chile. The division there is between the central region permanently colonized by the Spaniards and those lands to the south that remained in Araucanian hands or lay on the frontier exposed to their attacks. In the late sixteenth and early seventeenth century, Indian warfare had forced abandonment of the settlements of Arauco, Santa Cruz, Valdivia, Imperial, Angol, Villarica, and Osorno. Chillán and Concepción had been attacked, but the Christians had managed to re-establish their control in the country lying between the Rivers Maule and Bío-Bío. The policy of defensive war, begun late in the seventeenth century, consisted in holding the line of the Bío-Bío so as to protect the central part of the colony. Only missionaries were permitted to cross that line to deal with the natives. This important frontier, on which depended the conservation of Spanish power in the South Pacific, attracted the attention not only of the authorities of Chile but also of those of the viceroyalty of Peru and of Spain.

Like the war in northern Mexico, this struggle against the Araucanians went through several stages, expending troops and funds which during the seventeenth century came as a subsidy (*situado*) from Peru. This war, like the Mexican, alternated between attack and defense and led to the capture of prisoners on both sides. There was some mixing of blood due to unions between Spanish soldiers and Indian women and of Indians and captured Spanish women. Historians and students of Chilean literature point out that the war along the Araucanian frontier contributed unique features to the national culture. Among the themes brought forth in this literature as it has developed since the sixteenth century have been the glorification of the Araucanian war, begun by Alonso de Ercilla, and the recognition of the Indian's right to defend his land. The selection of these two themes is not meant as derogatory to any of the authors who praise the expansion of the Faith and of Christian rule or who exalt the deeds of

Spanish creole soldiers who fought the Indian wars.[5] As late as the nineteenth century, one can still note the dualism between the regard for the Araucanian's merits and for the final campaign that conquered him.

In the complex patterns of ideas about racial mixture, the vigor of the Araucanian is given credit as soon as it is seen to be a part of the racial stock just as European ancestry, particularly the Basque, is a matter for pride and distinction. Authors discuss the question of whether or not there has been an amalgamation of Spanish and Indian in the great oligarchic families. They speak of the balance attained between the various racial strains in the general population. Some believe in a Gothic origin of the pioneer Spaniards who came to Chile, while others prefer to stress the influence of the German migration of the late nineteenth century. They also single out certain forces drawn from ethnic and historical backgrounds to account for traits in the national character. For example, the laziness and improvidence of the people, their stoicism and courage, their martial spirit, inconstancy, and love of adventure are accounted for through the influence of war and their frugal frontier life. These ideas about the intermingling of peoples and the unity of feeling that results from blending a warlike history with qualities imputed to the national character throw into bold relief the influence of the southern frontier on the shaping of the personality of Chile.

Numerous writings about the plains of the Plata region deserve careful literary, social, and political analysis, and a few themes from the work of Domingo Faustino Sarmiento have been selected here to enable us to compare the image of this frontier with that of others in the New World.[6] Driven by his political desire to attack the tyrannical rule of the cattleman Juan Manuel de Rosas, Sarmiento contrasted the barbarism of the pastoral provinces with urban civilization of European origin. The passion of his argument did not blur the clarity of his description of gaucho life and he was well aware of the promise, implicit in the vigorous originality of this historical development in its American setting, for those who would treat it as a literary theme. As with Francis Parkman, the historian, and James Fenimore Cooper, the man of letters, Sarmiento was attracted by the American frontier. In the United States as in Argentina, he saw the dramatic interplay of civilization and barbarism between the European immigrant and the nomadic Indian. He saw these analogies clearly and was perhaps the first of New World writers to make the connection between North American and Spanish-American frontiers. However, there are in his pages some historical differences which make this parallel more complex. After all, the gauchos who inhabited the pastoral pampa and who are descendants of Spaniards, Indians, and sometimes also Negroes, were organized into a society already Europeanized during the colonial period. That society had conquered large tracts of the back country by use of cattle, horses, steel weapons, and firearms. It had founded the cities that Sarmiento pictured as oases of civilization in a cultureless plain.

Contrary to Sarmiento's point of view, we can properly speak of the existence of a historical frontier only where the Christian gauchos faced Indian enemies. That other frontier, conceived politically by Sarmiento as lying between the civilized and the barbarous, between urban and pastoral people, between European immigrants and gauchos—in short, between those who were politically disinherited as was Sarmiento and those who governed under the protection of Rosas—cannot be confused with the historical frontier that did lie between the wild Indians and the fortified line established during the colonial period. Here we see the dualism of Sarmiento's thought with respect to the urban and pastoral heritage of Spanish America. On the one hand, he saw this heritage as the fulcrum of tradition and civilized progress in Argentina, although he did try to distinguish between the Spanish colonial period with its backward society and the new policies directed toward economic progress, European immigration, religious tolerance, educational advances, and political democracy. On the other hand, he confused that older tradition with American barbarism—Indian, mestizo, gaucho, and colonial in origin— that was to be eliminated by advancing civilization. This dualism as lived and expressed by Sarmiento with dramatic intensity helps explain the historical position from which he viewed both the past and the future.

In explaining that the Argentine prairie wagons were drawn up in a circle for defense against Indian attack, he was well aware that the gauchos fought from within the defensive circle just as did the men of the western United States. Both represented to him the progress of European civilization on the American frontier in the face of the aborigines. The westward movement in the Argentine and in the United States began, however, in different centuries and followed different rhythms until a certain parallelism was reached in the nineteenth century. By that time, there already existed in South America a gaucho civilization, denoting an intermediate stage between the newly arrived European immigrant and the nomadic Indian.

The similarity between the frontiers of North and South America which Sarmiento saw derived from environmental conditions and from the tasks necessary to control these influences, that is, from factors peculiar to invasion of lands inhabited by nomads. His attention was drawn to the social and political aspects of life on the pampa, although the essential vigor of his writing stems from his poetic re-creation of the peculiar aspects of the countryside and the personality of the gaucho. He emphasized certain characteristics that may have been common to all men who pioneered in the new lands of America.[7] He was aware of the significance of the horse for the civilization of the New World, of the diversity between the mounted *vaqueros* of the pastoral regions and the peons or foot servants in the agricultural districts; and he knew the contributions made by the *llaneros* of Venezuela, for example, during the wars of independence. Nonetheless, his statements do not coincide with the thesis later formulated by Frederick Jackson Turner—this despite certain external similarities—since Turner found on the frontier not the cradle of pastoral despotism, as exemplified in the dictator Rosas of Argentina, but rather the seeds of democracy and social fluidity.[8] Sarmiento understood and admired the civilization of the United States. He knew how it differed from European society which he himself had seen, and he thought the American superior to the European. To him the frontier was the battleground between barbarism and civilization. The origin of democracy lay not on the frontier but in the European tradition transplanted there, the immigration of the Puritans, the freedom that rose out of the Reformation, and the life of the Atlantic coast and its expansion. He hoped the European immigrants would bring a reforming spirit to the Argentine and it mattered little to him that this might be done at the expense of gaucho customs which, in his general condemnation of barbarism, he inevitably treated as equivalent with the life of native nomads. Thus Sarmiento could perceive some of the problems which European immigration created for the United States and for Argentina, and in time he came to doubt the civilizing influence of these newly arrived people.[9] To achieve the goal of progressive virtues, he placed his best and final hopes in popular education.

The only Spanish-American writer I know who has tested Turner's frontier thesis for Spanish America is not Sarmiento, who died five years before Turner presented his paper of 1893, but the Peruvian Víctor Andrés Belaúnde.[10] He is of the opinion that the frontier appeared only rarely in the Spanish colonies. He points out the importance of the beginning of colonial occupation but believes that when that early period had passed, there was no free land on which a frontier might have been opened for the many. This was because of problems created by the Amazon River valley and the Andean range. From the geographical point of view, he sees nothing comparable to the opportunities held forth by the Mississippi Valley.

After examining the landholding situation in Chile, on the plains of the Orinoco, and in Mexico, Belaúnde pauses to consider the prairies of the Plata region and southern Brazil. Here the geography was more like that of the United States. The pampa, however, was occupied during the colonial period; later, the railroads and government land cessions further impeded the development of a frontier in a social sense, since large holdings prevailed. From this lack of a frontier stemmed a rigid social structure and an absence of vitality and youthful spirit. What Belaúnde emphasizes is the diversity of the situation, and he concludes that Turner's thesis does not apply.

In conclusion, I believe that the evidence is not all in, that the thesis may be examined in other regions and from other points of view. One case that deserves such study is the meeting of the Spanish-American frontier in northern Mexico with the westward-moving American frontier, not in its well-known political, military, and diplomatic aspects, but with reference to social exchanges and adjustments that occurred.

Notes

1. Alexander von Humboldt, *Political Essay on the Kingdom of New Spain*, vol. II, as cited in Ramos de Arizpe, *Discursos, Memorias, e Informes* . . . with notes by Vito Alessio Robles (Mexico, 1942), xvi.

2. Ramos de Arizpe, *Discursos, Memorias, e Informes* . . . , xix and 41.

3. See his *Ensayo Histórico de las Revoluciones de Méjico, desde 1808 hasta 1830* (2 vols.; Paris and New York, 1831–1832), II (New York, 1832), 171.

4. Ramos de Arizpe, *Discursos, Memorias, e Informes* . . . , 58.

5. After Ercilla's *Araucana*, the anonymous poem given in José Toribio Medina, *Historia de la literatura colonial de Chile* (3 vols.; Santiago, 1878), I, 259; Hernando Alvarez de Toledo, *Purén Indómito* (Leipzig, 1861: written after 1597); and Pedro de Oña, *Arauco Domado* (Santiago, 1917; orig. pub., Lima, 1596), among others.

6. For the most part I follow the fine selection in *El pensamiento vivo de Sarmiento*, comp. Ricardo Rojas (Buenos Aires, 1941). Quotations that follow in the text are mostly from *Facundo, ó Civilización i Barbarie* (orig. pub. at Santiago, 1845, in the newspaper *El Progreso*, as *Facundo*, then separately in the same year as *Civilización i barbarie. Vida de Juan Facundo Quiroga . . .*), and *Conflictos y Armonías de las Razas en América* (Buenos Aires, 1883). For a recent penetrating analysis, see Ezequiel Martínez Estrada, *Muerte y Transfiguración de Martín Fierro* (2 vols.; Mexico, 1948).

7. *El pensamiento vivo de Sarmiento*, 136: "Individualism was his very essence, the horse his exclusive weapon, and the immense pampa his theater"; on p. 132: "valor, boldness, dexterity, violence, and opposition to established justice"; and on p. 127: "The gaucho admired above all else physical force, skill in horsemanship, and courage."

8. See R. E. Riegel, "Current Ideas of the Significance of the United States Frontier," *Revista de Historia de América*, No. 33 (June 1952): 30: "These men were optimistic, nationalistic, and expansionist. They were individualistic and materialistic, with a sprinkling of the lawless, but withal brave, hardy and ingenious, willing to experiment until they overcame the difficulties of each new region. They were the primary source of such American traits as individualism, democracy, inventiveness, and materialism." Merle E. Curti, *Historiadores de América, Frederick Jackson Turner* (Mexico, 1949), 26, states that "the west-

ward movement, he [Turner] argued, developed the essentially American traits of restless energy, self-reliance, voluntary co-operation on the part of individuals, practical ingenuity and versatility, inventiveness, and a masterful grasp of material things. . . ." Note that in this listing of personal qualities there are as many coincidences as discrepancies with those ascribed to the gaucho.

9. *El pensamiento vivo de Sarmiento*, 77–78, 208. See Martínez Estrada, *Sarmiento* (Buenos Aires, 1946), 99. The nativist reaction as it was in 1870 is reflected in Lucio V. Mansilla, *Una excursión a los indios Ranqueles* (Buenos Aires, 1870).

For critical opinion of Sarmiento's historical position, see Martínez Estrada, *Sarmiento*, 94, and Ricardo Rojas' prologue to *El pensamiento vivo de Sarmiento*, 24–26.

10. *The Frontier in Hispanic America* (Rice Institute Pamphlets, No. X [October, 1923]), 202–213.

II

Latin America as a Frontier of Europe

6 Walter Prescott Webb ◆ The Great Frontier

Extending the argument of Frederick Jackson Turner, who saw the North American frontier as promoting democracy "here and in Europe," Walter Prescott Webb (1888–1963) regarded the entire Western Hemisphere (together with South Africa, Australia, and New Zealand) as a "great frontier" that profoundly transformed Europe.* Beginning with Columbus's discovery, Webb argued, the Great Frontier changed the Old World, contributing to the breakdown of feudal institutions and the rise of modern European capitalism, dynamism, and democracy. Most important, free land and easily exploitable gold and silver, Webb wrote, brought "windfall profits" into the European metropolis and sustained a prolonged period of growth from 1500 to 1900. Eurocentric like Turner, Webb regarded the great frontier as "a vast and vacant land." Also like Turner, he believed that the closing of the frontier would have severe consequences.

One of the most influential American historians of his generation, known especially for his book The Great Plains *(1931), the Texas-born Webb articulated the idea of* The Great Frontier *in a book published in 1952. He had conceived the idea for the book in the 1930s, however, when the Great Depression seemed a certain sign of the end of the four-century "boom."†*

From "Ended: 400 Year Boom—Reflections on the Age of the Frontier," *Harper's Magazine* (October 1951): 25–33. Reprinted with permission.

*Turner, "The Significance of the Frontier in American History," *Annual Report of the American Historical Association . . . 1893* (Washington: Government Printing Office, 1894), 221.

†For a brief biography, see Joe B. Frantz, "Walter Prescott Webb," in *Turner, Bolton, and Webb: Three Historians of the American Frontier*, ed. Wilbur R. Jacobs, John W. Caughey, and Joe B. Frantz (Seattle: University of Washington Press, 1965), 75–108. Necah Steward Furman, *Walter Prescott Webb: His Life and Impact* (Albuquerque: University of New Mexico Press, 1976), devotes little attention to *The Great Frontier*.

Many historians rejected Webb's thesis, or important parts of it, to which he responded, "the more revealing [the historian's] interpretation is, the more severe the criticism is likely to be."* The new economic boom after World War II, historian William McNeill suggests, seemed to invalidate Webb's gloomy view. So did the fact that the study of European expansion "was no longer a respectable field of academic endeavor."† Other historians, however, including McNeill himself, have found that Webb's thesis continues to provide an ample and cosmopolitan framework for interpreting the past. As Geoffrey Barraclough noted: "We shall never prove or disprove it in its totality; but in examining it, our knowledge of historical processes will be widened and deepened, our understanding made more secure."‡

It is difficult to discuss the frontier with an American audience because the literate American assumes that he knows what you are going to say in advance. It is difficult to expound the subject to a foreign audience for the opposite reason: the foreigner knows little about the subject, and because he cannot see that it touches his life, he is pretty indifferent to it. My purpose here is to show the American a phase of the frontier which he has not yet considered, and show the European that the frontier has for more than four centuries affected his life and well-being most profoundly. . . .

The movement of the American people into the frontier was unlike the movement of people from European nations into their equivalent frontier, and no doubt the simplicity of the American process explains why the historic force of the frontier was discovered first in the American context. Yet the American frontier was but a fragment of the Great Frontier, and the American process was but an example—the simplest and clearest, it is true—of a parallel but more complex development that was going on wherever European people were appropriating lands in the New World. Since America led the way in evolving the frontier process, and leads the world in the study of that process, we have no choice but to examine the American experience and to note briefly how scholars came to attend it

* Walter Prescott Webb, "The Great Frontier: An Interpretation," in *History as High Adventure*, ed. E. C. Barksdale (Austin: Pemberton Press, 1969), 183.
†McNeill, *The Great Frontier: Freedom and Hierarchy in Modern Times* (Princeton: Princeton University Press, 1983), 5.
‡Geoffrey Barraclough, "The Seminal Nature of Webb's Frontier Thesis," in Lewis and McGann, eds. *The New World Looks at Its History* (Austin: University of Texas Press, 1963), 168. Barraclough offered this remark when a panel in 1958 considered Webb's work. On that occasion, Keith Hancock, a historian of the British empire, assessed Webb's thesis favorably, while Arthur R. M. Lower, a Canadian historian, and José Honório Rodrigues, a Brazilian historian, regarded it more critically. See ibid., 135–64.

as a field of study. American historians assume that the frontier process began with the English settlement at Jamestown in 1607, and the year 1890 is usually taken to mark the date when there was no more frontier available, when the new land was no longer new. There may be some quibbling about the dates, but they do bracket the three centuries of American frontier experience and experimentation.

It was the magnitude and the unbroken continuity of the experience that gave the frontier major importance in American life. It made no difference what other tasks the Americans had on their hands at a given time, there was the additional, ever-present one or moving into and settling new country. They did it while they fought for independence, before and after; they did it while they hammered out the principles of a democratic government shaped to the needs of frontiersmen; and they did not cease doing it in the period of civil strife. They never reached the limits of the vacancy they owned before they acquired another vacancy, by purchase, by treaty, by conquest, and in every case the frontiersmen infiltrated the country before the nation acquired it. Like locusts they swarmed, always to the west, and only the Pacific Ocean stopped them. Here in this movement beat the deep overtone of a nation's destiny, and to it all kept step unconsciously.

To say that the people were unconscious of the force that moved them, and of the medium in which they moved, is to state a fact which is easy to prove but hard to explain. It may be said that they were emotionally aware of the frontier long before they were intellectually cognizant of it. People could not have as their main task for three centuries working with raw land without getting its dirt under their nails and deep into their skins. The effects were everywhere, in democratic government, in boisterous politics, in exploitative agriculture, in mobility of population, in disregard for conventions, in rude manners, and in unbridled optimism. Though these effects were present everywhere they were not understood anywhere by the people who felt and reflected them. The frontier still lacked its philosopher, the thinker who could view the whole dramatic experience and tell what was its meaning. This philosopher arrived three years after the experience ended and told the American people that from the beginning the American frontier had been the dominant force, the determining factor, in their history thus far.

This hypothesis was presented to the American Historical Association in a paper entitled "The Significance of the Frontier in American History." The date was 1893 and the author was a young and then little-known historian. That paper made Frederick Jackson Turner a scholar with honor in his own country; it altered the whole course of American historical scholarship, and it is recognized as the most influential single piece of historical writing ever done in the United States. The key to his thesis is found in this sentence: "The existence of an area of free land, its continuous recession, and the advance of American settlement westward, explain American development." The general acceptance of this frontier hypothesis, and the fame of its author, came about because the people in America were emotionally prepared to understand this rationalization and explanation of their own long experience. Turner's pupils—many of whom became disciples—flocked to the diggings and have worked out in every cove and valley the rich vein which he uncovered, but not one of them, not even the master himself, took the next step to point out or at least to emphasize that the American frontier was but a small fragment of the Great Frontier. On that Great Frontier was also an area of free land; it was in continuous recession; and the advance of European settlement into it should explain the development of Western civilization in modern times just as the American advance explains American development.

II

What happened in America was but a detail in a much greater phenomenon, the interaction between European civilization and the vast raw lands into which it moved. An effort will be made here to portray the whole frontier, to suggest how it affected the life and institutions of Western civilization throughout the modern period; and as a basis for this exposition four propositions are submitted for consideration:

(1) Europe had a frontier more than a century before the United States was settled.

(2) Europe's frontier was much greater than that of the United States, or of any other one nation; it was the greatest of all time.

(3) The frontier of Europe was almost, if not quite, as important in determining the life and institutions of modern Europe as the frontier of America was in shaping the course of American history. Without the frontier modern Europe would have been so different from what it became that it could hardly be considered modern at all. This is almost equivalent to saying that the frontier made Europe modern.

(4) The close of the Great Frontier may mark the end of an epoch in Western civilization just as the close of the American frontier is often said to have marked the end of the first phase of American history. If the close of the Great Frontier does mark the end of an age, the modern age, then the institutions designed to function in

a society dominated largely by frontier forces will find themselves under severe strain.

If we conceive of Western Europe as a unified, densely populated region with a common culture and civilization—which it has long had basically—and if we see the frontier also as a unit, a vast and vacant land without culture, we are in position to view the interaction between the two as a simple but gigantic operation extending over more than four centuries, a process that may appear to be the drama of modern civilization.

To emphasize the unity of western Europe, and at the same time set it off in sharp contrast to its opposite, the frontier, we may call it the Metropolis. Metropolis is a good name, implying what Europe really was, a cultural center holding within it everything pertaining to Western civilization. Prior to 1500 the Metropolis comprised all the "known" world save Asia, which was but vaguely known. Its area was approximately 3,750,000 square miles, and its population is estimated to have been about 100 million people.

There is no need to elaborate the conditions under which these people lived, but it should be remembered that by modern standards the society was a static one with well-defined classes. The population pressed hard on the means of subsistence. There was not much food, practically no money, and very little freedom. What is more important, there was practically no means of escape for those people living in this closed world. The idea of progress had not been born. Heaven alone, which could be reached only through the portals of death, offered any hope to the masses of the Metropolis.

Then came the miracle that was to change everything, the emancipator bearing rich gifts of land and more land, of gold and silver, of new foods for every empty belly and new clothing stuffs for every half-naked back. Europe, the Metropolis, knocked on the door of the Great Frontier, and when the door was opened it was seen to be golden, for within there was undreamed-of treasure, enough to make the whole Metropolis rich. The long quest of a half-starved people had at last been rewarded with success beyond comprehension.

Columbus has been accepted as the symbol, as the key that unlocked the golden door to a new world, but we know that he was only one of a group of curious investigators, Portuguese, Spanish, English, Dutch, and Scandinavian, men of the Metropolis and not of one country. Within a brief period, as history is told, Columbus and his prying associates pulled back the curtains of ignorance and revealed to the Metropolis three new continents, a large part of a fourth, and thousands of islands in oceans hitherto hardly known. They brought all of these—continents, oceans, and islands—and deposited them as a free gift at the feet of the impoverished Metropolis.

The Metropolis had a new piece of property and the frontier had a new owner. The Metropolitans were naturally curious about their property, and quite naturally began to ask questions about it. How big is it? Who lives on it? What is its inherent worth? What can *I* get out of it? They learned that the frontier had an area five or six times that of Europe; that it was practically vacant, occupied by a few primitive inhabitants whose rights need not be respected; that its inherent worth could only be guessed at. As to what can *I* get out of it?, the answer came in time clear and strong: You can get everything you want from gold and silver to furs and foods, and in any quantity you want, provided only that you are willing to venture and work! And more faintly came the small voice, hardly audible: Something all of you can get as a by-product is some measure of freedom.

The Metropolitans decided to accept the gifts. Instantly the divisions in Europe were projected into the frontier as each little European power that could man a ship seized a section of the frontier bigger than itself and tried to fight all the others off. Each nation wanted it all. The result was a series of wars lasting from 1689 to 1763 and from these wars England, France, and Spain emerged as chief owners of the frontier world. Their success was more apparent than real, for a spirit of freedom had been nurtured in the distant lands, and in less than fifty years England had lost her chief prize while Spain and France had lost practically everything.

But their loss, like their previous gain, was more apparent than real. True, by 1820 the Metropolis had lost title to most of the new land, but it had not lost something more precious than title—namely, the beneficent effects that the frontier exerted on the older countries. The political separation of most of North and South America relieved the Metropolis of responsibility and onerous obligations, but it did not cut off the abundance of profits. Europe continued to share in the riches and the opportunity that the opening of the golden door had made visible.

III

What was the essential character of the frontier? Was the direct force it exerted spiritual, intellectual, or was it material? The frontier was basically a vast body of wealth without proprietors. It was an empty land more than five times the size of western Europe, a land whose resources had not been exploited. Its first impact was mainly economic. Bathed in and invigorated by a flood of wealth, the Metropolis began to seethe with economic excitement.

With all the ships coming and going, the wharves of Europe were piled high with strange goods, the tables were set with exotic foods of delightful flavors, and new-minted coins of gold and silver rattled in the coffers of the market place. The boom began when Columbus returned from his first voyage, and it continued at an ever-accelerating pace until the frontier that fed it was no more. Assuming that the frontier closed about 1890, it may be said that the boom lasted approximately four hundred years. It lasted so long that it came to be considered the normal state, a fallacious assumption for any boom. It is conceivable that this boom has given the peculiar character to modern history, to what we call Western civilization.

Assuming that there was such a boom and that it lasted four hundred years, it follows that a set of institutions, economic, political, and social, would in that time evolve to meet the needs of the world in boom. Insofar as they were designed to meet peculiar conditions, these institutions would be specialized boomward. It is accepted that a set of institutions has developed since 1500, and we speak of them as modern to distinguish them from medieval institutions. Therefore we may well inquire whether our modern institutions—economic, political, and social, constituting the superstructure of Western civilization—are founded on boom conditions.

The factors involved, though of gigantic magnitude, are simple in nature and in their relation one to another. They are the old familiar ones of population, land, and capital. With the opening of the Great Frontier, land and capital rose out of all proportion to population, of those to share it, and therefore conditions were highly favorable to general prosperity and a boom. What we are really concerned with is an *excess* of land and an *excess* of capital for division among a relatively *fixed* number of people. The population did increase, but not until the nineteenth century did the extra population compare with the extra land and capital that had been long available.

For example, in 1500 the Metropolis had a population of 100 million people crowded into an area of 3,750,000 square miles. The population density for the entire Metropolis was 26.7 persons per square mile. For each person there was available about twenty-four acres, a ratio that changed little from 1300 to 1650. The opening of the frontier upset the whole situation by destroying the balance that had been struck between land and man. A land excess of nearly 20 million square miles became available to the same number of people, reducing population density to less than five, increasing the average area per individual to 148 acres instead of 24.

Capital may be considered in two forms, as gold and silver and as capital goods or commodities. The Metropolis was short of both forms of wealth throughout the medieval period, and the dearth of coin prior to the discoveries was most critical. It has been estimated that the total amount of gold and silver in Europe in 1492 was less than 200 million dollars, less than two dollars per person. Certainly there was not enough to serve the needs of exchange, which was carried on by barter, or to give rise to erudite theories of money economy. Then very suddenly the whole money situation changed.

By 1500 the Spaniards had cracked the treasure houses of the Great Frontier and set a stream of gold and silver flowing into the Metropolis, a stream that continued without abatement for 150 years, and that still continues. This flood of precious metals changed all the relations existing between man and money, between gold and a bushel of wheat or a *fanega* of barley. That changed relationship wrought the price revolution because temporarily—so fast did the metals come—there was more money than things, and so prices rose to the modern level. This new money was a powerful stimulus to the quest for more, and set the whole Metropolis into the frenzy of daring and adventure which gave character to the modern age.

Since our concern here is with the excess of wealth over population, we may examine with interest the rise in the quantity of gold and silver. Taking the 200 million dollars of 1492 as a base, we find that by 1600 the amount had increased eightfold, by 1700 it had risen nearly twentyfold, by 1800 it stood at thirty-sevenfold, and by 1900 at a hundred-and-fourfold over what was on hand when the frontier was opened. Obviously this increase of precious metals was out of all proportion to the increase in population. If we grant that an excess of money makes a boom, then here in this new treasure was the stuff a boom needed. It is safe to say that out of each $100 worth of precious metals produced in the world since 1493, not less than $85 have been supplied by the frontier countries and not more than $15 by the Metropolis, including Asia. The bearing of these facts on the rise of a money economy, of modern capitalism, is something for the economists to think about.

The spectacular influx of precious metals should not obscure the fact that they constituted but the initial wave of wealth rolling into the Metropolis from the Great Frontier. Wave followed wave in endless succession in the form of material things, and each deposit left the Metropolis richer than before. Unfortunately the quantity of material goods cannot be measured, but we know it was enormous. South America sent coffee, Africa, cocoa, and the West Indies sent sugar to sweeten them. Strange and flavorsome fruits came from the tropics. From primeval forests came ship timbers, pitch, and tar with which to build the fleets for merchants and warriors. North America sent furs for the rich and cotton for the poor so that all could have more than one garment. The potato, adapted to the Metropolis, became second to bread as the staff of life. The New World gave Indian corn or maize, and the rich lands on which to grow it, and in time hides and beef came from the plains and pampas of two continents. Everywhere in Europe from the royal palace to the humble cottage men smoked American tobacco and under its soothing influence dreamed of far countries, wealth, and adventure. Scientists brought home strange plants and herbs and made plant experiment stations in scores of European gardens. In South America they found the bark of a tree from which quinine was derived to cure malaria and another plant which they sent to the East Indies to establish the rubber industry. No, it is not possible to measure the amount of goods flowing into Europe, but it can be said that the Great Frontier hung for centuries like the horn of plenty over the Metropolis and emptied out on it an avalanche of wealth.

At this point let us turn to the growth of population, the number of people who in a rough sense shared the excess of land and of precious metals. As stated above the population in 1500 stood at about 100 million, and it did not increase appreciably before 1650. All the people of European origin, whether in the Metropolis or in the Great Frontier, had a little more than doubled by 1800. Not until the nineteenth century was the increase rapid. By 1850 the increase was more than threefold, by 1900 more than fivefold, but in 1940 population had increased eightfold over that of 1500. The significant fact is that between 1500 and 1850 the quantity of both land and capital stood high out of all proportion to the quantity of population. Equally significant, and somewhat disturbing, is the fact that the excess of land incident to opening the frontier disappeared in the world census of 1930. By 1940 the enlarged Western world was more crowded than the small world of Europe was in 1500. It was the observation of this fact which led Dean Inge to remark in 1938 that "the house is full." Much earlier William Graham Sumner commented on the man-land ratio: "It is this ratio of population to land which determines what are the possibilities of human development or the limits of what man can attain in civilization and comfort." To put the matter in another way, if the boom rested on a four-century excess of land over population, the land base of the boom disappeared in 1930.

The boom hypothesis of modern history may be summed up by stating that with the tapping of the resources of the Great Frontier there came into the possession of the Metropolis a body of wealth consisting of land, precious metals, and commodities out of all proportion to the number of people. . . .

IV

If the opening of the Great Frontier did precipitate a boom in Western civilization, the effects on human ideas and institutions must have been profound and far-reaching. In general such a boom would hasten the passing away of the ideas and institutions of a static culture and the sure appearance of others adapted to a dynamic and prospering society. There is no doubt that medieval society was breaking up at the time of the discoveries, that men's minds had been sharpened by their intellectual exercises, and that their spirits had been stirred by doubt. The thinkers were restless and inquiring, but what they lacked was room in which to try out their innovations, and a fresh and uncluttered soil in which some of their new ideas could take hold and grow. Their desires had to be matched with opportunity before they could realize on their aspirations, however laudable. The frontier offered them the room and the opportunity. It did not necessarily originate ideas, but it acted as a relentless sifter, letting some pass, and rejecting others. Those that the frontier favored prospered, and finally matured into institutions; those it did not favor became recessive, dormant, and many institutions based on these ideas withered away. Feudal tenure, serfdom, barter, primogeniture, and the notion that the world was a no-good place in which to live are examples of things untenable in the presence of the frontier.

Since we are dealing with the modern age, it would be very helpful if we could discover what it emphasized most. Where was the chief accent of modernity? What has been its focus? *Who* has held the spotlight on the stage of history since 1500? There can be little doubt, though there may be enough to start an argument, that the answer to all these questions is: the Individual. It is he who has been emphasized, accented; it is on him that the spotlight has focused; it is his importance that has been magnified. He is—or was—the common denominator of modern times, and an examination of any strictly modern institution such as democracy or capitalism will reveal an individual at the core, trying to rule himself in one case and make some money in the other. Not god nor the devil nor the state, but the ordinary man has been the favorite child of modern history.

Did the Great Frontier, which was his contemporary, have any part in giving the individual his main chance, the triple opportunity of ruling himself, enriching himself, and saving his own soul on his own hook? These three freedoms were institutionalized in Protestantism, capitalism, and democracy—whose basic assumption is that they exist for the individual, and that the individual must be free in order to make them work. The desire for freedom men surely have always had, but in the old Metropolis conditions prevailed which made freedom impossible. Everywhere in Europe the individual was surrounded by institutions which, whether by design or not, kept him unfree. He was walled in by man-made regulations which controlled him from baptism to extreme unction.

Then the golden door of the Great Frontier opened, and a way of escape lay before him. He moved out from the Metropolis to land on a distant shore, in America, Australia, South Africa. Here in the wild and empty land there was not a single institution; man had left them, albeit temporarily, far behind. Regardless of what befell him later, for an instant he was free of all the restrictions that society had put upon him. In short, he had escaped his human masters only to find himself in the presence of another, a less picayunish one.

The character of the new master, before whom he stood stripped of his institutions, was so in contrast with that of the old one as to defy comparison. Man stood naked in the presence of nature. On this subject, Alexander von Humbolt said, "In the Old World, nations and the distinction of their civilization form the principal point in the picture; in the New World, man and his production almost disappear amidst the stupendous display of wild and gigantic nature." The outstanding qualities of wild and gigantic nature are its impersonality and impassiveness. Nature broods over man, casts its mysterious spells, but it never intervenes for or against him. It gives no orders, issues no proclamations, has no prisons, no privileges; it knows nothing of vengeance or mercy. Before nature all men are free and equal.

The important point is that the abstract man we have been following did not have to *win* his freedom. It was imposed upon him and he could not escape it. Being caught in the trap of freedom, his task was to adjust himself to it and to devise procedures which would be more convenient for living in such a state. His first task was to govern himself, for self-government is what freedom imposes.

Of course there was not just one man on the frontier. In a short time the woods were full of them, all trained in the same school. As the years went by, they formed the habits of freedom, cherished it; and when a distant government tried to take from them that to which they had grown accustomed, they resisted, and their resistance was called the American Revolution. The American frontiersmen did not fight England to gain freedom, but to preserve it and have it officially recognized by the Metropolis. "Your nation," wrote Herman Melville, "enjoyed no little independence before your declaration declared it." Whence came this independence? Not from parliaments or kings or legislative assemblies,

but from the conditions, the room, the space, and the natural wealth amidst
which they lived. "The land was ours," writes Robert Frost, "before we
were the land's."

The other institution that magnified the importance of the individual
was capitalism, an economic system under which each person undertakes
to enrich himself by his own effort. It is only in the presence of great
abundance that such a free-for-all system of wealth-getting can long operate. There must be present enough wealth to go around to make such an
economy practicable. We have seen that the tapping of the frontier furnished just this condition, a superabundance of land, of gold and silver,
and of commodities which made the principle of *laissez faire* tenable. In
the frontier the embryonic capitalists of the sixteenth and seventeenth
centuries hit a magnificent windfall which set them up in business by
demonstrating that the game of wealth-getting was both interesting and
profitable. For four hundred years, to paraphrase Bernard DeVoto, "men
stumbled over fortunes looking for cows." . . . Free homesteads in Kansas, free gold claims in California, and free grass on the Great Plains are
examples of windfalls coming at the tag end of the frontier period, windfalls which come no more. In the larger sense the Great Frontier was a
windfall for Europe.

There is an unpleasant logic inherent in the frontier boom hypothesis
of modern history. We come to it with the reluctance that men always
have when they come to the end of a boom. They look back on the grand
opportunities they had, they remember the excitement and adventure of
it, they tot up their accounts and hope for another chance. Western civilization today stands facing a closed frontier, and in this sense it faces a
unique situation in modern times.

If we grant the boom, we must concede that the institutions we have,
such as democracy and capitalism, were boom-born; we must also admit
that the individual, this cherished darling of modern history, attained his
glory in an abnormal period when there was enough room to give him
freedom and enough wealth to give him independence. The future of the
individual, of democracy and capitalism, and of many other modern institutions are deeply involved in this logic, and the lights are burning late
in the capitals of the Western world where grave men are trying to determine what that future will be.

Meantime less thoughtful people speak of new frontiers, though nothing comparable to the Great Frontier has yet been found. The business
man sees a business frontier in the customers he has not yet reached; the
missionary sees a religious frontier among the souls he has not yet saved;
the social worker sees a human frontier among the suffering people whose
woes he has not yet alleviated; the educator of a sort sees the ignorance

he is trying to dispel as a frontier to be taken; and the scientists permit us to believe that they are uncovering the real thing in a scientific frontier. But as yet no Columbus has come in from these voyages and announced: "Gentlemen, there is your frontier!" The best they do is to say that it is out beyond, that if you work hard enough and have faith enough, and put in a little money, you will surely find it. If you watch these peddlers of substitute frontiers, you will find that nearly every one wants you to buy something, give something, or believe in something. They want you to be a frontier for them. Unlike Columbus, they bring no continents and no oceans, no gold or silver or grass or forest to you.

I should like to make it clear that mankind is really searching for a new frontier which we once had and did not prize, and the longer we had it, the less we valued it; but now that we have lost it, we have a great pain in the heart, and we are always trying to get it back again. It seems to me that historians and all thoughtful persons are bound by their obligation to say that there is no new frontier in sight comparable in magnitude or importance to the one that is lost. They should point out the diversity and heterogeneity, not to say the absurdity, of so-called new frontiers. They are all fallacies, these new frontiers, and they are pernicious in proportion to their plausibility and respectability. The scientists themselves should join in disabusing the public as to what science can be expected to do. It can do much, but, to paraphrase Isaiah Bowman, it is not likely soon to find a new world or make the one we have much bigger than it is. If the frontier is gone, we should have the courage and honesty to recognize the fact, cease to cry for what we have lost, and devote our energy to finding the solutions to the problems now facing a frontierless society. And when the age we now call modern is modern no longer, and requires a new name, we may appropriately call it the Age of the Frontier, and leave it to its place in history.

7 William H. McNeill ◆
The Great Frontier: Freedom and Hierarchy

*Although historian William McNeill has applauded Webb's idea of the
Great Frontier as "a great achievement," he also saw a darker side to the
"process of civilizational expansion" than Webb or Turner recognized.**
*"Progress and liberty, so dear to our forebears, played a part in the pro-
cess," McNeill argued, "but so did their opposites—slavery and the destruction of all those non-European cultures and societies that got in the
way."† As Europeans traveled to other continents, they brought deadly
diseases that decimated natives and created "free land," but left those
areas with a critical shortage of labor. In Turner's ideal world, Europeans responded to scarce labor by creating more egalitarian societies,
where each person worked with his or her hands; in much of North and
South America, however, Europeans filled the void of laborers by enslaving or indenturing others.*

One of America's premier historians, McNeill is widely known for his
Rise of the West: A History of the Human Community *(1963) and for
studies of large questions in a global framework, including* Plagues and
Peoples *(1976) and* The Pursuit of Power: Technology, Armed Force, and
Society Since A.D. 1000 *(1982). In the following excerpt from* The Great
Frontier: Freedom and Hierarchy in Modern Times *(1983), McNeill
argued that the egalitarian ideal was not the norm for Europe's overseas
frontiers.*

B efore 1750, therefore, the steppe and forest zones of Eurasia, together
with North and South America, constituted the principal regions
where frontier encounters assumed the extraordinary form familiar to us
from our own national history. This was where Europeans could and did
begin to occupy land emptied, or almost emptied, of older inhabitants by
the catastrophic juxtaposition of disease-experienced civilized populations with epidemiologically and culturally vulnerable natives.[1] Nothing
comparable had ever happened before. European expansion therefore assumed unparalleled proportions. The process gave birth to the two politically dominant states of our own time, the USSR and the USA, one east

From William H. McNeill, *The Great Frontier: Freedom and Hierarchy in
Modern Times*, 17–26. © 1983 by Princeton University Press. Reprinted by per-
mission of Princeton University Press.
  **The Great Frontier: Freedom and Hierarchy in Modern Times* (Princeton:
Princeton University Press, 1983), 8.
  †Ibid., 8–9.

and the other west of the older centers of European civilization. Brazil and the diverse states of Spanish America are likewise heirs of this frontier. So is South Africa; but the European encroachment on Australia, New Zealand, and other Pacific islands did not begin until after the middle of the eighteenth century and so does not yet enter our purview.

The most salient characteristic of the Great Frontier created by the combined ravages of civilized diseases, alcohol, and firearms on indigenous populations was that human numbers were or soon became scant in the contact zone. Anyone who wished to exploit the land agriculturally or sought to mine precious metals or extract other raw materials faced a problem of finding an adequate labor force to do the necessary work. Shortage of manpower meant that European skills and knowledge could not readily be brought to bear in frontier lands, no matter how richly they were endowed.

Carrying Europeans across the seas to remedy this situation was expensive. Relatively few ever made the crossing before the 1840s, when steamships began to cheapen passage and to enlarge passenger-carrying capacity. Estimates of transatlantic migration are very inexact, since early records of voyages across the ocean are spotty at best and seldom include passenger lists. A recent guess set the total of British immigrants to North America before 1780 at 750,000 and of French to Canada at only 10,000.[2] Further south no careful calculation of any general total of European immigration exists, though what scraps of evidence there are suggest that something like a million persons crossed the ocean to take up residence in the Caribbean and Latin America before 1800.[3]

Spaniards did, of course, employ Amerindians in the mines and for innumerable building projects and other enterprises in the first rush of their conquest. But the extreme vulnerability of such a labor force to epidemic disease led to heavy loss of life and soon made recruitment difficult. In most islands of the Caribbean the Amerindian population died out completely. Amerindians also disappeared almost totally from the coastal regions of the Caribbean, where African diseases reinforced the destructive power of those imported from Europe. Enslaved Africans, however, could and soon did provide a more disease-resistant labor force for plantation agriculture and other economic enterprises in the New World. Relatively precise calculation of the number of slaves carried from Africa is possible because the traffic came to be conducted by specialized slave ships, whose number and carrying capacity can be established with some accuracy. A recent estimate puts the number of Africans brought to the New World before 1820 at 7.8 million; and the same authority suggests that this figure is four to five times the contemporaneous total of European migration across the Atlantic.[4]

This perhaps surprising statistic ought to remind us of how important compulsory labor became and long remained in the New World. Compulsion bulks even larger in our perspective when we remember that most of the Europeans who crossed the Atlantic before steamships cheapened the cost of passage came as unfree indentured servants. Between 300,000 and 400,000 such persons left Britain for North America between 1650 and 1780, according to the best available estimates. This figure amounts to something between half and three-quarters of all the whites who came to North America from Europe before the American revolution.[5] Indentured servants could, of course, look forward to becoming free men if they survived the period of their indentured labor. But as long as their bondage lasted—often seven years—their legal position vis-à-vis their master was not much different from that of black slaves, though the absence of physical differentiation in outward appearance may have made it easier for them to run away before completing their contracts.

The free, egalitarian, and neo-barbarian style of frontier life, so dear to Turner and his followers, did of course exist in North America. It arose wherever export trade failed to thrive during the early stages of colonization. But in the more favored and accessible regions, where European skills proved capable of producing marketable wealth on a relatively large scale, frontier conditions ordinarily provoked not freedom but a social hierarchy steeper than anything familiar in Europe itself. The reason was that commercially precocious frontier societies usually found it necessary to assure the availability and subordination of a labor force by imposing stern legal restrictions on freedom to choose and change occupation. Hence, slave plantations and gangs of indentured servants in the Americas, as well as the serf-cultivated estates of eastern Europe, were quite as characteristic of the frontier as were the free and independent farmers and jacks-of-all-trades whom we habitually associate with frontier life.

One form of export trade that often played a prominent role on the frontier did impose a close symbiosis of equalitarian freedom with bureaucratic hierarchy. Capturing and collecting existing goods—whether furs, placer gold, raw rubber from the Amazon rain forest, or codfish from the Grand Banks—could only be done by a dispersed work force, operating beyond any manager's control. Trans-oceanic marketing of such goods, on the other hand, required comparatively large-scale organization.[6] Trading companies solved this problem by stationing agents at strategic locations, where they conducted a barter trade with the men who did the actual collecting. Commodities exchanged were sufficiently valuable to the parties concerned to bear the cost of transport; and even at remote locations, agents could still be controlled by their home offices since everyone knew

that if they failed to send back adequate amounts of the sought-after commodity, the flow of trade goods needed for barter would promptly dry up.

Though a few big trading companies thus managed to span the forbidding distances between European metropolitan centers and the frontier, it remained the case that frontier conditions could not sustain the
elaborately graded hierarchy that prevailed in the heartlands of European
civilization. Near the center, long tradition and market constraints combined to fit men and women into an elaborately interlocking and largely
hereditary pattern of occupations. Legal differentiation separated clergy,
nobles, and commoners, and defined membership in a great variety of
privileged corporations. In skilled trades, apprentices were bound to their
masters for a period of years under conditions that somewhat resembled
indentured labor in America. In all these senses, labor was subject to
legal coercion in Europe too. But slavery was unimportant; serfdom had
disappeared from the most active centers of European economic life long
before Columbus sailed; and the price system, acting through fluctuating
wages, was becoming increasingly effective in allocating and reallocating labor among competing occupations. Large-scale undertakings like
mining and shipping could recruit the necessary manpower by offering
appropriate rates of pay. Even soldiering had become a question of ful-
filling a contract freely entered into, at least in principle; though once
enlisted, a soldier, more even than an indentured servant or apprentice,
faced severe penalties for seeking to withdraw from his place in the ranks.

Western Europe's reliance on the market as a means of allocating and
reallocating labor among alternative employments was sustained by birth
and survival rates that were high enough to supply hands for existing
enterprises with a few left over for promising new ventures as well. Legal
compulsion, backed by force, became quite unnecessary when enough
labor presented itself spontaneously for carrying out all the tasks that the
rulers and managers of society felt were really necessary and important.
Under such circumstances, compulsion became a waste of time and effort, and a needless provocation as well.

The balance of supply and demand for labor was always precarious.
The Black Death in the fourteenth century set back European population
for more than a century and altered wage rates abruptly. Thereafter,
recurrent epidemics, concentrated especially in towns, frequently cut back
on local populations, sometimes very sharply.[7] But such perturbations were
rapidly made good by accelerated influx from the healthier countryside,
where all those youths who were unable to count on inheriting rights to
enough cultivable land to live as their parents were doing constituted a
pool of ready recruits for any venture that promised escape from what

was, within the village confines, a radically unsatisfactory career prospect. Europe's remarkable record of expansion at home and abroad, dating back to about A.D. 900, rested on a demographic pattern that regularly provided a surplus of rural youths for export to towns and armies, with a few left over for migration to more distant frontier zones as well.

But Europe's demographic balance, elaborate social hierarchy, and the well-established interdependence of social classes could not be reproduced on the frontier. Local population was inadequate. Large-scale enterprise that required major input of labor could not be carried on without compulsion. This was as true of the overland as of the overseas frontier. The legal enserfment of Russian peasants in the seventeenth century differed only slightly from the slavery of American plantations; and debt peonage imposed on Amerindians in the New World, as well as English indentured labor, had the same practical effect, even if the obligated human beings retained rights under these legal systems that were denied to black slaves.

The whole point was to keep slaves, serfs, indentured servants, and peons at work on tasks a managerial, owning class wanted to see accomplished. In proportion to their success, a flood of new goods—sugar, cotton, silver, wheat, indigo, and many more—entered European and world markets. Income thus accruing to enterprising landowners, mine operators, and resident factors for wholesale merchants based in Europe allowed them to buy expensive imported European products so that they could live like gentlemen—more or less. In this fashion a slender simulacrum of European polite society quickly arose in American and European frontier lands. Subsequently, in proportion as local population grew so that labor became available for various crafts and retail commercial occupations, an approximation to European forms of society could gradually develop in the shadow of the planter-landowner-managerial class.

The prominence of slavery and serfdom in European frontier expansion did not foreclose the egalitarian alternative entirely, even in societies dominated by compulsory labor. Runaways and individuals who had worked out their indenture could and did take off into the backwoods to carve out a life free of any obligation to social superiors. Such pioneers often cut themselves off from any but sporadic contacts with civilization. But, like planters and landowners of the frontier, they continued to depend for some critically important items on sources of supply far in the rear. Guns and ammunition, as well as iron for tools, were things that even the most remote frontiersmen found it hard to do without. How they got possession of such goods is often unclear. Hand-to-hand swapping could reach far beyond organized markets; and incentive to swapping was real enough since the frontier could usually be made to yield something precious and portable—furs, placer gold, or the like—that commanded a high enough price on world markets to justify its carriage across many miles of plain and mountain.

Hence, even the most remote and barbarous *coureurs de bois* of North America, the *bandeirantes* of Brazil, the *gauchos* of the pampas, the *vortrekkers* of South Africa, and the Cossacks of Siberia retained a significant and vitally important link with the nearest outposts of civilization. Like the slave-owners and serf-owners of the frontier they, too, participated in the world market system that centered in western Europe. Their participation shrank in proportion as their mode of life descended toward local self-sufficiency. But complete autarky meant loss of the margin of superiority newcomers enjoyed vis-à-vis older native inhabitants. Those who cut loose entirely from Europe-centered and -managed trade nets simply merged into local indigenous populations, and thereupon ceased to act as agents of frontier expansion. Such persons were always few, since the status of a man without access to a gun (and other European-made goods) diminished drastically in remote communities.

The sharp polarization in frontier society between freedom and hierarchy should therefore be understood as arising from alternative responses to the overriding reality of the frontier, to wit, the drastic shortage of labor. For this reason, one social structure was capable of abrupt transmutation into its opposite. Runaway slaves or serfs who made good an escape from their master's control at once became egalitarian frontiersmen. The maroons of Jamaica constituted the most famous such community, but were only one of many. On Europe's other flank, Cossack hordes in their early days recruited runaway serfs as a matter of course; later, after the hordes were themselves captured by the Russian state, such escape became illegal, though successful flight into the depths of Siberia continued to occur as long as Russian serfdom endured.

The opposite transmutation from egalitarianism to legally imposed hierarchy was even more common. In the east, wholesale enserfment of once-free peasant populations was the order of the day when frontier expansion into the steppelands got seriously under way in the seventeenth and eighteenth centuries. In the New World, the rise of peonage in Mexico in the sixteenth and seventeenth centuries was analogous. Efforts to transplant reinvigorated forms of manorial jurisdiction to Canada and New York met with scant success; and indentured labor provided only a precarious basis for gentlemen farmers in Virginia and Maryland in the seventeenth and eighteenth centuries. But such efforts show that the urge to impose legal bonds on free men operated in English, Dutch, and French colonial society as well as on the Russian and Spanish frontiers.

We are accustomed to thinking of the egalitarian alternative as the norm of frontier life. Both Turner and Webb, for example, skip over the role of slavery in the frontier history of the United States. I suppose this remarkable omission arose from the fact that they cherished an ideal of American liberty and equality, and also felt nostalgia for the days of their youth when residues of the Wisconsin and west Texas forms of frontier life still dominated local society. By noticing only one aspect of frontier reality, Turner and Webb were able to combine these sentiments uninhibitedly. But this kind of wishful thinking deserves to be subjected to skeptical examination. If one does so, it seems to me that a neutral observer would have to conclude that compulsion and legally reinforced forms of social hierarchy were more generally characteristic of frontier society than were equality and freedom.

Notes

1. Drastic disorganization of traditional cultural values invited self-destructive escape into alcoholism among native peoples of the frontier. Cf. Mark Twain, *Life on the Mississippi*, chapter 60, "Speculations and Conclusions":

> How solemn and beautiful is the thought that the earliest pioneer of civilization, the van-leader of civilization, is never the steamboat, never the railroad, never the newspaper, never the Sabbath-school, never the missionary—but always whisky! Such is the case. Look history over: you will see. The missionary comes after the whisky—I mean he arrives after the whisky has arrived; next comes the poor immigrant, with ax and hoe and rifle; next the trader; next the miscellaneous rush; next the gambler, desperado and highwayman, and all their kindred in sin of both sexes; and next the smart chap who has bought up an old grant that covers all the land; this brings the lawyer tribe; the vigilance committee brings the undertaker. All these interests bring the newspaper; the newspaper starts up politics and a railroad; all hands turn to and build a church and a jail—and behold! civilization is established forever in the land.

2. Stanley L. Engerman, "Servants to Slaves to Servants: Contract Labor and European Expansion," in *Colonialism and Migration: Indentured Labour Before and After Slavery*, ed. H. van den Boogaart and P. C. Emmer (The Hague: Martinus Nijhoff/Leiden University Press, [1984] Comparative Studies in Overseas History, Vol. VI).

3. David Eltis, "Free and Coerced Transatlantic Migrations: Some Comparisons," *American Historical Review* [88 (April 1983): 251–80]. Table 3 gives a grand total of 1,250,000 Europeans as emigrating to Brazil and Spanish America, excluding Peru, prior to 1825; but this total rests on a collocation of very flimsy estimates. Peter Boyd-Bowman, "The Regional Origins of the Earliest Spanish Colonists of America," *Modern Language Association Publications* [71 (1956): 1152–72], calculates that 200,000 Spaniards reached America by 1600. James

Lockhart, *Spanish Peru, 1532–1560* (Madison, 1968), p. 12, says that 8,000 Spaniards reached Peru within the first 25 years of the conquest. These were the only statistically careful estimates I found.

4. Engerman, *op. cit.*, p. 11. The landmark study was Philip Curtin, *The Atlantic Slave Trade: A Census* (Madison, 1969). Engerman's figure represents only minor modifications of Curtin's original calculations.

5. David W. Galenson, *White Servitude in Colonial America* (Cambridge, 1981), p. 17 and *passim*. I owe my chance to see Engerman's unpublished essay, cited above, to Professor Galenson's kindness in acting as intermediary.

6. Codfish were exceptional inasmuch as even small fishing ships could sail back to Europe at the end of the season and market their salted catch without any centralized management whatsoever.

7. Cf. Roger Mols, *Introduction à la démographie historique des villes d'Europe du XIVe au XVIIIe siècle*, 2 vols. (Louvain, 1955), for telling examples of the frequency and severity of local disease disasters in early modern centuries.

8 Walter Nugent ◆ New World Frontiers: Comparisons and Agendas

During the nineteenth century the attraction of America's frontiers intensified as news spread through Europe that land was good, cheap, and available. Population pressures, low wages, unemployment, and the replacement of sailing ships by more reliable steamships encouraged millions of people to try their luck in the New World. As Professor Alfred W. Crosby has noted, "the greatest transoceanic migration in human history" took place between 1851 and 1960, when more than 61 million Europeans migrated to continents other than that of their birth. In the following essay Walter Nugent considers one important phase of this movement by comparing the experiences of the 33 million immigrants who began new lives on the frontiers of Argentina, Brazil, Canada, and the United States in the half century before World War I.*

Nugent shows that while all four countries actively recruited Europeans, built railway networks to open up the wilderness, and removed the aboriginal inhabitants from the frontiers with various degrees of harshness, a key element in the appeal of a New World destination was the possibility of owning land. Deeply rooted traditions of latifundia in Argentina and Brazil soon forced the majority of their immigrants to become sharecroppers or to seek work in the cities. In the United States and Canada, however, the central governments were able to retain ownership of land as public domain "until it was transferred to private hands —not always but usually actual settlers." This helps to explain why 60 percent of all immigrants during this period came to the United States and, as Nugent points out, demonstrates that in some respects American and Canadian governments maintained stronger control over their frontiers than did their Latin American counterparts.

Frontier history is inherently comparative history, and Nugent's essay reveals the insights that can be gained when researchers move beyond the narrow boundaries of national history. His list of eleven avenues for further research underscores the open-endedness of historical inquiry, and his call for a new discipline of comparative peace history seems especially appropriate in the aftermath of the sometimes rancorous quincentennial celebrations of Columbus's first trans-Atlantic voyage.

Tackes Professor of History at Notre Dame since 1984, Walter Nugent completed his Ph.D. in American history at the University of Chicago in

From a paper originally delivered at the Historical Society of Israel's June 1992 conference on the Discovery of America. © 1992, 1993 by Walter Nugent. Reprinted by permission of the author.

*Alfred W. Crosby, Jr., *The Columbian Exchange: Biological and Cultural Consequences of 1492* (Westport, CT: Greenwood Press, 1972), 214.

1961. He has taught at institutions including Indiana University, the Hebrew University of Jerusalem, and Warsaw University. Author of many books and articles, he is currently interested in demography and comparative history, as is suggested by his most recent book, Crossings: The Great Transatlantic Migrations, 1870–1914 *(Bloomington: Indiana University Press, 1992), and this wide-ranging essay, published here for the first time.*

E mpires and frontiers have many similarities.[1] Imperial outposts, considered from a demographic viewpoint, were frontiers that failed to take hold. Over the past five hundred years of European history, and most intensively in the late nineteenth century, several European states conquered and ruled various parts of the rest of the world—sometimes briefly, as was the case of the Belgian king in the Congo, sometimes as long as three or four centuries, as with Spain in the Americas and the Philippines. In the aftermath of the two world wars of this century, virtually all these imperial outposts disappeared, with governance reverting to the people who live there.

Frontiers of settlement, however, have remained, most notably in the Americas and in Oceania (including Australia and New Zealand), where European languages and cultures overwhelmed the native peoples to an irreversible degree. In the long view, "empires proved transient and frontiers evolved into permanent societies."[2] In places where the European presence was superimposed on an existing population, especially a large and long-developed one as in China, India, or Indochina, the imperial presence (no matter how temporarily mighty) withered and withdrew. Where the European presence became a self-sustaining, growing demographic regime, it either mixed with or pushed aside the indigenous peoples and supplanted them culturally.

The Europeans and their descendants considered this the frontier process. It seldom happened overnight. The Spanish and French presence in North America gradually became more secure, but less purely European, through intermarriage with native people. Such intermarriage remained rare in the English colonies, and the English settlements along the Chesapeake required reinforcement through immigration for almost a hundred years after their founding. By the 1780s, however, the British-stock American frontier of settlement crossed the Appalachians and through force of numbers overwhelmed the native peoples, who previously matched or outnumbered the Spanish, French, and English intruders.[3] By the 1880s domination of the American continents by European-descended peoples was virtually complete. It remained in place, while various empire-building European conquests of the 1880s, in Africa, Southeast Asia, and the Pacific, have disappeared. The difference was in numbers rather than attitude, for both settlers and imperial administrators assumed that their European presence was legitimate and beneficial.

Much of the focus in New World migration history has been on urban migrants, although most Europeans who migrated to the New World before 1900 were peasants, leaving one rural situation and entering another. They arrived in frontiers of settlement, the great mass of them going to Argentina, the United States, Canada, and Brazil. In the first three, the frontier of rural settlement lasted well past 1900, and in Brazil it is still going on. Without minimizing the significance of European migration to urban places in the New World (and cities were in many respects frontiers also, of both opportunity and exploitation), the settlement frontiers of those four major receiving countries bear comparison. These rural and chiefly agricultural areas took in the majority of the Europeans who migrated between 1870 and World War I, when steamships and steam railroads greatly magnified the flow in all directions between Europe and the Americas. As we now know, mass migration *out of Europe* never resumed on the same scale except for the half-dozen years between 1919 and 1924; economic and political dislocations, together with a tide of restrictionism in all major American receiving countries, halted the traffic despite continuing improvements in the means of travel.[4]

A brief sketch will provide a sense of migration and settlement patterns in Argentina, Brazil, Canada, and the United States in the half-century before World War I.[5] Of the fifty-five million migrants who left Europe for the Americas during this period, about 60 percent, or thirty-three million, remained, while the other 40 percent returned to spend their lives in Europe, many of them having secured what they went to America to find—namely, the means to a better life back home.[6] Of the thirty-three million who either failed in that aim or for other reasons decided to stay in the New World, more than 60 percent went to the United States, about 11 percent to Canada, another 11 percent to Argentina, and 8 percent to Brazil, with the remaining 10 percent scattered among the other republics and colonies, particularly Cuba. As the period opened, the United States already was home to a larger population than the other three countries combined, and in 1870 it stood reunited politically and on the brink of a startling economic and demographic expansion that was simultaneously industrial-urban and rural-agricultural. But the size of the United States within the entire spectrum of migration and settlement should not obscure the others' presence.

Argentina took in twice the number of migrants, relative to existing population, as did the United States. Between 1869 and 1914 the Argentine population nearly quadrupled (while that of the United States did not quite triple), much of the increase coming from immigration to the great port city and capital of Buenos Aires and to the central and northern provinces, the apparently limitless pampas. But, like the American Great Plains, the pampas were not limitless; within two generations they were filled with agricultural colonies producing wheat and beef for sale on world markets. By 1914, more than 30 percent of Argentina's people were European-born or the children of Europeans—a level twice that of the all-time peak of foreign-born and foreign-descended U.S. residents of just under 15 percent in 1910.[7] If ever a country was a "nation of immigrants," it was Argentina. More than half those immigrants were Italian, the majority from the north; a quarter were Spanish; and the rest belonged to a scattering of other European nationalities. Few in number, Britons played a disproportionately large economic role in Argentina, overseeing capital investment in railroads and in extractive enterprises. Italians appeared in every occupation and status level.

More so than in North America, Argentine land was "free"—that is, after 1879, the pampas were free of native inhabitants and for a brief time virtually cost-free for the taking. In that year an Argentine army "conquered the desert" by driving off or exterminating the Araucanians and other native groups who had thwarted Spanish and (after independence) Argentine invaders since the first contacts in the sixteenth century. Mendoza, on the eastern slope of the Andes, had been inaccessible from the Atlantic settlements since its founding in the late 1500s, but soon after the "conquest" it became the western terminus of a railroad spanning the seven hundred miles of pampas between it and Buenos Aires.

Railroads began running northward as well. What might have been called "the great Argentine desert" became home, by 1895, for several hundred thousand Italians and other European-descended people. The similarities to the former "great American desert" of the United States, particularly central Kansas, Nebraska, and Dakota Territory, were striking: population booming eight- to tenfold in twenty years, families of small farmers working the land either independently or in colonies, production funneling into exportable wheat and cattle, the railroad as a lifeline to regional, national, and world markets. The winters were milder on the pampas than on the Great Plains, and people spoke Italian or Spanish, rather than German or English, but otherwise the 1880s in northern Argentina and along the ninety-eighth meridian in North America were not so different.

Later, however, the differences became clearer. They were many, but among them, after the mid-1890s, were changes in Argentine settlement and migration patterns. Even in the fluid days of the 1880s and early 1890s, much of the pampas was legally owned by *latifundistas*, or *estancieros* if they ran cattle ranches, in large tracts. In J. Valerie Fifer's trenchant phrase, Argentina defied earlier expectations and became, after 1914, "not a 'new West' but an 'Old South'."[8] As land values and demand increased, these grandees became reluctant to sell to new settlers, instead preferring to lease to them. New settlers became tenants or sharecroppers. Migration to Argentina shifted from the land toward the cities, and changed in source from northern to southern Italy, becoming much more like the contemporaneous Italian migration to the United States. The Indians were gone by 1880, but by 1900 so were freehold opportunities. By 1914 Argentina enjoyed the best standard of living in the southern hemisphere, but it relied heavily on its service sector, continued high exports of foodstuffs, and imported capital. The guns of August 1914 changed much of that, and Argentina never recovered its momentum. Its "frontier" phase was over by 1914, indeed in many ways by 1900.[9]

Migration and settlement in Brazil involved sizable numbers but took shape differently from anywhere else in the Americas. Indians continued to live in the country and still do (as the world now knows about the Yanomami) but were too few and disorganized to present any hindrance to white advance in the areas that were "frontiers" in the late nineteenth century—chiefly the state of São Paulo. The "far west" (and north) of Mato Grosso, Rondônia, Amazonas, and Goias were frontiers of the twentieth-century future. Agricultural settlements, some dating back to 1824, of tens of thousands of Germans, Italians, and Poles, occupied parts of Rio Grande do Sul and the other southern states by the 1880s. They formed ethnic enclaves whose cultural assimilation still continues.

A more massive migration, however, began as soon as slavery was abolished in 1888. The coffee-planter elite of São Paulo state, the *fazendeiros*, eager to extend cultivation hundreds of miles inland, pressured the state government to replace the former slave labor force with European migrants, particularly northeastern Italians, to be recruited and transported with state subsidies. More than 1.3 million arrived in the next decade, 60 percent of them Venetians (Venezia was one of the hardest-hit provinces of Italy in its agrarian crisis of the 1880s) brought over as families, of whom more than 60 percent went to the coffee fields of São Paulo state. A few thousand who came with moderate capital were able to enter "nuclear colonies" and become freeholders, but the great majority worked as sharecroppers on the plantations (*fazendas*), achieving owner-operator status only rarely and with great difficulty. Conditions became so notorious that the Italian government conducted an investigation, and in 1902 it prohibited further contract recruitment of Italians. So-called spontaneous—that is, nonsponsored—migration to Brazil continued, including Italians, then Portuguese, Spanish, Japanese, and other groups.

But Brazil, despite its size, attracted the fewest Europeans of the four leading New World countries of migration and settlement. European migration slowed in the 1920s and virtually stopped after restrictive laws went into effect in 1930. But Brazil's settlement frontier never really ended. The struggle for turf among cattle ranchers, rubber gatherers, would-be farmers, and others continues. The environmental damage generated by this struggle receives frequent attention in the world press. Similar damage generated on eighteenth- and nineteenth-century frontiers in North America, now well disguised by the passage of time, has received less attention.[10]

Migration and settlement in Canada approached and then stopped at the rocky swamps of the Canadian Shield at the beginning of this period; newly cultivated land in Ontario became scarce after 1860. In Canada, relations between Indians and whites had been marked at times by harsh conflict, as late as the Second Riel Rebellion in Manitoba in 1885. But since Europeans began arriving in the early 1600s, French, English, and various Indian groups often accommodated each other. These relations were seldom wholly secure for either side, but they permitted Canada to avoid the near-constant conflict so characteristic of Indian-white relations in the United States. Throughout the nineteenth century, French-speaking Lower Canada (Quebec) grew in population much more from natural increase than from immigration. But Upper Canada, later Ontario, whose first white settlers were Loyalist refugees from the American Revolution, took in tens of thousands of British and Irish migrants from the 1820s to the 1860s. The frontier of farm settlement in Ontario in those decades closely resembled, in its economic and demographic characteristics, the farm frontier in Ohio, Michigan, and other Great Lakes states of the United States at that same time.

But the occupation of Ontario's potential farmland was nearly complete by the 1860s. The line of settlement had to stop at Lake Huron, Lake Erie, and the edge of the Canadian Shield. If the Anglo-American peace treaty of 1783, concluding the American War of Independence, had reflected the disposition of military forces at that moment, Michigan and Wisconsin would have become Canadian, and the settlement frontier of Canada would have simply pushed west, as happened in the United States. As it was, many young Canadians after 1860 did cross into Michigan and, in the 1870s and 1880s, westward into Kansas and Nebraska. The Canadian government devised what it called its "National Policy" in the early 1870s, involving a system of distributing its public lands to actual settlers (copying some of the better features of the Homestead Act of 1862 in the United States), who could also buy contiguous acreage from the

Canadian Pacific Railway then being built to link eastern Canada and the Pacific (it opened in 1885).

Only after 1900, when migration and settlement in the United States began filling up North Dakota and Montana, was the Canadian Shield circumvented. Migrants either came directly by the Canadian Pacific Railway to the potential farm and grazing land of the prairie provinces or scuttled northwestward from Minnesota and the Dakotas, regarding the forty-ninth parallel border as an administrative inconvenience rather than a real barrier. More than three hundred thousand Americans (many of them, or their parents, Canadian-born) moved to Canada between 1901 and 1911. Nearly half a million more arrived during that decade from Britain and Ireland, and from eastern Europe. The prairie provinces— Manitoba, Saskatchewan, and Alberta—were truly the last North American frontier. The migration continued until 1930, when prairie population reached its practical limit and the central government declared the end of its "Dominion Lands" policy. Throughout this period, immigrants to Canada chiefly sought land rather than wage-labor jobs, in contrast to many migrants to the United States after 1880 or to Argentina after 1900.[11]

Migration and settlement in the United States differed from the other three New World receivers in size (it captured 60 percent of all European trans-Atlantic migrants); in diversity of source (every group was represented, while Canada mainly took in British, Irish, Germans, and east Europeans, and Argentina and Brazil mainly Mediterraneans); and in diversity of destination (after 1850 Europeans avoided the South but went everywhere else—West, Midwest, and Northeast). Migration to large cities has received so much attention that one can overlook the fact that more new farms (mostly on the Great Plains) were created in the United States between 1900 and 1915 than between 1862 (the Homestead Act) and 1900, and many of these new farms were the work of German-Russians, Norwegians, Irish, British, and many other kinds of migrants.

A crucial characteristic, shared with Canada but not with Argentina or Brazil (at least not after 1900), was that in the United States a migrant settler could become a landowner. Latifundia scarcely existed outside certain parts of the South. The central government retained ownership of land as "public domain" until it was transferred to private hands—not always but usually actual settlers. For all their flaws, the American and Canadian land policies did succeed in creating more equitable wealth distribution, a more fluid class structure, and a sounder rural economy. Considering the reputation of Iberian regimes for absolutism and Anglo-Saxon ones for individualism (read, on the American frontier, near anarchy), it is ironic that with regard to land policy, the American and Canadian governments maintained much stronger central control than did the Argentine or Brazilian. Ownership and distribution of public land was tightly controlled and enforced by state and federal legal systems in North America, whereas in Argentina and Brazil the effective power rested with local magnates—the *estancieros* and *fazendeiros*.

What was different and what was similar among these four countries of migration and frontier settlement? They all carried out Indian removal with greater or lesser degree of harshness—Argentina probably the harshest, Canada the mildest—but in all cases the indigenous people were either to be transformed into small farmers, just like white ones (as in the American Dawes Severalty Act of 1887), or replaced by whites who would, in their own estimation, put the land to "better use." All four countries built railroad networks that brought settlers to their respective "Wests" and conveyed staple products to urban consumers and seaports; even recent migrants became parts of a world capitalist economy. The traditional semisubsistence frontier family farm became a thing of the past in the United States and elsewhere, except the more remote interior of Brazil. All four countries recruited Europeans, either directly through labor contracts and agents, or indirectly by promotional devices—state boards of immigration and tourism, railroad pamphleteering and land agents, and other means.

A great difference between the North American and South American receivers lay in how (or whether) migrant settlers acquired land. In Argentina freehold was possible in the first fifteen to twenty years after the "Conquest of the Desert," but not after 1900. In Brazil it was difficult any time during the period, with only the minority of migrants—those living in "nuclear colonies" and a few others—ever achieving it. In Canada and the United States, rectilinear land surveys and enforceable contracts greatly benefited the migrant settler despite flaws in the system, such as undependable credit markets and enticement into areas too arid or cold to farm successfully. The requirement that one be a citizen in order to gain full and final title to public-domain land—a condition absent in Argentina and Brazil—had great (and largely unintentional) stabilizing effects on the two North American societies.

All four countries, in different ways and contexts, decided by the middle or late 1920s that European immigration should be restricted. The methods varied but the signal was the same: Europeans (and Asians and Africans) should stay home. The American national-origins quota laws of 1921 and 1924 were by no means unique. Canadian policy took various twists during the 1920s but finally opted for limiting immigration to people from "preferred" countries. Brazil effected restriction in 1930 and Argentina in 1931. By then most of the industrialized world and countries deeply involved in world commodity markets were slipping into the

Great Depression. Migration from Europe to the Americas never resumed
on its previous scale.

Much remains to be done in comparing the histories of New World
migration and settlement. The foregoing is no more than suggestive. It
does indicate, however, that national histories usually thought to be exceptional or unique may be compared; that comparisons often serve to
blunt self-praise but sometimes blunt self-criticism (for example, North
American land laws, despite their well-known flaws, were preferable to
South American latifundia from almost any standpoint). Yet many other
avenues of historical exploration remain to be traveled. For example:

1) The treatment of native peoples. How were laws and policies
   shaped, how were they executed, and what were the consequences
   for both the native and the European-descended peoples involved?
   In the cases of Brazil and the United States the situation of
   African-origin people should be factored into the history of
   race relations.

2) How were laws made regarding settlement and specifically the
   getting and keeping of land—by whom and to whose benefit?
   Homestead-type laws (liberally granting land to settlers) were
   passed in Brazil in 1850 and other times, but never became
   effective; why? Were there ever realistic alternatives to latifundia,
   and could it have been transformed into something different as
   the antebellum slave plantations were transformed after 1860 in
   the United States (the closest North American parallel to the Brazilian coffee plantations)?

3) What forces—social, economic, or otherwise—brought about
   the era of unrestricted migration, and what ended it after World
   War I? Why were migrants encouraged to become citizens of their
   countries of settlement in some cases, discouraged in others?

4) The demographic characteristics of settlement frontiers have yet
   to be fully worked out. At what point were European-descended
   populations able, through more massive numbers, to shift from
   accommodation with native peoples to simply overwhelming them
   culturally? Rates of population increase appear to have been in
   the range of 300 to 500 percent per decade in settlement-frontier
   areas of Canada, the United States, and Argentina; was that also
   true of Brazil, and if not, why not? Were the demographic profiles of settlement frontiers and frontiers of resource exploitation (gold rushes, oil booms, long cattle drives, and so on) as
   different in other countries as they were in the United States?

5) What were the human experiences on these settlement frontiers; how did family, birth and death, sex and marriage, disease and nutrition, compare? Women could homestead under American and Canadian law—where did they stand in Argentina and Brazil and did laws make much difference? Do the demographic profiles of frontiers of settlement and frontiers of resource exploitation differ elsewhere as much as they did in the United States?

Most of these questions involve the familiar categories of race, class, and gender. In addition one might inquire into

6) the political integration of peripheries and minorities, and instances of successful and unsuccessful assimilation, nation-building, and multiculturalism;
7) to what extent frontiers involved opportunities as well as exploitation, both of people and environmental resources, and which was the rule; and how the histories of frontiers of resource exploitation in the past differ or shed light on the Brazilian frontier still in process;
8) how nationalism relates to sectionalism or regionalism as a force in the frontier-imperial experience;
9) what role the frontier area played in the national culture, and what (if any) national creation myths developed elsewhere in parallel to that of the United States;[12]
10) how have the major American receiving countries regarded their natural environments? What are their environmental histories, from the standpoints of bio-ecology, cultural attitudes, and public policy; how do they compare?
11) and what has been the nature, in historical experience, of the imperialist urge, and what evidence exists of anti-imperialist, anti-exploitative patterns of migration and settlement?

Since Frederick Jackson Turner stated so clearly in 1893 what Americans have believed about themselves before and since—that the interaction of themselves and their Anglo-Saxon ancestors with the North American frontier environment produced an exceptional people, virtuous and democratic—exceptionalism and frontier history have been welded together.[13] Turner's biographer and latter-day exponent, Ray Allen Billington, was a believer in American exceptionalism, of a benign variety.[14] But the gentle, democratic Turner has not been the only source of America's mythology of exceptionalist expansion; less benign was

Theodore Roosevelt, for whom the "winning of the West" was an interracial struggle, of which "overseas imperialism . . . [was] the necessary continuation."[15] Here, exceptionalism was not benign. People who think themselves exceptional, and possessed of an exceptional message to give to (or if need be, to force on) other people, more cheerfully adopt imperialist methods. Turner called the frontier line the border between "civilization" (us) and "savagery" (them). Such bluntness is now rarely voiced; some sensitivity to the rights and cultures of native peoples and other races permeates all but the most aggressive monoculturists.

Nonetheless it is always easy to fall into "us-them", "friend-enemy," "preceptor-client" ways of thinking, and the imperialist tendencies and associations of the frontier idea reinforce such thinking. The frontier idea is not an inevitable or necessary reinforcement to imperialist thinking; the British, French, and other European imperialists carried out their empire-building quite well without it. Yet they and earlier European colonizers and empire-builders were each convinced of their own exceptional culture and civilizing mission. It is not the frontier idea in itself but its tendency to degenerate into aggressive expansionism that should be carefully watched. At the close of the twentieth century, the latter half of which has been "the American Century" if there ever was or will be such a time, Americans need to examine carefully whether their so-called frontier heritage does not blind them to their own aggressiveness and disrespect for others' rights. Comparative frontier studies as well as the emerging school known as the "New Western History" are and will be helpful and important in this regard.[16]

Americans need to develop a new area of inquiry called comparative peace history. Europe-centered histories of expansion since 1492 have been overly triumphalist and celebratory. The tone of the 1992 observances, in contrast to 1892, revealed widespread appreciation that new approaches are needed. Developing new approaches is not always easy. An eminent historian of the Spanish Borderlands, David J. Weber, recently spoke to this point:

> How, then, are we to comprehend the Spanish frontier in North America? For those with an aversion to ambiguity or a strong need for absolute truth, the current answer is not comforting. There are many viewpoints, some of them contradictory and all of them valid, even if not of equal merit. This is not to deny the existence of an objective past. . . . The past itself, however, has ceased to exist. What remains of importance is only our understanding of it, and that understanding, as historian Peter Novick has squarely put it, "is in the mind of a human being or it is nowhere." Lacking omniscience and possessing only a partial record of the past, we humans reconstruct time and place in highly imperfect ways, recounting stories that often tell us more about the teller than the tale.

The Spanish past in North America, then, is not only what we have imagined it to be, but what we will continue to make of it. Like all historical terrain, the Spanish frontier seems destined to remain contested ground, transformed repeatedly in the historical imaginations of succeeding generations.[17]

The same may be said of many other frontiers and areas of contact in the New World.

Comparative peace history offers hope that Americans will not always be self-blinded by triumphalist history proclaiming and assuming the exceptionalism of their or any other history. Instead it opens the possibility of understanding that one can learn, from history, how to avoid exploitation of resources and of other people and learn to survive with each other and with the environment.

Notes

1. In a slightly different version, this paper was first presented at the conference on the Discovery of America organized by the Historical Society of Israel and held in Jerusalem in June 1992. The author is grateful to Professor Miriam Eliav-Feldon, the Historical Society of Israel, and the Zalman Shazar Center for Jewish History for permission to publish the essay here.

2. Concerning the frontier-empire relationship, see Walter Nugent, "Frontiers and Empires in the late Nineteenth Century," in *Religion, Ideology and Nationalism in Europe and America: Essays in Honor of Yehoshua Arieli,* ed. Michael Heyd et al. (Jerusalem: Historical Society of Israel and the Zalman Shazar Center for Jewish History, 1986). A revised version appeared as "Frontiers and Empires in the Late Nineteenth Century," in *Western Historical Quarterly* 20 (November 1989): 393–408; the quotation is on 394.

3. Excellent histories of contact in Transappalachia include Richard White, *The Middle Ground: Indians, Empires, and Republics in the Great Lakes Region, 1650–1815* (New York: Cambridge University Press, 1991), and Andrew R. L. Cayton, *Frontier Indiana, 1700–1850: A History* (New York: Kraus International Publishers, forthcoming).

4. Post-1945 migrations have been massive—out of Asia, out of Latin America, and within Asia and Europe—but never again resumed at the pre-1914 levels from Europe to the Americas.

5. For a more extended discussion of migration to the New World in the 1870–1914 period, see Walter Nugent, *Crossings: The Great Transatlantic Migrations, 1870–1914* (Bloomington: Indiana University Press, 1992), esp. chapters 4 (Migration in general), 12 (Argentina), 13 (Brazil), 14 (Canada), and 15 (the United States).

6. Estimates vary and exact figures will never be known. For a recent and reasonable estimate see Norman J. G. Pounds, *An Historical Geography of Europe, 1800–1914* (Cambridge, England: Cambridge University Press, 1985), 79.

7. Gino Germani, *Política y sociedad en una epoca de transición: de la sociedad tradicional a la sociedad de masas* (Buenos Aires: Editorial Paidos, 1965), 179; United States Bureau of the Census, *Historical Statistics of the United*

States, Colonial Times to 1970 (Washington, DC: Government Printing Office, 1975), chapter A.

8. J. Valerie Fifer, *United States Perceptions of Latin America, 1850–1930: A "New West" South of Capricorn?* (Manchester and New York: Manchester University Press, 1991), 178; see esp. pp. 4–5 and "Conclusion," pp. 165–85.

9. A first-rate comparative history of Argentine and Canadian development in this period is Carl E. Solberg, *The Prairies and the Pampas: Agrarian Policy in Canada and Argentina* (Stanford: Stanford University Press, 1987). Samuel L. Baily compares urban migrants in "The Adjustment of Italian Immigrants in Buenos Aires and New York, 1870–1914," *American Historical Review* 88 (April 1983): 281–305. Very helpful for understanding Argentine migration and settlement are James Bryce, *South America: Observations and Impressions* (New York: Macmillan, 1912); Roberto Cortes Conde, *El progreso argentina 1880–1915* (Buenos Aires: Editorial Sudamericana, 1979), and "The Growth of the Argentine Economy, c. 1870–1914," in *The Cambridge History of Latin America*, ed. Leslie Bethell (Cambridge: Cambridge University Press, 1986), V:327–57; and Ezequiel Gallo, *La pampa gringa: la colonización agrícola en Santa Fe (1870–1895)* (Buenos Aires: Editorial Sudamericana, 1892), and Gallo, "Argentina: Society and Politics, 1880–1916," in Bethell, ed., *Cambridge History*, V:359–91.

10. Relevant chapters in volumes 4 and 5 of the *Cambridge History of Latin America* are helpful for understanding Brazil's migration and settlement history. Also helpful are Jose Fernando Carneiro, *Imigração e Colonização no Brasil* (Rio de Janeiro: Universidade do Brasil, 1950); Pedro Calderan Beltrão, *Demografia: Ciencia da População, Analise e Teoria* (Porto Alegre: Libraria Sulina Editora, 1972); Paul Hugon, *Demografia Brasileira: Ensaio de Demoeconomia Brasileira* (São Paulo: Atlas, 1973).

11. Particularly helpful on Canadian settlement patterns are Gerald Friesen, *The Canadian Prairies: A History* (Lincoln: University of Nebraska Press, 1984); Norman Macdonald, *Canada: Immigration and Colonization 1841–1903* (Aberdeen: Aberdeen University Press, 1966); and Chester Martin, *"Dominion Lands" Policy* (Toronto: McClelland and Stewart Ltd., 1973). On migration patterns the basic work remains Nathan Keyfitz, "The Growth of Canadian Population," *Population Studies* 4 (June 1950): 47–63.

12. William H. Goetzmann, Richard Slotkin, and others have discussed American Western and/or "frontier" history as the national "creation myth." A classic and still provocative exploration of national development myths in Brazil, contrasted with the United States, is C. Vianna Moog, *Bandeirantes and Pioneers* (New York: Basic Books, 1964).

13. Frederick Jackson Turner, "The Significance of the Frontier in American History," a paper first read on July 12, 1893, and reprinted many times since; a recent reprinting and commentary is Martin Ridge, *History, Frontier, and Section: Three Essays by Frederick Jackson Turner* (Albuquerque: University of New Mexico Press, 1993).

14. Martin Ridge, "Ray Allen Billington, Western History, and American Exceptionalism," *Pacific Historical Review* 56 (November 1987): 495–511.

15. Richard Slotkin, *Gunfighter Nation: The Myth of the Frontier in Twentieth-Century America* (New York: Atheneum, 1992), 51.

16. Leading examples and discussions of the "New Western History" include Patricia Nelson Limerick, *Legacy of Conquest: The Unbroken Past of the American West* (New York: W. W. Norton, 1987); Patricia Nelson Limerick,

Clyde A. Milner II, and Charles E. Rankin, *Trails: Toward a New Western History* (Lawrence: University Press of Kansas, 1991); William Cronon, George Miles, and Jay Gitlin, *Under an Open Sky: Rethinking America's Western Past* (New York: W. W. Norton, 1992).

17. David J. Weber, "The Spanish Legacy in North America and the Historical Imagination," *Western Historical Quarterly* 33 (February 1992): 23–24.

....
....
....

....
....

III

Frontier Peoples and Institutions

9 David G. Sweet ◆ Reflections on the Ibero-American Frontier Mission as an Institution in Native American History

Frontier missions in Latin America have long been assessed through the eyes of Iberian missionaries themselves, who left behind written records and who regarded their work as an extension of their superior culture and religion to benighted natives. As historian David Sweet reminds us, however, the missionization process involved two active parties: Indians as well as missionaries. Those Indians who accepted European missionaries acted in their interests as they understood them—to avoid punishment, gain spiritual benefits, or acquire European imports. Those benefits came to Indians at a cost, however, as Sweet explains, for among the European imports were fatal new diseases and new modes of social control including physical punishment. Acculturation, the goal of missionaries, implied deculturation for Indians. If padres were to play the part of missionary "fathers," Indians would have to adopt the role of children. For Indians to accept the extraterrestrial god of the Christians meant losing touch with their natural world. Indians often refused to pay these costs and resisted or rebelled.*

David Sweet has taught Latin American history at the University of California, Santa Cruz, since 1971. He holds a Ph.D. from the University of Wisconsin, where he studied in the Comparative Tropical History Program. Among his publications is Struggle and Survival in Colonial America

From *The New Latin American Mission History*, ed. Erick Langer and Robert H. Jackson. © 1994 by the University of Nebraska Press. Reprinted by permission of the University of Nebraska Press.

*See also David Block, "Themes and Sources for Missionary History in Hispanic America," in *Latin American Frontiers, Borders, and Hinterlands: Research Needs and Resources*, ed. Paul Covington (Albuquerque, NM: SALAM, Inc., 1990), 62–71.

(1981), edited with Gary B. Nash. He has recently completed a book-length study, "A Rich Realm of Nature Destroyed: The Central Amazon Valley, 1540–1750."

These remarks are intended to suggest a reconsideration by scholars, Christian activists, and others of the role of a classic institution in colonial Latin American history—the Roman Catholic frontier mission.[1] In pursuing this goal, I have sought to shift the perspective from which the history of missions has customarily been studied: to view it not "over the shoulders" of the missionaries and government officials who left the documents from which this history is reconstructed, but from the vantage point of the "missionized" Indians. To attempt to do this is not to presume to be able to think as the colonized Native Americans did about their experiences in the missions. It is simply to recast the discussion of mission history so as to make Indian experience rather than missionary experience its subject.

We are handicapped in doing this, of course, by the almost total absence of Indian testimonies in the documentary record, by the ethnocentrism and the self-serving character of most missionary reports, and by the universal missionary view of Indians as children barely capable of reason. All these have left deep marks on both scholarship and popular writing in this field since the beginning and, through them, on the public memory. But now it is high time that the old-fashioned missionary view of Indian culture and history, like that of the agents of colonialism, be left behind by thinking people who have rejected colonialism itself and who would reject as well a pre-Enlightenment view of human nature and of the role of religion in society. With the help of the ethnohistorians, the historical archaeologists, and others, it is now possible at least to experiment with some Indian-centered generalizations about mission Indian history. As we do so, it behooves us to strain our ears to listen for such Indian voices as may still come to us faintly through the missionaries' documents, and through the material remains and the dispersed yet still vital cultural heritage of the "mission Indian" societies themselves.

The canonical text for this discussion is the brilliant faculty research lecture on the "mission as a frontier institution," which was given by Professor Herbert Bolton at the University of California in 1917. Bolton was a distinguished historian who wrote extensively on the history of what he called the "Spanish borderlands," from Florida to California. At Berkeley he trained or influenced a generation of graduate students (among them several Catholic clergy), whose dissertations explored aspects of mission history in those regions. Late in life, he helped launch the lamentable but so far successful campaign for the elevation to sainthood of the pioneer

California Franciscan missionary Fray Junípero Serra. The extraordinary impact of this life's work enabled Charles Gibson to write that "few persons have created and defined a historical field so sucessfully as Bolton," while noting that the work of his school was "weakest in social and economic history."[2]

Bolton and the Mission Frontier

Bolton invited his readers to move beyond the romantic hagiography and the Californian focus of the English-language mission histories of his day, to see the frontier mission as a key institution of Spanish colonialism throughout the Americas—one parallel in importance to the fur trading post in French Canada or the homestead in English North America. That was the broad scope of his "ideal type," although except for a fleeting reference to Paraguay, Bolton drew all his illustrative examples from the missions of New Spain's northern frontier. The importance and effectiveness of the frontier mission, he argued, was attested by the continuing vigor of Spain's language, culture, and religion in all the regions in which it had been established.

The central purpose of the frontier mission, as Bolton described it, was threefold: "to convert, to civilize" (elsewhere to "discipline" and "instruct"), and "to exploit" its Indian inhabitants in the service of the Spanish crown. In classic liberal scholarly fashion, Bolton viewed the religious function as self-evident (or perhaps not susceptible to scrutiny); he had almost nothing to say, for example, about the character of religious instruction or the circumstances of baptism. The exploitative function he also apparently saw as unexceptional and therefore unworthy of critical examination. His own emphasis was on the "civilizing" function: missions served "not alone as a means of control, but as schools in self-control as well." Here he gave voice, perhaps unconsciously, to the prevailing North American educational philosophy of his day—one that looked to a formal and unapologetically Eurocentric system of public instruction, relying heavily on "hands-on" learning as well as discipline, to produce the mentally resourceful, mechanically skilled but politically uncritical, even obedient citizenry required by an emerging North American imperial capitalist regime.

To "civilize" had been the ostensible role of the *encomienda* in densely settled central Mexico, where the native peoples were "fairly docile, had a steady food supply and fixed homes, were accustomed to labor, and were worth exploiting." But the Indians the Spaniards found on the expanding frontier were less tractable; they "had few crops, were unused to labor, had no fixed villages, would not stand still to be exploited, and

were hardly worth the candle," in Bolton's unfortunate phrase. Subject-
ing them required a new approach, because the settlers in those regions
simply refused to accept responsibility as *encomenderos* for the incorporation into colonial society of "wild tribes which were as uncomfortable
burdens, sometimes, as cub-tigers in a sack."

The religious orders were therefore assigned to this important work.
As they understood it, the tasks of "converting, civilizing, and exploiting" the frontier Indians were one. It could be accomplished, they
decided, by congregating as many of the widely scattered barbarians as
possible into a few new settlements under missionary administration, in-
structing them there in the basic principles of Christian vassalhood, re-
training them for sedentary living and productive labor, and finally putting
them to work in mission farms and workshops that would provide subsistence and self-sufficiency for the missionaries and for themselves. In this
way the "unexploitable" savages might be transformed into a labor force
that would some day be of use to European enterprise. . . .

Bolton admired the frontier mission for having spread the Faith and
taught the Indians "good manners, the rudiments of European crafts,
agriculture, and even self-government." It had preserved them, in sharp
contrast to the wanton destruction characteristic of the Anglo-American
frontier, "improving the natives for this life as well as for the next." If
sometimes it had failed to achieve its own objectives, its lasting glory
was that it had introduced European civilization to the ancestors of
millions of people who were alive still in his day.

Reframing the Discussion

This classic picture of the mission was in some respects accurate as far as
it went, faithful to its missionary sources and to the nineteenth-century
liberal-cum-Spanish colonialist perspective from which it was drawn. It
also had its severe limitations, focusing as it did on the temperate zone
rather than on the tropics, within which most of the Ibero-American frontier missions were found; disregarding the severe epidemiological and
demographic consequences of life in the missions on every frontier; and
not even attempting to take Indian culture and know-how, Indian labor,
or in general Indian "agency" into account as determining factors in the
history of missions. But despite these limitations, its heuristic effect must
be recognized in the lasting influence it has had on both scholarship and
textbook writing.[3] Something akin to the Bolton view (because derived
from the same sources, read with a similar ideological disposition) is
found, moreover, in all the modern Spanish-language histories of the
church in Latin America—including, surprisingly enough, the monumen-

tal *Historia general de la iglesia en America Latina*, which was written during the 1970s and 1980s and partially under the influence of the new "liberation theology." The image of the mission as a benignly paternalistic educational institution has also recently been "immortalized" on the silver screen by the shameless fabricators of an apologetic film called *The Mission*.[4]

Historians both religious and secular, and their readers in every language, have become attached to Bolton's (and to the religious historian's) ideal-typification of the frontier mission as a religious and educational institution, and as a moral alternative within the tawdry chronicle of colonialism in the Americas. In the meticulously reconstructed mission-museums of California, for example, one looks in vain for signs of the whipping post and stocks, which were standard equipment in frontier missions everywhere, or of the *monjerías* in which young girls were isolated from family and friends for the protection of their virginity.[5] In these circumstances it is difficult for the modern student to think critically about the mission as a frontier institution and context for the colonization of frontier peoples, or to form an accurate impression of its role in the formation of Latin American societies.

The most serious problem with the conventional history of the mission in colonial Latin America is that its subject, however soberly and "objectively" represented, is always the missionary. Missionaries to the Indian frontiers were often enough men of strong character and fascinating personality, to be sure, men capable of extraordinary deeds. . . . Nonetheless, it must be remembered that for the most part the vast spiritual and socio-economic projects of these men, and their mighty individual endeavors—admirable as they were, in many respects—came to naught.

The missionaries' indefatigable labors did, however, have a great (if largely unintended) impact on the historical development of many peoples and vast territories.[6] The real effect of the missions can in fact only be seen in the experience of the peoples they were established to serve. It therefore seems reasonable to ask that mission history be concerned from now on primarily with the consequences of that institution for the Indian inhabitants of missions, over both the short and the long terms—and that it concern itself only incidentally with the lives of the missionaries themselves. To return to Bolton's definition of the purpose and character of the frontier mission, the traditions of the field leave us hard put at present, in particular to understand how much "conversion" actually took place in these institutions, what aspects of "civilization" were actually assimilated in them, by what means and with what results "exploitation" was actually practiced, with what impact on the lives of the exploited.

Mission history needs to be freed of its obsession with missionaries and their affairs. This shift in perspective does not require that we deprecate or downgrade the good padres or their accomplishments, as has sometimes been done in angry response for example to the Serra canonization campaign. There is no need to demean the motives or debunk the remaining claims to fame of these stalwart servants of the state religion of colonialism. Their experiences are still worth recounting, if only as a contribution to the little-studied social history of the religious orders themselves in colonial America. But their story is not, as Bolton thought, that of the origins of modern Christian mestizo society in the frontier regions of Latin America. Those origins are to be found in the harder-to-get-at stories of the Indian followers, subjects, or "neophytes" who surrounded every missionary priest. To put mission history into balance, therefore, we must somehow gently remove the missionaries from the center of the stage. We must reread their accounts more critically than has sometimes been done, with an eye primarily to what they have to say about the dimly viewed Indian "other"; and we must learn to distinguish their high ideals and aspirations, the inflated claims of their fund-raising appeals, and the well-meaning instructions regularly given to them by their superiors, from what we can reconstruct of their actual practice.

In trying to do these things, it will be helpful to keep in mind a few a priori propositions that, though inoperative among traditional mission historians, seem self-evident today. The first is that real day-by-day Indian experience, though severely constrained by the missionary and in some crucial respects deeply informed by him, was never in fact lived out, guided, or defined—and certainly never fully understood—by any missionary. People lived their own lives, even in the mission. Another proposition is that adult Indians were never the children the missionaries imagined them to be, never "clay" in the missionary's hands. Not even Indian children could be indoctrinated more than partially, or persuaded more than partially to distrust and disregard their parents' wisdom and values, by even the most zealous of missionary educators. This was because the living mission community that existed around every missionary was a chronically resistant, only conditionally cooperative, decidedly restrictive context for his work (as is attested by the universal missionary complaints about recalcitrance and ungratefulness in their charges). The relationship of missionary to neophyte was, therefore, not simply an action but an *interaction*—not a "conversion," says a young historian of missions in another part of the world, but a "conver*sation*."[7] These propositions, increasingly supported by the ethnohistories of once-missionized Indian peoples and others, are essential tools for the reframing that this subject requires.[8]

Frontier missions were operated at one time or another between the late sixteenth and the early nineteenth centuries, by most of the religious orders at work in Ibero-America. Franciscans and Jesuits had the greatest number of them over the widest area during the longest period of time; but Dominicans, Augustinians, Capuchins, Mercedarians, and Calced Carmelites also contributed substantially. The mission territories during that long period included the entire northern tier of New Spain from California, Sonora, and Nayarit across to Tamaulipas and Florida; several regions of Central America, including the Petén, southern Honduras, and southern Costa Rica; the Orinoco valley and much of the rest of modern Venezuela; the Colombian *llanos*; the eastern slopes of the Andes from Colombia to northwest Argentina; the entire Amazon valley and most of the Paraguay-Paraná basin, the Chaco, much of coastal Brazil, the Argentine pampas, and southern Chile—at least half the entire geographical area of today's Latin America. These were the least populous and the least successfully colonized regions of the Spanish and Portuguese empires, by and large and by definition. Nevertheless, their total population at the beginning of the colonial era must have been somewhere between five million and ten million people, divided between several hundreds of distinct societies. Millions of people died in the frontier missions, and some regions are even less densely inhabited today than they were before the arrival of the Europeans; but in most of them some ex-mission peoples survive. These peoples everywhere practice Christianity in one form or another, just as they display a wide variety of other beliefs, behaviors, and artifacts appropriated and adapted by them from Europeans through the agency of the mission. The frontier mission therefore represents a very significant episode in Native American history. . . .

Impassioned denigrators of the frontier mission enterprise sometimes confuse genocide with ethnocide when appraising its disastrous consequences for Native American history; but such incendiary argumentation casts more heat than light on our subject. Missionaries everywhere sought to exterminate Indian culture, not Indian people. Their policy toward the Indians themselves was one of stern but "paternalistic," systematic re-education. Yet in the mission environment, appallingly, the people proved even more vulnerable than their cultures; and cultural resistance was itself greatly undermined by demographic decline. Those who died in the missions succumbed for the most part to biological and socio-economic forces operating largely beyond the missionary's control, and of which the missionary himself had very little understanding—a situation that led one mission historian to characterize the wholesale destruction of humanity within this system as "inexcusable but not intentional."[9]

One curious and lamentable feature of the "genocide" school of criticism is that in effect it perpetuates Bolton's perspective on the history of the frontier missions, by reaffirming the primary agency of the missionaries in mission Indian history. But the Indians of mission history, like other historical peoples, were always more actors than acted upon. They constructed their own histories, though they did so within exceptionally severe constraints. These constraints were erected for them by missionaries, by the political economy of colonialism, and by the Euroasiatic disease microorganisms, working in unintended collaboration with one another. It is therefore a waste of ammunition to attack the missionaries for the genuine and unprecedented demographic and cultural catastrophe that was mission history on every frontier.

The historical demography of mission territories has recently gone a long way, at least in the Californias, toward rectifying both the whitewashed romantic and the more political Boltonian version of mission history; even more important, it has contributed in significant ways to laying the groundwork and raising some key questions for future reconstructions of the social and cultural histories of missionized peoples.[10] Not even the groundwork has yet been laid for a rethinking of most of the other mission histories of colonial America. But in the long run, what world historians and others will be interested in knowing about mission Indian history is less when and why or in exactly what numbers so many people died, but what those who had not yet died did with the mission system while they were still alive in it, what their survivors did with what was left to them of their forebears' culture and patrimony, and especially what that history has to say to people alive today.

When the history of native Americans in the mission system is written from an Indian perspective, employing categories derived from the reconstruction of Indian experience such as those with which we have been working here, it will presumably become even clearer than it is today that that system's constraints on the autonomous activity of Indians vastly outweighed the opportunities it provided for them.[11] This is the opposite of what Bolton concluded, by focusing his thought on the missionary himself, on the mission as a constructive and rational enterprise, and on the interests of the Spanish colonial state. Bolton and subsequent historians have taken the language and the conceptual frameworks for their discussions of mission history mostly from the missionaries themselves. A sign of this is the curious persistence in the writings even of liberal secular historians on the colonial mission of terms such as "conversion," the "saving" of "souls," and "protection."

"Conversion" cannot be done to people. It is undergone voluntarily by rational adults who have learned something new that makes sense to them and that seems to them so important as to cause them to want to adjust the rest of their thinking and behavior to it. It is an active and not a passive experience. Children may be separated from their families, taken to boarding schools where they are taught by missionary teachers to hold beliefs different from those of their parents, and thereby raised up as believing Christians (something that was seldom feasible on the frontiers of colonial America). But no one could "be converted" through an act of another's will, no matter how artful or kindly. Conversion, then, is not an accurate term for the real transformations that took place among Indians in the frontier missions. The missionary record makes it clear that Indians were frequently persuaded or even required—at least as a survival strategy—to accept the Catholic rite of baptism. It reveals that those who outlived the disease and hardships that followed on incorporation into the mission regime, and who found reasons to continue to endure it, also generally managed to accommodate themselves to the mission's conventlike regimen, including frequent attendance at Catholic rituals and the daily recitation of Catholic prayers. Yet the record provides little evidence that adult Indians in the missions ever stopped believing what their previous lives and their parents and respected leaders had taught them, in order to begin believing what the missionaries had taught them instead.

If "conversion" has little to do with what transpired in missions, what about the "salvation" of the "soul"? Whatever one understands "souls" to be, to attribute their "salvation" to missionary labors in the present context requires a leap of faith that few secular historians today, if examined closely on the point, would probably be willing to make. Similarly, "protection" was in practice usually a euphemism for hegemonic control. The conventional language of mission history is a therefore serious handicap to understanding. It reifies an archaic notion of Christian spirituality and Christian praxis; and it dehumanizes, infantilizes, and "otherizes" the Indian just as did the missionary enterprise itself. Yet so prevalent is this language that it has become difficult even to talk about the colonial frontier mission without making use of it. The social history of missions needs to be freed from this mission historian's language and from the anti-Indian bias and perspective that it embodies. Nothing about the mission enterprise is self-evident; and in view of its terrible consequences for the Indian populations it was designed in principle to benefit, nothing about it should still be taken for granted or at face value by serious historians.

Seen from the perspective of Indian experience, the frontier mission appears to have been an institution within which religious "conversion" was all but impossible, in which the "civilization" process was rather more forbidding than inviting, and in which "exploitation" itself was severely handicapped by Indian resistance as well as by demographic decline. Its major features were sickness, death, forced labor, flogging, deculturation, infantilization, and alienation from nature. It was therefore scarcely a benign context for the assimilation of intractable natives into the colonial socioeconomic order, or into the process of the construction of new mestizo cultures and nationalities. Few people, in fact, survived it long enough or healthy enough to flourish and multiply within that order; for most, it was a bitter disappointment, a dead end, and an early grave. These features were intrinsic to the mission regime, and they may be attributed to its ideology, its ecology, and its political economy as well as to its epidemiology. They were also very little affected by the character and practice of individual missionaries, no matter how high-minded or saintly.

At the same time, this same regime offered survival to a limited number of the beleaguered Indian inhabitants of the colonial frontiers. For the survivors it offered access to, and a prolonged period of exposure in which to assimilate, some of the more valuable aspects of European culture: superior tools, some useful domestic plants and animals, some usable notions of community and of production for exchange in the world market, some Biblical visions of justice and loving community. Mission at its best was a context for the appropriation of these cultural features on the surviving and half-reeducated mission Indians' own terms—and with lingering results for themselves and their mestizo descendants. The importance of this function, where the mission indeed succeeded in performing it, survived and transcended the mission regime itself.

Notes

1. Research for this essay was assisted by a grant from the Committee on Faculty Research of the University of California, Santa Cruz. Rick Warner provided invaluable assistance by searching the literature of California mission history for material on the essay's themes, and by discussing the project with me at length at each stage of its development. Useful criticism of the manuscript itself was provided by Frank Bardacke, Guillermo Delgado, Robert Jackson, Noel Q. King, Erick Langer, and Rick Warner.

2. Herbert E. Bolton, "The Mission as a Frontier Institution in the Spanish-American Colonies," *American Historical Review* 23 (1917):42–61. Cf. John F. Bannon, ed., *Bolton and the Spanish Borderlands* (Norman, 1964), and "The Mission as a Frontier Institution: 60 Years of Interest and Research," *Western Historical Quarterly* 10 (1979):303–22; Lewis Hanke, ed., *Do the Americas Have a Common History?* (New York, 1964); James A. Sandos, "Junipero Serra's Canonization and the Historical Record," *American Historical Review* 93, no. 5 (December 1988):1253–69, and his "Junipero Serra, Canonization and the California Indian Controversy, *Journal of Religious History* 15, no. 3 (June 1989):311–29; Charles Gibson, *Spain in America* (New York, 1966), 231.

3. E.g., Bailey W. Diffie, *Latin American Civilization: Colonial Period* (Harrisburg, 1945), 577–87; C. H. Haring, *The Spanish Empire in America* (New York, 1963), 182–88; and Gibson, *Spain in America*, 80–83 and 185–89. Mark A. Burkholder and Lyman L. Johnson, *Colonial Latin America* (New York, 1990), 897–98, pay scant attention to the institution; only James Lockhart and Stuart B. Schwartz, *Early Latin America* (Cambridge, 1983), provide a context for understanding the frontier mission phenomenon in their imaginative chapter 8 on "The Fringes." Cf. J. Fred Rippy and Jean Thomas Nelson, *Crusaders of the Jungle* (Chapel Hill, 1936); Alistair Hennessy, *The Frontier in Latin American History* (Albuquerque, 1978), esp. 54–60; and brief references in the chapters on church history by Eduardo Hoornaert and Josep Barnadas in *Cambridge History of Latin America*, vol. I, ed. Leslie Bethell (Cambridge, 1984), 511–56 and 616–23.

4. Enrique Dussel, ed., *Historia general de la iglesia en América Latina* (11 vols.; Salamanca, 1965–). E.g., the treatment of the Jesuit Orinoco mission by P. José del Rey Fajardo in vol. VII, pp. 96–121. For a revealing memoir of the making of the film, see Daniel Berrigan, S.J., *The Mission: A Film Journal* (San Francisco, 1986).

5. Maynard Geiger, O.F.M., *Indians of Mission Santa Barbara in Paganism and Christianity* (Santa Barbara, 1968), 27.

6. For a reasoned discussion of such an impact, see James Schofield Saeger, "Another View of the Mission as a Frontier Institution: The Guaycuruan Reductions of Santa Fe, 1743–1810," *Hispanic American Historical Review* 65, no. 3 (1985):493–517.

7. Vincent Díaz, personal communication, 1990. Díaz's doctorate in the History of Consciousness program at the University of California, Santa Cruz, focused on the seventeenth-century Spanish Jesuit missionary to Guam P. Diego Luis de Sanvitores and the twentieth-century campaign for his canonization.

8. An especially good example is the history of the Yaqui of northwestern Mexico as studied by Edward H. Spicer, in *The Yaquis: A Cultural History* (Tucson, 1980), and many other works. . . . by Evelyn Hu-Dehart, in *Missionaries, Miners and Indians: Spanish Contact with the Yaqui Nation of Northwestern New Spain, 1533–1820* (Tucson, 1981), and others, and by José Velasco Toro, *Los yaquis: historia de una activa resistencia* (Xalapa, 1988). Cf., for some very different themes in book-length ethnohistorical studies of other frontier peoples: Florence Shipek, "A Strategy for Change: The Luiseño of Southern California" (Ph.D. dissertation, University of Hawaii, 1977); Mary W. Helms, *Asang. Adaptations and Culture Contact in a Miskito Community* (Gainesville, 1971); Nancy C. Morey, "Ethnohistory of the Colombian and Venezuelan Llanos" (Ph.D. dissertation, University of Utah, 1975); Stéfano Varese, *La sal de los cerros* (*una aproximación al mundo Campa*) (Lima, 1973); Robin Wright, "The History and Religion of the Baniwa Peoples of the Upper Rio Negro Valley" (Ph.D. dissertation, Stanford University, 1981); Branislava Susnik, *El indio colonial del Paraguay* (3 vols.; Asunción, 1965–71), and *Los aborígenes del Paraguay* (8 vols.; Asunción, 1978–87); Juan Friede, *Los andakí, 1538–1947: historia de la aculturación de una tribu selvática* (Mexico, 1953); Neil L. Whitehead, *Lords of the Tiger Spirit: A History of the Caribs in Colonial Venezuela and Guyana, 1498–1820* (Dordrecht, 1988); and Jean-Marcel Hurault, *Français et indiens en Guyane, 1604–1972* (Paris, 1972).

9. Robert Archibald, *The Economic Aspect of the Hispanic California Missions* (Washington, 1978), 184.

10. E.g., Homer Aschmann, *The Central Desert of Baja California: Demography and Ecology* (Ibero-Americana 42; Berkeley, 1959); Sherburn F. Cook, *The Indian vs. the Spanish Mission* (Ibero-Americana 21; Berkeley, 1943); and reprinted in his *The Conflict between the California Indian and White Civilization* (Berkeley, 1976). The most detailed and suggestive reconstruction since Cook's of demographic decline in a frontier mission population is found in the series of articles by Robert H. Jackson on Alta and Baja California in the *Journal of California and Great Basin Anthropology* 3, 4, 5, 6, and 9 (1981–87), *Southern California Quarterly* 63 (1981), and *The Americas* 44 (1985). Work of this kind is notably absent for frontier mission populations elsewhere in colonial America.

11. The bulk of the text from which these excerpts are taken is devoted to an analytical discussion of what I take to have been the constraints (disease, malnutrition, regimentation, discipline and punishment, deculturation, infantization, and alienation from nature) and the opportunities (survival; new tools, cultigens, and techniques; new forms of community; Christianity; and challenges to resistance) that the mission regime offered as a context for Native American historical experiences.

10 Elman R. Service ◆ The *Encomienda* in Paraguay

The encomienda was perhaps the most durable and characteristic insti-
tution of Spanish colonial rule. First introduced in the early sixteenth
century, it was a system by which groups of Indians were assigned to
Spanish colonists or conquerors. The Indians were required to perform
labor and give tribute to their lord, or encomendero, who, in return, was
obliged to protect and Christianize his charges and render military ser-
vice in defense of the colony. Intended as a way to reward deserving colo-
nists and integrate Indians into Hispanic civilization, all too often the
system became one of disguised exploitation that isolated natives from
acculturative influences and enabled "a thin surface of dominant, class-
conscious Spaniards to spread over Spanish America."*

Such was the case in the heartlands of Mexico and Peru but, as
Elman R. Service points out, on the Paraguayan frontier "local condi-
tions of geography, kinds of available wealth, and types of native popula-
tion" modified the nature of the institution. Instead of separating the races
in the region around Asunción, the encomienda speeded their amalgam-
ation. It promoted the racial and cultural integration of the Guaraní In-
dians and Spanish colonizers into a uniquely self-sufficient society.

First published in 1951, this classic essay shows how the blending of
anthropological and historical research methods can enhance our under-
standing of frontier processes during the colonial era. In collaboration
with Helen S. Service, Professor Service went on to publish Tobatí: Paraguayan Town *(Chicago: University of Chicago Press, 1954). Now profes-*
sor emeritus at the University of California, Santa Barbara, he also has
written Origins of the State and Civilization: The Process of Cultural Evolution *(New York: Norton, 1975) and* A Century of Controversy: Ethno-
logical Issues from 1860 to 1960 *(Orlando: Academic Press, 1985).*

In the Spanish colonization of the New World, the *encomienda* system
and the mission system were the two most important means of institutionalized control of the native population, especially during the early
years of the colonial period.[1] Sometimes side by side, competing, sometimes widely separated and alone, these two types of agencies each succeeded in varying degree, and by varying methods, in bringing the New
World natives into a place within the orbit of Spanish colonial society. It
seems probable that the several kinds of Spanish-Indian relations which
were implicit in these institutions may help to account for certain

From *Hispanic American Historical Review* 31, no. 2 (May 1951): 230–52
passim. © 1951 by Duke University Press. Reprinted by permission.
*Charles Gibson, *Spain in America* (New York: Harper & Row, 1966), 67.

features of subsequent cultural developments in particular regions of Spanish America, and to some extent, for some of the cultural and racial distinctions which exist in our own day.

The *encomienda* system, as it operated in certain areas of the New World, has been described in some detail by modern historians. With respect to Paraguay, however, it is the mission organization of the Jesuits which is the best documented colonial institution, and which has even been the subject of many popular works. The area of primary Spanish settlement in Paraguay, however, was the region around Asunción, and from here the *encomienda*, rather than the Jesuit missions, rapidly extended the area of Spanish control over the aborigines throughout the whole central region. The later Jesuit "state" of thirty mission towns was situated mainly in the Alto Paraná basin, a region remote and nearly inaccessible from central Paraguay, where the nucleus of the later nation of Paraguay was in the process of formation. It is the purpose of the present paper to offer some data descriptive of the Paraguayan *encomienda*, and to suggest a few of the possible long range effects implied in this type of Spanish-Indian association.

The *encomienda* system of exploitation and control of indigenous populations which the Spaniards employed in different parts of the New World was general in conception and intent. Since the laws regulating this institution were promulgated by the Spanish king and his Council of the Indies, they were usually formulated to apply to all of the Spanish possessions in the New World. They were, however, often modified in practice by local conditions of geography, kinds of available wealth, and type of native population. Exceptions in the application of these rules in Paraguay, as compared to other areas, emphasize and make explicit those features which were unusual in the relationship of Spaniards and Paraguayan Indians in the early colonial period.

At the time of the first Spanish exploration of the La Plata region, Guaraní-speaking Indians occupied a large area extending from the Atlantic coast westward to the Paraguay River, covering much of the present-day Brazilian state of Rio Grande do Sul, Paraná, Misiones Territory in Argentina, and virtually all of Paraguay east of the Gran Chaco. This part of Paraguay and the Alto Paraná basin to the east were occupied almost exclusively by Guaraní.

Guaraní culture was roughly similar to the generic culture type called "Tropical Forest" in the classification used in *The Handbook of South American Indians*.[2] Subsistence activities were based on widespread tropical forest agricultural techniques. There was no irrigation nor fertilization of cultivated fields, so that every two or three years the fields were abandoned in favor of more productive virgin areas. The usual tropical foods were grown, sweet manioc and maize being the important staples. Several kinds of sweet potatoes, beans, peanuts and pumpkins were also cultivated. There were no domesticated animals, with the possible exception of the Muscovy duck, and meat was therefore obtained by hunting such animals as the tapir and deer. Fishing and gathering wild forest products were important supplementary activities. The digging-stick was the basic agricultural tool, and the bow and arrow the important hunting weapon. As with most tropical forest peoples, the women concentrated on horticultural labor, the men on hunting and warfare.

Villages were usually composed of large thatched communal buildings, each housing the several families which formed one patrilineal lineage. Often a whole village consisted of a single house.[3] Each of these units had a headman or chief, and if the village were composed of more than one lineage, these chiefs may have been subordinate to a village chief. The Guaraní headman's power over his kinsmen was quite limited compared to that wielded by chiefs in the higher cultures of the Andes and circum-Caribbean areas, for Guaraní society was not class-structured with an hereditary hierarchy of chiefs whose authority extended over great numbers of conquered or federated villages. This feature was to be an important determinant of the type of Spanish control system, for the Spaniards could not simply replace the top-level native rulers and govern through an intermediate bureaucratic class. Control had to be immediate and specific, reaching the individual Indian, in contrast to the situation in Peru and Mexico.

There is evidence, however, of a status system which suggests an incipient trend in the direction of socio-political classes. The chief's crops were planted and harvested by the members of his community, and, additionally, chiefs or important people commonly had plural wives or concubines, the number of which corresponded roughly to his prestige. The lack of political power of the leaders continually impressed the Spaniards, who often referred to the general anarchy and lack of authority.[4]

The original expedition of Spaniards to the La Plata region was inspired by false beliefs that the region was very wealthy in gold and silver. This was the great Mendoza expedition, which was a powerful force for its time but was so reduced by hardship and battles with Charrúa and Querandí Indians near Buenos Aires and by subsequent losses suffered in various attempts to reach Peru via the Gran Chaco that those who finally formed the settlement near Asunción, even when reinforced by the remainder of the garrison from the original settlement of Buenos Aires, numbered altogether three hundred and fifty Spaniards.[5] The first and only important reinforcement the colony ever received was that of Cabeza de Vaca's group, which brought the greatest number of Spaniards to about six hundred.[6] This was a small number of soldiers for the huge area they hoped to dominate. Asunción was a thousand miles from the mouth of the La Plata and much of the intervening area was populated by hostile tribes. The fort at Asunción was especially threatened by a great number of enemies in the nearby Chaco. It is plain that the Spaniards would have been in a strategically untenable position had the Guaraní of Paraguay proper also been at war with them, for under these circumstances it would have been more difficult to conquer and rule than in a region of relatively united "empires" like Mexico and Peru.

It was, perhaps, entirely fortuitous that just as the first group of Spaniards arrived in the vicinity of Asunción, in 1537, the agricultural Guaraní, who were hard-pressed by warlike Indians of the Chaco, preferred to welcome the newcomers as potential allies rather than enemies. The Spaniards, who had already suffered grievously from Indian warfare, formed an alliance with certain Guaraní chiefs and built the fort at Asunción. Asunción soon became the Spanish headquarters and base from which further explorations were made in search of the fabulous "Sierras de la Plata." The Spaniards were now settled in a region where the Indians were friendly, and useful, and they took great care not to "violate the customs or wound the sensibilities of the Guaraní."[7]

During the first twenty years of the settlement at Asunción, the assignment of lands and establishment of *encomiendas* was not considered, because the Spaniards still hoped to find gold and silver mines, or Indians with treasure, and had no intention of forming a permanent settlement. In the absence of *encomiendas*, the Spaniards acquired large numbers of Guaraní women, who served not only as wives and concubines, but also as servants and food providers. The relatives of these women also helped provide food and labor for the Spaniards in the same way that they customarily provided for their own chiefs. The Guaraní apparently considered this situation a normal consequence of the alliance.

Numerous coöperative military expeditions were carried out during the first years of the settlement. Under Spanish leadership, the Guaraní won a number of victories over their Chaco enemies, the Guaycurú and Payaguá tribes. Spanish prestige grew as a consequence of these military victories, and the Guaraní contributed very large contingents on subsequent expeditions to the west. This kind of military coöperation and the acceptance of Spaniards as in-law relatives with the status of chiefs was of utmost importance in determing the character of the later, permanent colonization of Paraguay.[8]

This rather casual adaptation of the two peoples to each other was typical of the pre-*encomienda* period, and has often been considered one of the most notable aspects of the early colonial period in Paraguay.[9] In later times, the *encomienda* system appeared, and was a more characteristic Spanish institution, but the concubinage-kinship-labor pattern was never entirely replaced, and it imparted its flavor to the whole subsequent history of Spanish-Guaraní relations.

In 1556, in accordance with a crown order, Governor Irala divided the Indians in the vicinity of Asunción into *encomiendas*, and turned the attention of the colonists from the fruitless search for wealth to the task of permanently settling the land.[10] This new orientation resulted in the rapid extension of the *encomienda* system to new areas of Paraguay, and even to parts of present-day Argentina, where new Spanish towns were established as well. Santa Fe, Corrientes, and Buenos Aires, and Santa Cruz, in what is now eastern Bolivia, were all founded within thirty years after the original *encomienda* grants, and so were many villages in Paraguay proper. Most of the Paraguayan settlements were not created to be populated by Spaniards but by *encomienda* Indians. A total of thirty-eight of these towns were formed, and many of them are still in existence in modern Paraguay.[11]

This expansion of colonization which began after the issuance of *encomienda* grants in 1556 was made possible by the increasingly important role of mestizos. The number of original peninsular Spaniards in Paraguay had diminished greatly in the second half of the sixteenth century, but there had been a great increase in the numbers of their mestizo sons and daughters as a consequence of the extensive polygyny of the conquistadores and the Guaraní women. Santa Fe was founded by nine Spaniards and seventy-five creoles, and Buenos Aires by ten Spaniards and sixty-three creoles.[12] A great many sources from the latter half of the sixteenth century indicate that the mestizos not only greatly outnumbered the Spaniards, but held offices and *encomiendas* and were already displaying a very independent attitude toward Spanish rule. Several scattered rebellions were already called *comunero* movements and presaged the revolts which in later years culminated in the independence of the Latin American states.[13]

The transitional period following the 1556 grants involved the formation of new *encomiendas* in remote areas, and the adaptation of Irala's decrees to the already existing patterns of Spanish-Indian relations which we have described as characteristic of the pre-*encomienda* period. By about 1580, or one generation later, the colony had taken on the most important local characteristics which were to influence the adaptation of the *encomienda* Indians to Paraguayan colonial life. By this time, the influence of the earlier patterns and the exigencies of economic life had developed two quite separate types of institutions of Spanish-Guaraní association—the *originario* and the *mitayo encomiendas*—which retained their stability for the remainder of the colonial period.

The rigid royal laws relating to the *encomienda*, which did not take account of cultural and ecological differences in the various areas of Spanish settlement, were never entirely enforced in Paraguay, despite repeated attempts by several governors to create a system which would conform to crown intentions.[14] As we shall see, some of the laws which had originally grown out of the crown's experiences in the West Indies, Mexico, and Peru had unforeseen consequences in Paraguay, while others had to be modified or disregarded.

The *encomienda* laws most generally ignored in Paraguay were those designed to prevent unpaid, unregulated exploitation of the labor of the natives. The restrictions on Indian labor had been judged by the Spanish crown and its advisers to be the most important means of preventing the rise of a powerful feudal class in America and of protecting the Indians. The frank violation of this prohibition was always one of the characteristics of both the *originario* and *mitayo encomiendas* in Paraguay.[15]

There were many factors in the Paraguayan situation which may have been responsible for this practice, but the most direct and influential imperative was the nature of the Paraguayan economy. Lack of mineral wealth, isolation, and limited commerce meant that Guaraní labor-power was exploited in terms of a subsistence economy, and that tribute of money, agricultural produce, or a native trade ware could not develop in place of labor services, for there was no export market of any importance. . . .[16]

The poverty and scarcity of markets, which reduced the colony to a barter economy, helped bring the Spaniards and Indians into a symbiotic relationship in subsistence activities and were, therefore, very important in promoting the mixing of the two cultures. The limited economy also had the effect of reducing the great gulf which has always existed between the philosophy and attitudes of Europeans and American Indians in economic matters. In other parts of Latin America, the profit-seeking motives of the Spanish entrepreneurs as opposed to the native conception of production-for-use was, and often still is, an important factor inhibiting a mixture of the two cultures.[17] In Paraguay, circumstances never permitted the growth of a class of traders and financiers whose interests and ideals would necessarily be opposed to the Indian viewpoint. The Spaniards in Paraguay were, truly enough, the exploiters, and the Indians were exploited, but as this occurred within a subsistence economy, it was a situation at least comprehensible to the Indians, and probably even a more acceptable one than it might have been under the conditions of a commercial economy.

In addition to these economic characteristics, the adaptation of the Spanish conception of *encomienda* to Paraguay was also affected by such factors as the previously mentioned simplicity of Guaraní socio-political structure and the lack of large population centers when contrasted with the native "empires" of Mexico and Peru. To these must be added the important circumstance that the *encomiendas* were not established in a formal sense until the Spaniards and Indians had already undergone a period of about twenty years of expedient, informal adjustment during which the newcomers acted as allies rather than as conquerors of the Guaraní. As the settlement at Asunción gradually came to be regarded as permanent, the original system of year-round personal service by the "harems" of Indian women and their relatives came to be regarded as an *encomienda*, and was called the *encomienda originaria*. This *originario* had such a firm basis in Paraguayan life that, despite the crown's attempts to limit or abolish it from time to time, it remained a characteristic of Paraguay throughout most of the colonial period.[18]

The more formal *encomienda* created by Irala's ordinances of 1556, was used to extend Spanish control to villages of Indians in areas at some distance from Asunción. This latter system was called the *encomienda mitaya* because the Indians were brought to Asunción periodically as laborers, hence *mitayo* after the *mita* or *corvée* labor system of Peru. Certain main features of both the *originario* and *mitayo* were influenced by the factors outlined above. The specific differences between them will become apparent below where each type of *encomienda* is discussed separately.

The *originario* was not created by decree but was merely the gradual institutionalization of the Guaraní customs of polygyny and kinship obligations. . . .

Specific details are lacking on the manner of life of the *originarios*, but there is evidence indicating that these Indians were regarded as permanent residents of the homes and *estancias* of the Spaniards. Some of the *originarios* were simply domestic servants living all the time at the residence of the *encomenderos* in the Spanish towns.[19] Other whole families of Indians lived as permanent laborers on the outlying *estancias* and farms of the *encomenderos*, and were often passed on in inheritance with the land they worked.[20]

As might be expected, the few sketchy descriptions of life in the *originario* vary, picturing it as either heavenly or hellish. It is difficult, and probably profitless, to attempt to make a judgment—probably some Indians were well-treated and others were not. Writers were partisan in their defense or opposition to the system because the question of personal servitude of Indians was full of political significance. It is notable, however, that Francisco de Alfaro, visiting inspector (*veedor*) of the crown, and great opponent of the *originario*, indicated that he did not believe that the Guaraní considered themselves victimized. . . .

There was little real attempt to indoctrinate the *originario* Indians to the extent the crown considered necessary. We have seen that it was common for the Indians to work on fiesta days and Sundays. Ramírez de Velasco attempted to remedy the lack of religious instruction by ordering that each *encomendero* should have on his estate two native boys and two girls who knew the doctrine in order that they teach the *originario* men and women who were to be brought together each night to hear evening prayers.[21] Alfaro also indicated his dissatisfaction with the failure of the Spaniards to indoctrinate their Indians.[22] One of the factors related to this state of affairs was the notable lack of clerics during the whole period from the conquest until the arrival of the Jesuits. In fact, this is suggested as one of the reasons why the Jesuits were finally asked to come to Paraguay. . . .[23]

The *mitayo encomienda*, unlike the *originario*, extended Spanish influence to Indian villages which were far from Asunción and brought Indians who had been relatively untouched during the exploratory phase of the colonization into a regulated colonial system. The *mitayo* Indians retained the integrity of their society longer than did the *originario* Indians because they still lived together and tilled their own village lands, so that their culture was altered less as a result of breakdown than of slower modification. Although the *mitayo* system allowed the Indians less independence than the crown desired, the Indians were, nevertheless, more protected than in the *originario* system.

The *mitayo encomiendas* were not large at the time of their inception in 1556, and they became even smaller as the Indian population declined during the first hundred years of the colony. Irala stated that twenty thousand Indians were placed in the first *encomiendas*, divided among "320 or more Spaniards."[24] This would be about sixty-two Indians per Spaniard, though they were not apportioned equally. There was a storm of complaints about this, the original colonists feeling that the Indians were too few to be divided among so many *encomenderos*.[25] There are references to two epidemics which killed great numbers of Indians, one in 1558 or 1560, and another in 1605–1606.[26] By the time of Alfaro's ordinances in 1611, many documents stressed that the *encomiendas* often had fewer than ten Indians.[27]

The usual crown policy that *encomiendas* were to be held for only two generations was not observed in Paraguay, so this cannot be considered a cause of the diminution in numbers of *encomienda* Indians. Alfaro and the Council of the Indies attempted to establish this rule in Río de la

Plata in 1611, but although it was observed in Buenos Aires, Santa Fe, and Corrientes, it never was in Paraguay.[28] The right of the first *adelantados* to grant *encomiendas* was retained by subsequent governors, and even Philip II gave permission to Governor Ortiz de Zarate in 1579 to regrant *encomiendas* and also to grant them for three generations.[29]

The small average size of the *encomiendas* helps to explain why *encomienda* labor was always used instead of tribute; there were simply not enough Indians from whom to collect tribute in any substantial amount. It is also probable that the small number of Indians per *encomienda* was a circumstance which contributed directly to their acculturation. As the proportion of Indians to *encomenderos* grew smaller, the amount of personal control over individual Indians increased; Spaniards and Indians were in closer and more immediate contact. There seems to be no evidence that the size of the Indian villages decreased, so some may have been combined as the general population declined—thus more *encomiendas* and more *encomenderos* appeared in each village. This would increase the amount of Spanish influence in each village, or at least contribute to the disruption of native village organization. . . .

The Guaraní, in their aboriginal condition, lived in extended family groups in small villages which shifted their location every few years. One of the important effects Spanish control had on their culture was the change induced by grouping them into larger permanent villages, "reducing" them to easier control and indoctrination. . . .

Spanish control of the daily life of the village Indians was also considerable. The authority of the *encomendero* was virtually unhampered, as the crown laws which were supposed to limit his prerogatives were largely ignored in Paraguay. Additionally, the Paraguayan *encomendero* customarily placed Spanish administrators, *pobleros* or *mayordomos*, in residence in the villages to rule the Indians. These men apparently had considerable authority and freedom of action. Repeatedly, ordinances by Ramírez and Hernandarias complained that they misused authority, kept Indian girls in concubinage, and set a bad example in general. Alfaro, of course tried to abolish *pobleros* altogether, as their use conflicted with law.[30] The Indian officials who actually should have been in charge of the villages had little power. Except for the native chief, or *cacique*, there was not even a legal provision for Indian town officers until Governor Hernandarias attempted to institute *fiscales* in 1603, and Alfaro, in 1611, required that Indian officials be appointed after the Spanish pattern.[31]

We may expect that certain aspects of aboriginal village life were altered in the interest of efficiency of control by the *encomenderos* and local administrators. As examples, we may cite ordinances 1 and 15 of Irala's *encomienda* rules which stated that the Indians were to remain permanently in their own villages, and that the *encomendero* did not have rights to the land of his Indians, nor could he interfere with its use.[32] This rule was general in Spanish America, and grew out of the problems the crown faced in protecting the Indians of Mexico and Peru, regions of dense aboriginal population and large permanent towns.[33] There, the greatest disruptive effect occurred when the scarce and valuable Indian lands were encroached on by Spaniards, and when the Indians were dislodged from their towns. In Paraguay, however, there was plenty of cultivable land, thus there was no necessity to dislocate Indian villages by progressive encroachment. On the contrary, the aboriginal Guaraní practiced a shifting agriculture which involved periodic relocation of their villages, so that as the Spaniards enforced stability of Guaraní villages, they interfered with aboriginal techniques of land use. Thus, ordinances which, when enforced, tended to preserve aboriginal village and land systems in Mexico and Peru, had the effect of altering them in Paraguay.

Ordinance 15 specifically changes one aboriginal custom by ordering that on the death of an Indian husband, his wife, or wives (and children, of course), must continue to occupy the house of the deceased, instead of returning home to her consanguineal family "as was the ancient custom." Like the previously mentioned ordinances, it seems likely that this one was enforced, as the *encomendero* would naturally be loath to lose any of his Indians as a consequence of such an "ancient custom." It should be noted here that it is a characteristic of primitive society that the unilateral consanguineal family is the stable unit through which property is inherited, and in which the security of the individual is provided through mutual aid; the conjugal relationship of men and women of different blood lines is a fragile one, and property is not inherited by the surviving spouse.[34] The above ordinance, however, forces property to be retained by the widow, thus adding a characteristically European element to the Indian marital relationship. We might also expect that the Spaniards would discourage the aboriginal tendency toward easy "divorce," both for reasons stemming from Christianity, and for the practical necessity of maintaining permanence of residence among the *encomienda* Indians.

There were probably many other kinds of disturbances to the native village organization. Through the years, small *encomiendas* were probably combined occasionally or growing ones divided. Epidemics reduced some villages, and the depletion caused by the Spaniards' practice of taking away women must also have been disruptive. All of these occurrences would disturb the delicate balances of house size, population size, subsistence coöperation, and marriage customs, which keep a unilateral kinship group a smoothly functioning unit. Every disturbance would tend to strengthen the conjugal family at the expense of the consanguineal unit, which was larger, more complex, and thus less able to withstand strains.

Probably the most profound acculturative effects resulted from the use of the Guaraní as a labor force in the *mita*. Irala's ordinances of 1556 stated that the Indians were obliged to serve their *encomenderos* in building houses, repairs, agricultural work, hunting and fishing, or any other enterprises, and that they must obey in what they were ordered to do. The sole restriction on the amount of labor was that only one-fourth of the *encomienda* could be used at one time. If work were divided equally, therefore, an Indian was expected to serve three months of the year. The ordinances said nothing about age limits, nor did they forbid the use of women.[35]

Subsequent evidence indicates that abuse of the Indians as laborers was characteristic of the early period. Governor Ramírez de Velasco, in 1597, expressly issued his ordinances to alleviate the hardships of the Indians, ordering that only one-fourth of the *encomienda* be used except during the grain harvests, when half might be used. Further, the labor force was to include men only, between the ages of fifteen and fifty.[36]

Inasmuch as these ordinances were designed, as stated, to correct abuses, it can be argued that in Paraguay prior to 1597 the Indians were probably used as a labor force more than three months of the year, and that women, and children under fifteen, were probably also used at the convenience of the *encomendero*. The validity of this inference is strengthened when we consider the ordinances of Hernandarias, issued six years later. Governor Hernandarias, like Ramírez, complained of the "great lack of regulation in the treatment of the Indians." His ordinance 5 required that boys under fifteen, girls under thirteen and people over sixty should be exempt from work. Ordinance 12 provided that no more than one-third of the Indians of a village could be taken for the *mita*, except for the grain and grape harvest, when one-half could be taken.[37] These ordinances are less restrictive than Ramírez's earlier ones. It seems reasonable to judge, therefore, that inasmuch as Hernandarias was trying to help the Indians, the actual situation must have been quite out of hand.

In addition to the general farm labor required of *mita* Indians, there were several more specialized tasks. Indian women, for example, were required to work four days of each week for ten months, spinning and weaving cloth for the *encomendero*.[38] In regions where the *yerba mate* grew wild, Indians were employed intensively in the labor of cutting and curing it, and carrying it to market. The *yerba* was one of the first of the few cash crops ever developed in Paraguay, and it came to be Paraguay's most important commercial crop. Ruiz de Montoya, writing of the early years of the seventeenth century, notes that the lack of money in Paraguay caused *yerba mate* to become the principal medium of exchange.[39] The transportation of products from the farms to the city markets was another usual kind of labor service. Apparently, the Indians were so commonly used as carriers that both Ramírez de Velasco and Alfaro saw fit to prohibit this practice, though Ramírez admitted that human carriers were necessary in the interior regions where carts were handicapped by lack of roads.[40] Indians were also used as oarsmen for the river craft which carried cargoes between towns.[41]

The farm labor of *mita* Indians under close supervision of the *encomendero* or Spanish *mayordomos* resulted in a blending of Spanish and indigenous subsistence items at an early date. . . .

Most of the European garden vegetables apparently never found favor in Paraguay, even in modern times, although the country is well-suited to many of them, nor was rice adopted in the early colonial period. Wheat was necessary for the sacrament, but as daily fare it never competed with manioc.[42] Sugar cane and citrus fruits, especially favored by the Paraguayan climate, were accepted almost immediately. Such domestic animals as chickens and pigs had become part of the Indians' diet as early as 1556, and were of great importance as subsistence items, for aboriginally most of the meat had been obtained by hunting.[43] Horses and cattle, goats and sheep, were very useful and fitted well into the Paraguayan ecology.[44] The use of these animals probably did not require the cultivation of feed since large areas of excellent pasturage were available all year, nor were the Indians crowded from their best agricultural lands by the herds, as in the Andes.

The addition of so many useful Spanish elements to the native inventory was undoubtedly of great importance. The new skills in agriculture and animal husbandry merged with the native technology, first among the *originario* Indians, and eventually in the *mitayo* villages, and resulted in a new and higher level of productivity. The introduction by the Spaniards of various domestic animals abolished the most important lack in the native food economy. Improved tools, transportation by wheeled vehicles, and the use of horses, burros and oxen, together with a more productive and secure food economy, permitted the larger and more stable population aggregates which were prerequisites for the effective participation of the Indians in Paraguayan colonial culture. . . .

Notes

1. The present article is a condensation of one aspect of a larger work, which is available in microfilm at the Columbia University Library under the title

"Spanish-Guaraní Acculturation in Early Colonial Paraguay," Ph.D. dissertation, 1948. The author wishes to thank the University of Texas for making available certain manuscripts of its Gondra Collection of documents pertaining to early Paraguayan history.

2. The most important source for the following data on the Guaraní is by Alfred Métraux, "The Guaraní," in Julian H. Steward, ed., *Handbook of South American Indians* (Bulletin 143, Bureau of American Ethnology) (6 vols., Washington, 1946–1950) III, 69–94.

3. Nicolás del Techno, "The History of the Provinces of Paraguay, Tecumán, Río de la Plata, Paraná, Guairá, and Urviaca," in Awnsham Churchill, *A Collection of Voyages and Travels* (6 vols., London, 1744–1746, IV, 680–807), pp. 717–718.

4. For example, see Governor Irala's statement in R. de Lafuente Machain, *El Gobernador Domingo Martínez de Irala* (Buenos Aires, 1939), p. 42; and Pedro Dorantes, "Requerimiento del factor Dorantes para que poblase y encomendase indios y su respuesta por el teniente de gobernador Irala," *ibid.*, appendix, p. 486.

5. Alonzo Cabrera, Veedor, quoted in Enrique de Gandía, *Historia de la conquista del Río de la Plata y del Paraguay* (Buenos Aires, 1932), p. 89.

6. Cecilio Báez, *Historia colonial del Paraguay y Río de la Plata* (Asunción, 1926), p. 26. There were subsequent attempts at reinforcement, by Sanabria and Rasquín, but they ended disastrously.

7. Julián María Rubio, *Exploración y conquista del Río de la Plata. Siglos XVI y XVII* (Barcelona and Buenos Aires, 1942), p. 154.

8. *Ibid.*, p. 135, and Carlos Pereyra, *Historia de la América española* (8 vols., Madrid, 1920–1927), IV, 78.

9. For example, Gandía states:

La mezcla de españoles e indígenas se realizó en forma ejemplar en el Paraguay. Domingo de Irala fué el colonizador perfecto que supo fusionar un ejército de pocas decenas de españoles con un pueblo de miles y miles de indios. Los restos de la brillante armada de don Pedro de Mendoza se salvaron en el Paraguay cuande el veedor Alonso Cabrera, atacado de manía destructora, hiza destruír Buenos Aires en 1541. La vida en la Asunción fué comparada con la del paraíso de Mohoma porque cada español disponía de un número de mujeres que iba desde cinco y diez a un centenar. Entre ellas había madres, hijas y hermanas y todas solían hacer vida marital con el conquistador que las dirigía. Los clérigos ponían el grito en el cielo; pero los españoles sellaban alianzas de familia con los innumerables parientes de las indias y así cada uno de ellos podía llamarse cuñado, *tovaya'*, de cientos de indios. El hogar hispanoindígena del Paraguay, en esta forma, llegó a estar constituído por varios miles de indios e indios guaraní, y por unos pocos cientos de soldados españoles. La paz fué asegurada y gracias a las *inmoralidades* de los españoles la colonización pudo salvarse de los asaltos de los guaycurús y payaguás.

Enrique de Gandía, *Francisco de Alfaro y la condición social de los indios* (Buenos Aires, 1939), pp. 33–34. Rubio, *Exploración y reconquista*, p. 181, makes similar remarks.

10. Pedro Dorantes, "Requerimiento . . . . ," 483–490.

11. Félix de Azara, *Viajes por la América meridional* (2 vols., Madrid, 1923), II, 129.

12. Ricardo Levene, *A History of Argentina* (Chapel Hill, 1937), pp. 41–42.

13. *Ibid.*, pp. 41–42; Enrique de Gandía, *Los primeros Italianos en el Río de la Plata y otros estudios históricos* (Buenos Aires, 1932), pp. 93–94.

14. See Domingo Martínez de Irala, "Ordenanzas sobre repartimientos y encomiendas—14 de Mayo, 1556," in Lafuente Machain, *El Gobernador Domingo Martínez*, appendix, pp. 511–524; "Ordenanzas dadas por el Gobernador D. Juán Ramírez de Velasco, sobre el gobierno y trato de los indios, 1 de enero, 1597," in Juán Carlos García Santillán, *Legislación sobre indios del Río de la Plata en el siglo XVI* (Madrid, 1928), appendix, pp. 356–375; "Ordenanzas dadas por el Gobernador y Capitán General, Justicia Mayor y Juez de Residencia de las Provincias del Río de la Plata, Don Hernán Arias de Saavedra, sobre el tratamiento de los indios, 29 de diciembre de 1603," *ibid.*, pp. 376–388; "Ordenanzas de Alfaro," Pablo Hernández, *Organización social de las doctrinas guaraníes de la Compañía de Jesús* (2 vols., Barcelona, 1913), II (Appendix 56) 661–677; "Decisión real confirmatoria," *ibid.*, II (Appendix 57) 677–681.

15. This is not to say, of course, that Indians were not forced to labor in other parts of Spanish America. The extent to which *encomienda* laws after 1542 were violated in other regions is a question which lies outside the scope of this paper.

16. Silvio Zavala has made a good argument to this effect. See "Apuntes históricos sobre la moneda del Paraguay," *El Trimestre Económico* XIII (1946), 126–143.

17. Lesley Byrd Simpson, "New Lamps for Old in Latin America," in *The Civilization of the Americas* (Berkeley, 1938), pp. 3–24.

18. See the following sources, which mention the *originario* system as of 1679, 1780, and 1801: Cédula Real, "Redúzcanse los indios originarios á mitayos, y júntense como los demás en pueblos," Hernández, *Organización social . . .* , II (Appendix No. 61), 688–690; Juán del Pino Manrique, "Informe del protector de naturales del Paraguay sobre encomiendas . . . ," Andrés Lamas, ed., *Colección de memorias y documentos para la historia y jeografía de los pueblos del Río de la Plata* (Montevideo, 1849), pp. 457–465; Félix de Azara, *Descripción e historia del Paraguay y del Río de la Plata* (Buenos Aires, 1943), p. 168.

19. Félix de Azara, *Viajes . . .* , II, 16–17.

20. Juán del Pino Manrique, "Informe . . . ," Lamas, ed., "Colección de memorias . . . ." Evidence is unclear, however, as to whether the rule that *encomiendas* could be held for only two generations of Spaniards was successfully enforced. See Hernandarias de Saavedra, "Ordenanzas," ordinance 27; "Carta de Pedro Dorantes al Consejo de Indias, 8 de Abril, 1573," in Blas Garay, ed., *Colección de documentos relativos a la historia de América y particularmente á la historia del Paraguay* (Asunción, 1899–1901), pp. 138–139; "Carta del Capitan Martín de Orue para S.M., Asunción, 14 de Abril, 1573," *ibid.*, p. 165.

21. Ramírez de Velasco, "Ordenanzas . . . ," ordinance 17.

22. Francisco de Alfaro, "Ordenanzas . . . ," article 7.

23. Félix de Azara, *Viajes . . . ,* II, 120.

24. Domingo Martínez de Irala, "Relación breve . . . ," Lafuente Machain, *El Gobernador Domingo Martínez*, p. 544.

25. See, as examples: "Carta de Juan de Salazar al Consejo Real de Indias, dando cuenta de su expedición al Paraguay, y pidiendo, como primer poblador,

que se le concediese a perpetuidad cierto numero de indios, Asunción 20 de Marzo, 1556," in *Cartas de Indias* (2 vols., Madrid, 1877), I (Documento XCVIII) 579–582; "Memoria de Juán Salmerón de Heredia a S.M.," Blas Garay, *Colección de documentos . . .* , pp. 232–238.

26. Juán López de Velasco, *Geografía y descripción universal de las indias* (Madrid, 1894), p. 552; "Request of Manuel de Frias . . . , 1617," Ms., Manuel E. Gondra Collection, University of Texas, Ms. 38a.

27. See, as examples: "Certificación . . . , Asunción, 1612," in Gandía, "Francisco de Alfaro . . ." (Documento XXIV), p. 459; "Alegatos presentados . . . ," Madrid, 1618, *ibid.*, (Documento XLII), pp. 513, 517; Cabildo of Asunción to King, April 20, 1612, Gondra Collection, University of Texas, Ms. 1442; Request of Manuel de Frias, 1617, *ibid.*, Ms. 38a; Sebastián de León to King, Asunción, September 7, 1639, *ibid.*, Ms. 209a; Report to Procurador General, Asunción, April 3, 1643, *ibid.*, Ms. 209c; Petition to Lieutenant General, Asunción, March 3, 1640, *ibid.*, Ms. 209d.

28. Félix de Azara, *Descripción e historia del Paraguay . . .* , p. 168; Miguel Lastarría, *Colonias orientales del Río Paraguay o de la Plata.* (*Documentos para la historia argentina*, III, Buenos Aires, 1914), 28–29.

29. Antonio de León Pinelo, *Tratado de las confirmaciones reales* (*Biblioteca argentina de libros raros americanos*, I, Buenos Aires, 1922), p. 101. Philip II to Captain Ortiz de Çarate, Madrid, July 10, 1579 (Gondra Collection, University of Texas, Ms. 515i).

30. Ramíres de Velasco, "Ordenanzas . . . ," ordinance No. 32; Hernandarias de Saavedra, "Ordenanzas . . . ," ordinance No. 20; Francisco de Alfaro, "Ordenanzas . . . ," ordinance No. 13.

31. Hernandarias de Saavedra, "Ordenanzas . . . ," ordinance Nos 6, 8; Alfaro, "Ordenanzas . . . ," ordinance No. 8.

32. Domingo Martínez de Irala, "Ordenanzas sobre repartimientos y encomiendas," Lafuente Machain, *El Gobernador Domingo Martínez*, pp. 511–524.

33. See Silvio Zavala, *De encomiendas y propriedad territorial en algunas regiones de la América española* (Mexico, 1940); F. A. Kirkpatrick, "The Landless Encomienda," *The Hispanic American Historical Review*, XXII (1942), 765–774.

34. Ruth Benedict, "Marital Property Rights in Bilateral Society," *American Anthropologist*, N.S., XXXVIII (1936), 368–373.

35. Domingo Martínez de Irala, "Ordenanzas sobre repartimientos y encomiendas . . . , 14 de Mayo, 1556," Lafuente Machain, *La Gobernador Domingo Martínez*, appendix, pp. 511–524.

36. *Ibid.*, ordinance 9.

37. Hernandarias de Saavedra, "Ordenanzas . . . ."

38. Ramírez de Velasco, quoted in Enrique de Gandía, *Francisco de Alfaro*, p. 89.

39. Antonio Ruiz de Montoya, *Conquista espiritual hecha por los religiosos de la compañía de Jésus en las provincias del Paraguay, Paraná, Uruguay y Tapé* (Bilbao, 1892), pp. 16–17.

40. Ramírez de Velasco, "Ordenanzas . . . ," ordinance 19; Alfaro, "Ordenanzas . . . ," ordinance 33.

41. Alfaro, "Ordenanzas . . . ," ordinance 11.

42. Ruiz de Montoya, *Conquista Espiritual . . .* , p. 17.

43. See Irala, "Ordenanzas . . . , 1556," Lafuente Machain, *La Gobernador Domingo Martínez*, pp. 511–524, ordinance 9.

44. "Carta de . . . Martín de Orue . . . ," Blas Garay, *Colección de documentos . . .* , p. 164.

11 Louis de Armond ◆
Frontier Warfare in Colonial Chile

*On the frontiers of colonial Latin America, Indians who resisted mission-
aries and encomenderos often met representatives of another Iberian frontier institution, the military. Although European soldiers arrived with iron
weapons and gunpowder, they failed in some areas to subdue Indians by
military force alone. Louis de Armond explains why in the celebrated
case of Araucanians in Chile. The Araucanians found numerous ways to
adopt and adapt to Spanish military techniques, and thereby maintained
their independence until the end of the colonial era.*

*In writing from the point of view of the Araucanians in this essay,
which appeared in 1954, de Armond was ahead of his time.* Much of the
traditional scholarship on frontier warfare in Latin America had focused
on Iberian militaries and the ways in which they did or did not adapt to
frontier conditions, rather than on Indian adaptations.†*

*Louis de Armond (b. 1918), who served as a Foreign Service officer
in Chile from 1942 to 1944, received a Ph.D. in history from the University of California at Berkeley in 1950. He enjoyed a long teaching career
at California State University, Los Angeles, from 1950 until his retire-
ment in 1979.*

W arfare between Indians and Spaniards in sixteenth-century Chile
saw a very nearly regular rise in the warrior capacity of the Araucanians and a steadily declining military potential on the part of the Spaniards.[1] Factors quite apart from numbers account for the changing fortunes
of the contenders. The 150 troops who accompanied Pedro de Valdivia on
his first trip to Chile were but a handful compared with the Spanish army
of the early seventeenth century, which numbered well over a thousand.[2]
Conversely, the Araucanian population had diminished notably by the end

From *Pacific Historical Review* 23, no. 2 (May 1954): 125–32. © 1954
by the Pacific Coast Branch, American Historical Association. Reprinted by
permission.

*For a more recent treatment of this subject, with a theoretical context and
guidance to literature, see Nathan Wachtel's discussion of war and acculturation
among the Araucanians in *The Vision of the Vanquished: The Spanish Conquest
of Peru through Indian Eyes, 1530–1570*, trans. Ben and Sian Reynolds (1st ed.,
1971; New York: Barnes & Noble, 1977), 192–96.

†See, for example, Max L. Moorhead, *The Presidio: Bastion of the Spanish
Borderlands* (Norman: University of Oklahoma Press, 1975), and Alfred J. Tapson,
"Indian Warfare on the Pampa During the Colonial Period," *Hispanic American
Historical Review* 42 (February 1962):1–28.

of the sixteenth century. Nonetheless, a competent observer estimated that the area south of the Bío Bío River still held something more than twenty thousand Indian warriors.[3]

Whatever the accuracy of the population estimates extant, they clearly indicate that the Araucanians, despite the recurrent ravages of smallpox and other diseases, still enjoyed an overwhelming numerical advantage over the Spaniards. Given this preponderance, one wonders why they did not expel the small and miserably poor Spanish population.

Paradoxically, the very circumstance which made it virtually impossible for the Spaniards to end the war with the Indians seems also to have rendered the Indians incapable of ousting their European enemy. This factor was the basic nature of the Indian social order, which was characterized by an extraordinary degree of individualism and, in a manner, rude democracy. The Spaniards were quite unable to find any single individual or group against whom they could direct their energies in an effort to conclude the war. The correspondence of governors, judges of the audiencia, and army officers is replete with annoyed references to the fact that there was no Indian chieftain responsible for the conduct of all the natives of Chile. Conversely, the Araucanians were never able, if ever they sought, to mass their entire potential against the Spaniards. Thus the early seventeenth century found the war in Chile in a state of uneasy equilibrium. The Spaniards were unable to push deeper into Indian territory, while the natives engaged mostly in limited raids across the frontier of the Spanish area.

A major cause bringing about this balance was that the Araucanians soon surpassed the Chilean Spaniard in equestrian ability and acquired the talents that make today's Chilean *huaso* in every respect the equal of Argentina's now-disappearing Gaucho. From the time they stole their first horses from Pedro de Valdivia, the Araucanians steadily augmented their mounted troops and came to place growing reliance on cavalry in encounters with the Spaniards. Clear proof of the fact would seem to lie in their penchant for stealing horses from the Spaniards.

Not alone through their adoption of the horse did the Indians enhance their fighting potential. Other facets of acculturation had raised their individual capacity to meet the second-rate Spanish troops in Chile. Most of the changes, however, occurred in strategy rather than in the weapons used. The weapons of Araucanian infantry in the seventeenth century remained largely those of the pre-Spanish period and comprised pikes, arrows, and clubs. The pikes, though not as durable as their Spanish counterpart, were formidable weapons from twenty to twenty-two feet long. The bows were smaller and heavier than those used in many other parts of America, for they were only about three and a half feet long; the arrows were comparably short, and were customarily tipped with a variety of materials that often remained in the wound. Used less frequently were the clubs, shaped roughly like a hockey stick, in cross section as large as a man's wrist, and perhaps seven feet long.[4]

In their attacks on Pedro de Valdivia and his men, the Indians had displayed heroic valor but their superior numbers were neutralized by the Spanish soldier's lance, sword, and, above all, discipline. Within a very few years, however, the Araucanians had learned their first lesson. In the attack that led to the capture and death of Pedro de Valdivia, instead of attacking *en masse*, the Indians formed in several squadrons. The first descended on Valdivia and his men and fought until forced to break and run. It was at once replaced by another, which was then replaced by a third. While successive squadrons were engaging the Spanish troops, the first groups reformed and, in turn, attacked. Thus through sheer force of numbers and despite heavy losses, the Indians fought without cease until the Spaniards were literally so tired they could not lift their sword arms and fell under the weight of Indian numbers.[5]

Soon thereafter the Araucanians used lassos of *liana*, with considerable effect, to pull Spanish troops from their horses and bring them within reach of Indian hand weapons.[6] A change in tactics as well quickly became apparent. In 1555 occurred the first instance in which the Araucanians took a leaf from the Spaniards' book and used fortifications. In December of that year they overnight silently occupied an excellent defensive position overlooking Concepción, prepared a rude stockade of poles they had carried with them, and then waited for the Spaniards to attack. The Spaniards did attack, but despite their horses and arquebuses they failed completely to dislodge the enemy. Retiring to their own stockade, the Spaniards found themselves besieged and finally were forced to retire over trails made difficult by trees the Indians had felled.[7]

As early as 1558 the natives had lost their fear of firearms. Thereafter, though grossly inaccurate in their aim and usually short of powder, they used firearms whenever circumstances permitted. Soldiers of the Spanish army, usually mestizos from the ranks, from time to time fled to join the Indians. According to one Spanish officer, these renegades afforded the Araucanians a limited force of arquebusiers who were effective only to the extent that powder could be taken from the Spaniards.[8]

Refinements in Indian methods of fortification soon included the practice of digging trenches and camouflaged holes to trap the Spanish horses. The effectiveness of the practice became evident in a pitched battle of 1563, which also gave clear evidence of the deterioration of the Spanish military. In that year a group of ninety Spaniards attacked such an Indian fort with disastrous results. As they approached the palisade, many of the horses and their riders fell into the holes prepared for them. Thrown from their mounts, the Spaniards were easy targets for Araucanian arrows. Thus the Spanish attack was promptly converted into a rout from which the attackers fled in complete disorder and with heavy toll of lives.[9]

The same year witnessed other instances of the inventiveness of Indian resistance. An excellent illustration of this adaptability is in their laying siege to Arauco fort. They took up position just beyond the range of the few artillery pieces in the Spanish fort and there waited for the Spaniards to exhaust their scant food supplies. Finding that the enemy was getting water from a ravine within the cover of his artillery, the Indians under cover of darkness threw bodies and other decaying matter into the pool. The extremity of the Spaniards was such, however, that they continued to use the water despite its contamination. The Araucanians thereupon dug a ditch and drained the pool.[10]

Finally, the natives attacked the besieged soldiers with a grisly form of psychological warfare. Another body of Indians had felled part of a group of Spanish troops who sought to lift the siege of Arauco. The heads of the hapless Spaniards were promptly brought to Arauco and lifted high on pikes. Seeing them, the trapped Spaniards were assured that Concepción had fallen and that they were the only Christians remaining in all of southern Chile. Whatever the effectiveness of this unusual bit of strategy, the Araucanians maintained such a tight siege that Arauco fort was abandoned after two months of isolation.[11]

In all these engagements the Indians were gaining increasing quantities of Spanish matériel, including swords, pikes, and guns, as well as protective helmets and leather jackets that rendered the Spanish soldiers' swords less dangerous. Most important, however, were the horses which the Indians were taking in steadily increasing numbers. As a single instance, when the Spaniards evacuated Arauco (re-established after its loss in 1563) and Cañete forts in 1566, they left behind 360 horses and a quantity of saddles.[12] Within a relatively brief span these and other horses gained by the Indians enabled them to mount cavalry forces far superior to those of the Spaniards. The first governor of Chile in the seventeenth century lamented that "all the enemy who can, move on horseback and therefore enter and leave our territory with increasing ease and speed. . . ."[13] The maximum body of cavalry the natives could mass, according to an authoritative estimate of 1614, was an impressive six thousand.[14] By this time the native cavalry could boast of defensive armor for both horse and rider that was fully the equal of the Spaniards'. The only weapon carried by the Indian cavalryman was a lance.[15]

The Indian military position in Chile was further enhanced by the nature of Spanish soldiery. Letters and reports of the early seventeenth century unvaryingly speak of the exceptionally low moral and military level of troop reinforcements that reached Chile, whether they came from Peru or, much less often, from Spain. One of the most serious penalties assessed for wrongdoing in Peru was exile to Chile and service in the army there. Thus many of the soldiers sent from Lima were habitual criminals.[16] Whether criminals or not, they were of little or no value in the struggle with the Araucanians.

The practice of allowing these soldiers to winter in Santiago was a major reason for the regular diminution of the army's numbers and the need for its aperiodic reinforcement. Indeed, more soldiers were lost to the army in peaceful Santiago than were lost in the war. Statistical details are not available for the rate of attrition of the army in the period as a whole. But there is record that from November, 1591, to late 1593 thirty-two soldiers died from causes growing out of action against the Indians, while at least three times that number were lost in Santiago through death from disease, flight from the country, or escape into a religious order.[17]

The fact that fewer soldiers were lost to the army in the war than in Santiago was a direct result of the deplorable conditions under which the soldiers lived. One army officer, writing in 1594, asserted that "the name Chile grows daily more hateful" and "today not one man of those who serve there and are not settled would remain if he were given permission to leave. . . ."[18] The men were ill-clothed, ill-fed, and ill-equipped. They were the victims of exploitation by merchants, *encomenderos*, and their own officers. Competition among these persons for a share of the soldiers' wage was keen, but competitive price-cutting was not a feature of this contest.

The supply situation of the garrison troops in the more remote frontier forts was particularly difficult. Sometimes rations were completely exhausted and they were forced to forage for food in the area surrounding the forts. They were usually forced to remain near the forts for fear of Indian ambush if they ranged too far afield. The hardships that resulted were sometimes extreme, as is illustrated by the account given by one officer of the plight of the garrison of a small fort near the junction of the Laja and Bío Bío rivers.

> When the reduced rations of wheat and barley were exhausted I first ordered that, of the two companies I had with me, one should go out each day into the unproductive and barren countryside to bring back thistles . . . , which were the most substantial thing to be found. . . . When these were gone we collected other unfamiliar plants, from which some became ill. . . . I went out daily in a little boat we had there and went upstream [collecting] the leaves, larger than a shield, of a plant called *pangue*. . . . It was necessary to distribute these leaves with sword in hand. . . . Finally the state of hunger reached such extremes that no shield

or other thing made of leather remained. . . . Even the palisade of the
fort was torn apart for the leather thongs, rotted by sun and water, with
which the timbers were lashed together. . . . Despite the precaution of
seeing that no soldier who guarded the wall at night should carry a knife
or sword . . . we woke one morning to find the fort torn apart and open
in a score of places . . . and [soldiers] roasting the thongs over the coals
of a fire.[19]

In the light of these multiple problems, army leaders in the late sixteenth century initiated a battle strategy which became the norm. An un-
stable frontier roughly paralleling the Bío Bío River had come into being.
Now the *maloca*, or summer campaign, was initiated. It was essentially
defensive, for it sought to prevent the Araucanians, through destruction
of their crops and their homes, from mounting any major attack. In the
main, the strategy was effective, for only once in the next twenty years
did the Indians coalesce their forces into a general movement that for a
brief time threatened the entire Spanish position south of the Maule River.
During the rest of this period the Araucanians for the most part confined
themselves to guerrilla raids by small groups of mounted troops.

Perhaps a more important reason for the success of the *maloca* in
maintaining relative peace north of the Bío Bío was that the Indian rebels
soon came to look upon it with what amounted to approval. They noted
that the campaign began at approximately the same time from year to
year and usually followed a rather closely prescribed route through the
central valley. They continued to plant some corn within reach of the cam-
paigning Spanish army, but they also planted larger crops far back in
mountain valleys where the Spaniards feared to go. Most of the Indians
retired to these same mountain retreats.

The circumstances suggest that the Indians continued plantings in
the central valley only as bait designed to persuade the Spaniards to
continue their annual campaign. The truth is that the Indians promptly
made of the *maloca* a positive benefit to themselves. Wrote one Spanish
soldier:

> Each year [they] look forward to our *campeada* as an excellent and
> abundant fair where they know they can abundantly replace whatever
> time has consumed. . . . From our campaigns they provide themselves
> with many horses . . . , as well as so many bridles, spurs, and stirrups
> that they have stopped using those . . . made of whale bone and wood. . . .
> The offensive arms the Indians gain in greatest numbers . . . are swords
> which provide them with iron for their pike and lance [tips]. But now
> they have so many that . . . their infantry attach [complete swords] to
> the long and pliable poles of their pikes. . . . Besides the swords, they
> get knives, machetes, mattocks, and axes in great quantity. Among all
> the tools they esteem the axes most, for they are very useful to them.

[With them] they speedily fell trees that fall across . . . the trails and hinder the passage of our cavalry. . . .[20]

Not alone by dint of seizure did the Araucanians gather Spanish artifacts. At once suggesting the advantage enjoyed by the Indians as a result of these campaigns and indicative of the extraordinarily low position of the Spanish army was the willing part played by Spanish soldiery itself. Many of the Spanish troops participated in an unusual trade with the enemy wherein they bartered their swords and even the matchlocks and supporting hooks of their arquebuses in exchange for a little fruit or grain meal. Sometimes their hunger reached such extremes that they even handed gunpowder to the enemy in return for food.[21] It might be added parenthetically that the clandestine trade gave clear evidence that the Araucanians were completely familiar with the functioning of the arquebus. They readily took matchlocks in this commerce, not because of any intrinsic value, but because the Spanish firing pieces were thus very effectively immobilized.

Such were some of the aspects of warfare in colonial Chile. It was a war that by the seventeenth century found the Spaniards on the horns of a dilemma. On the one hand, they did not have the strength to deal the Indians a definitive blow. On the other, much as they might suffer directly or indirectly, they felt they had to continue the war in an effort to prevent the Indians from becoming predominantly stronger, to keep in force the royal subsidy of the army in Chile, and to provide some replenishment of encomienda labor. As the seventeenth century wore into the eighteenth and as the European population of Chile mounted—albeit very slowly—there emerged what was essentially a stalemate broken by brief flurries of warfare. This unhappy situation was not to end until the diplomacy of an independent Chile finally brought solution in the late nineteenth century.

Notes

1. This article treats but one aspect of Araucanian culture and acculturation. Those wishing a fuller treatment of Araucanian habits are referred to John Montgomery Cooper, "The Araucanians," *Handbook of South American Indians* (6 vols., Washington, 1946–1950), II, 687–760. Comprehensive in its own right, this article has appended to it a very full bibliography. Romantics would probably enjoy the less academic but still classic *La Araucana* of Alonso de Ercilla y Zúñiga or the less well known *Arauco domado* of Pedro de Oña.

2. In 1611 the army totalled 1,838 men ("Discursos i apuntamientos sobre las cosas de la guerra deste reino hecho por el capitan don Diego de Mercado," Santiago, April 19, 1613, in Medina transcripts, Chilean National Library, Vol. 112, folio 314), while the governor of Chile indicated his actual fighting force in

1614 numbered 1,344 (Alonso de Rivera to the king, Buena Esperanza, February 18, 1615, in Medina transcripts, Vol. 112, folio 342).

3. Alonso González de Nájera, "Desengaño y reparo de la guerra del reino de Chile . . . ," in *Colección de documentos inéditos para la historia de España* XLVIII (Madrid, 1866), 151, 180.

4. *Ibid.*, 177–178.

5. For a full account of the capture and death of Valdivia see Diego Barros Arana, *Historia general de Chile* (16 vols., Santiago, 1884–1902), I, 432–437.

6. *Ibid.*, II, 23.

7. *Ibid.*, 73–75.

8. González de Nájera, "Desengaño y reparo . . . ," 219.

9. Barros Arana, *Historia general de Chile*, II, 314–315. Frequently the Indian enhanced the frightfulness of these traps by placing in the bottom upright pointed stakes as large as a man's arm (González de Nájera, "Desengaño y reparo . . . ," 297, note 1).

10. Barros Arana, *Historia general de Chile*, II, 319–320.

11. *Ibid.*, 320.

12. *Ibid.*, 398–399.

13. Alonso de Rivera to the king, Concepción, October 18, 1613, in Medina transcripts, Vol. 112, folio 94.

14. Testimony of Fray Juan Falcón de los Angeles, Santiago, April 18, 1614, in Medina transcripts, Vol. III, folio 205.

15. González de Nájera, "Desengaño y reparo . . . ," 210–211.

16. *Ibid.*, 431.

17. Report of Miguel de Olaverría, Lima [?], 1593, as cited in Barros Arana, *Historia general de Chile*, III, 126, note 7.

18. Memorial of Miguel de Olaverría, Lima [?], 1594, in Claudio Gay, *Historia física y política de Chile. . . . Documentos sobre la historia, la estadística y la geografía* (2 vols., Paris, 1846–1852), II, 53.

19. González de Nájera, "Desengaño y reparo . . . ," 337–338.

20. *Ibid.*, 303–306.

21. *Ibid.*, 308–309.

12 Franklin W. Knight ◆
"Black Transfrontiersmen": The Caribbean Maroons

Indians were not the only people to resist the expansion of European fron-
tiers in colonial Latin America. African slaves who ran away from plan-
tations took refuge in the uninhabited hinterlands outside Spanish and
Portuguese towns. Known as maroons, these fugitives formed their own
communities, called palenques *in Spanish America and* quilombos *or*
mocambos in Brazil. Many palenques, *consisting of just a handful of*
maroons, were ephemeral, but others numbering in the hundreds or thou-
sands proved difficult to destroy. * Palmares, the most famous* quilombo
in Brazil, was founded in 1605 in the backlands of Pernambuco. When it
expanded to include more than thirty thousand residents in ten villages
by mid-century, it presented a serious threat to the Portuguese slave soci-
ety on the coast. Palmares successfully resisted six Portuguese military
expeditions sent out against it in the 1680s, but it was eventually
destroyed in 1695 after a two-year campaign waged by an army launched
from São Paulo.†

In this cogent excerpt from his book The Caribbean: The Genesis of a
Fragmented Nationalism, *Franklin Knight examines the Caribbean*
maroons as "transfrontiersmen," or "people who chose to operate out-
side the conventional confines of the colonies." He distinguishes between
"petit" and "gran marronnage" and describes the characteristics of
palenques *that sprang up in isolated areas of the Caribbean islands, the*
Guianas, Colombia, and Venezuela. Knight shows that successful maroons
were able to establish a semisymbiotic relationship with the societies from
which they had withdrawn, enabling them to procure firearms, tools, food,
and intelligence. Yet in the end, cooperation with the organized and for-
mal colony proved their undoing, sapping the very integrity, cultural dis-
tinctiveness, and vitality of their existence. Those maroons who achieved
the ultimate goal—legal recognition through the signing of treaties—
unwittingly relinquished their independence and reduced their appeal as
an alternative frontier state.

From Franklin W. Knight, *The Caribbean: The Genesis of a Frag-*
mented Nationalism, Second Edition, 90–96. © 1990 by Oxford University Press,
Inc. Reprinted by permission.
   *Alistair Hennessy, *The Frontier in Latin American History* (Albuquerque:
University of New Mexico Press, 1978), 68.
   †For an in-depth study of Palmares, see R. K. Kent, "Palmares: An African
State in Brazil," *Journal of African History* 6 (1965):161–75. This essay is in-
cluded in Richard Price's edited volume, *Maroon Societies* (1st ed., 1973; Balti-
more: Johns Hopkins University Press, 1979), which offers essays on *marronnage*
throughout Spanish America, Brazil, and the Caribbean.

The Jamaican-born Knight is a professor of Latin American and Caribbean history at the Johns Hopkins University. He has published extensively and is perhaps best known for his monograph Slave Society in Cuba during the Nineteenth Century *(Madison: University of Wisconsin Press, 1970).*

As late as 1700—and much later on the larger islands and mainland possessions—the European colonies in the Caribbean constituted expanding enclaves with moving frontiers. Until the Peace of Utrecht in 1713, there were two general types of society existing in alternating harmony and discord. The first type comprised the boisterous, violent society of struggling settlers, prospering planters, exasperated officials, machinating merchants, suffering slaves, and ambivalent free persons of color. Together these constituted the organized and formal colony. They were the true colonists who accepted, albeit often under duress, the rules, regulations, and interventions of the metropolises and subscribed to varying degrees to the political integrity of the different imperial systems. The second social type generated by the considerable sociopolitical flux of the times consisted of a variegated group of individuals, commonly considered transfrontiersmen—people who chose to operate outside the conventional confines of the colonies. Such transfrontier groups ranged from the highly organized communities of Maroons, or escaped slaves, to the defiant, stateless, peripatetic collectivity of buccaneers or free-booters. These two groups—Maroons and buccaneers—were not primarily a threat to settled, organized society in the Caribbean but represented a temporary alternative to the formal colonial social structure.

The Maroons formed the most successful alternative to organized European colonial society. Born of the innate resistance to slavery, they were essentially communities of Africans and their descendants who escaped individually and collectively from the plantations and households of their masters to seek their freedom, thereby continuing a tradition begun by the indigenous Indians. The word "maroon" was first used to describe the range cattle that had gone wild during the first attempts at Spanish colonization on the island of Hispaniola. It was also applied to Indians that had escaped from the established Spanish compounds. By the middle of the sixteenth century, it was already being applied to African slaves. In any case, *marronnage*—the flight from servitude—became an intrinsic dimension of American slavery, enduring as long as the institution itself.

American plantation society spawned a variety of forms of resistance to enslavement. Acts of resistance could be categorized into two forms. The first was the temporary desertion of individual slaves. This form of escape, frequently called *petit marronnage*, reflected the strong individual inclination on the part of the slave to resist forced or unpleasant labor, to procrastinate, to defy a master or a rule, or to visit friends, family, or acquaintances in the neighborhood without the requisite permission. *Petit marronnage* was eventually accepted with due reluctance as one of the inescapable concomitants of the system and was punished with less severity than other infringements of local regulations or other patterns of behavior that jeopardized the social order. At its most serious, *petit marronnage* remained a personal conflict between the master and the slave.

This was not true of the second form of resistance, *gran marronnage*, which constituted a fully organized attempt to establish autonomous communities, socially and politically independent of the European colonial enclave. This pattern of conduct was potentially subversive to the entire socioeconomic complex of colonial life. Such independent communities— variously called *palenques* in the Spanish colonies, *quilombos* or *mocambos* in the Portuguese, and Maroon towns in the English colonies— encompassed varying numbers of individuals. Some communities lasted only for very short periods of time. Others endured for centuries. In their construction and their survival may be deduced the eloquent articulation of the Africans and Afro-Americans on the real conditions of slavery and their opinions of it. Organized bands of Maroons prevailed for centuries in Jamaica, outlasting the determined communities of Bahía and Palmares in Brazil, Esmeraldas in Ecuador, or Le Maniel in French Saint-Domingue.

Detested and vehemently opposed by the European slave-owning colonists, these misnamed towns taxed the ingenuity and resourcefulness of all the participants, both for their sustenance and for their survival. Considering the extreme disadvantages under which the Maroons labored, it is most surprising that so many communities survived for such long periods of time, often in close proximity to operating plantations. The principal ingredients of success seemed to be the nature of their social organization and the physical location of the communities.

Maroon villages were composed predominantly of young able-bodied adults, although as Barry Higman points out in his study of the slave populations of the British Caribbean, *marronnage* involved slaves of all ages and both sexes. Until the eighteenth century, Africans tended to predominate among the Maroon communities, but gradually the composition reflected the changing demographic structure, with an increasing number of Creoles. Indeed, with the cessation of official English participation in the transatlantic slave trade after 1807, both the slave and Maroon communities acquired an increased proportion of Creoles.

During the eighteenth century, Maroons acquired a fearsome reputation. Bryan Edwards wrote a curiously admiring description of the

Maroons of Jamaica in the later part of the eighteenth century which reveals as much about the writer and his society as his subject:

> Savage as they were in manners and disposition, their mode of living and daily pursuits undoubtedly strengthened their frame, and served to exalt them to great bodily perfection. Such fine persons are seldom beheld among any other class of African or native blacks. Their demeanor is lofty, their walk firm, and their persons erect. Every motion displays a combination of strength and agility. The muscles (neither hidden nor depressed by clothing) are very prominent, and strongly marked. Their sight withal is wonderfully acute, and their hearing remarkably quick. These characteristics, however, are common, I believe, to all savage nations, in warm and temperate climates; and like other savages, the Maroons have only those senses perfect which are kept in constant exercise. Their smell is obtuse, and their taste so depraved, that I have seen them drink new rum fresh from the still, in preference to wine which I offered them; and I remember, at a great festival in one of their towns, which I attended, that their highest luxury, in point of food, was some rotten beef, which had been originally salted in Ireland, and which was probably presented to them, by some person who knew their taste, *because it was putrid.*

Like banditry, successful Maroon communities depended on good fortune and the quality of their leadership. Leadership seemed to have been determined partly by military and partly by political ability, qualities which were not exclusively male. One of the most successful of the Jamaican Maroon leaders was a formidable lady called Nanny, of the Windward Maroons near Port Antonio. The most successful leaders, such as Nanny and Cudjoe in Jamaica; Macandal or Santiago in Saint-Domingue; or Ventura Sanchez, otherwise known as Coba, in Cuba, combined religious roles with their political positions, thereby reinforcing their authority over their followers. Good leaders also showed an unusually keen understanding of settled colonial society that facilitated their ability to deal with the white political leaders. Prior to the eighteenth century, most leaders tended to be rigidly authoritarian and needlessly cruel. New recruits to Maroon communities were scrupulously tested, and deserters, wanderers, and suspected spies were brutally killed. Maroons, however, had no monopoly on brutality. In 1819, Brigadier Eusebio Escudero, the military governor of Santiago de Cuba, captured Ventura Sanchez through deception. Rather than be jailed, or re-enslaved, Sanchez committed suicide. Escudero then had his head displayed in an iron cage outside the city of Baracoa for a long time, presumably as a macabre form of intimidation. Maroon communities were vulnerable to internal feuds or disenchanted defection from the ranks.

Security was a constant preoccupation of Maroon villages. The physical setting of the village became a prime ingredient in its survival and eventual evolution. All successful villages in the Caribbean depended, at least initially, on their relative inaccessibility. They were strategically located in the densely forested interior of the Sierra Maestra, in the sparsely settled areas of Pinar del Río and Las Villas, or in the rugged northern coastlands of Oriente in Cuba; on the conical limestone ridges of the Cockpit Country in western Jamaica; on the precipitous slopes of the Blue Mountains in eastern Jamaica; in the formidable *massifs* of northern and southern Haiti; in the rugged *cordilleras* of Santo Domingo; on the isolated slopes of the Windward and Leeward islands and in the jungle interiors of the Guianas and Suriname. Where geography was not conducive to hiding, such as in cities—and urban Maroons were a serious problem in the nineteenth century—or on small islands or in less rugged terrain such as found in Barbados, Antigua, Martinique, or Guadeloupe, *petit marronnage* rather than *gran marronnage* seemed to be the order of the day.

Early Maroon communities seemed to have suffered from a shortage of women, not a surprising occurrence given the male preponderance of the rural slave cohorts from which they mainly drew their recruits. The scarcity of women and the observed polygamy and polygyny of some of the leaders forced some unusual practices during the formative years of the community. One such practice was raiding for the express purpose of capturing women, usually Indian women, as occurred in the Guianas and other areas on the mainland. Another was enforced sharing of females, as was reported for some Jamaica Maroons. As the communities endured and stabilized, however, sexual imbalance adjusted itself, especially as Maroons were able to produce and nurture to adulthood their own offspring. By the nineteenth century, the Maroons appeared to have achieved a more normal sexual balance. Barry Higman reports that in 1817 all the slaves reported "at large" in Kingstown, St. Vincent, were females; and in Bridgetown, Barbados, twice as many females as males were in Maroon communities. Between 1827 and 1831, about 49 percent of the Maroons on the small island of Anguilla were female. The presence of women was crucial for the survival of any Maroon community.

Given the inhospitable environment in which most Maroons chose to set up their communities, only the fittest and luckiest survived. Starvation, malnutrition, dysentery, smallpox, and accidental poisoning from unfamiliar herbs and leaves took a high toll of the villagers. The threat of discovery and attack by the organized colonial society remained constant. Throughout the Caribbean, large-scale military expeditions to seek and destroy Maroon villages that had become too prominent were sporadic, though important, activities. Colonists in Cuba and Jamaica employed specially trained dogs to hunt and recapture Maroons; and on the mainland, the Indians were rewarded for returning Maroons, dead or alive, to the colonial authorities. Notwithstanding the hazards, Maroon communities recruited and trained enough manpower to defy local authorities, wage successful wars, and secure their own peace treaties, as the Jamaica Maroons did in 1739 and 1795. Or they secured a modus vivendi with the local communities and de facto recognition from the political rulers as they did in eastern Cuba and Le Maniel in southern Saint-Domingue.

Successful *marronnage* required the concealed cooperation of slaves, free persons of color, and free whites within the settled societies. This communication with the established societies enabled the Maroons to get firearms, tools, utensils, and, in some cases, food, and this assistance was often crucial in the early stages of subduing the forest and building the community. Later the Maroons could obtain intelligence of impending raids or, in times of cooperation, could conduct free commerce with the neighboring towns, plantations, or islands. Not only urban Maroons but also a large number of rural Maroons gradually developed a semisymbiotic relationship with the societies from which they had withdrawn their support and revoked unilaterally their servile status.

With unfortunate irony, it was this very semisymbiosis that proved most lethal to the integrity, cultural distinctiveness, and vitality of Maroon existence. Once the Maroons succeeded in gaining legal or quasi-legal recognition, their structure, internal organization, methods of recruitment, and political attitudes underwent significant changes. In the treaties that they signed, they accepted severely limited territorial concessions, restricting their mobility. The legal status that they got in return was at the cost of some internal power and control. For example, by treaty obligations, runaway slaves could no longer be ascripted to the group but had to be handed over to the planter societies, often for a fee. This practice not only restricted the physical size of the community but insidiously undermined the political appeal of the Maroons as a viable alternative to the organized slave society. The Maroons of Jamaica signed treaties with the English government in the eighteenth century allowing them to trade in slaves or to own slaves and obliging them to return runaway slaves to their owners—a deed that incurred a lot of ill will among the slaves. If the Maroons viewed the treaties as a form of collective security, they nevertheless represented a strengthening of the very sociopolitical structure that they had formerly despised. Formal treaties with the Maroons (and other free communities surrounding slave plantations) strengthened the system of slave control by removing, reducing, or otherwise restricting one option of personal escape from slavery to freedom. Maroon communities, by agreeing to the external legal controls over basic aspects of their life, even regarding the succession of leaders, may have done themselves more harm than good in the long run. Increased interrelations with the slave society exacted its penalty. In the familiar tradition of all groups crossing a common frontier, the various Maroon societies gradually became indistinct from their neighboring slave communities. They lacked adequate facilities and autonomous infrastructures for long-term economic and social success, a condition common to most transfrontier groups. Eventually, the Maroons, like the French Huguenots, ultimately were unable to overcome the severe limitations and internal contradictions of a state within a state.

13 Alida C. Metcalf ◆ Family, Frontiers, and a Brazilian Community

Alida C. Metcalf's recent book Family and Frontier in Colonial Brazil: Santana de Parnaíba, 1580–1822 *is a case study of a community to the west of São Paulo examining how peoples were shaped by the frontier and how they exploited it over a period of two hundred and fifty years. Mining a rich cache of archival sources such as censuses, wills, property inventories, and parish registers of births, marriages, and deaths, Metcalf shows that in the seventeenth century, the frontier initially provided some opportunity for social mobility. By the eighteenth century, however, Parnaíba had become a "society clearly stratified into the social classes of planters, peasants, and slaves." She analyzes the effects of the frontier on each of these classes, concluding that, much like the American frontier as described by Turner, it brought independence and self-sufficiency to the peasants, but, unlike Turner's American frontier, it did not promote equality. Elite families, Metcalf tells us, discovered ways to exploit resources and labor on the frontier to gain wealth and to dominate the community and surrounding region economically and politically. In contrast, slaves benefited hardly at all from its presence.*

Metcalf holds a Ph.D. in history from the University of Texas at Austin and is associate professor at Trinity University in San Antonio. The following excerpt, taken from the introduction to the book, summarizes her thesis and the historiographical context of her work. The processes she describes of how Brazilian families proceeded into the wilderness and sought to recreate a world they had known have continued to the present. (For a stirring fictional account of the conquest of the cacao frontier in Bahia in the nineteenth century, see Jorge Amado's masterpiece, Terras do Sem Fim *[1943], translated by Samuel Putnam as* The Violent Land *[New York: Knopf, 1964].)*

The strategies of families, in relation to the frontier, are critical to understanding the colonization of this region of Brazil. Not only does this relationship help to explain the process of colonization but it also holds the key to understanding the origins of social stratification. Power and wealth in this region have come from the frontier, but not all have had equal access to it. Those families and social classes that controlled the development and exploitation of the frontier came to dominate the region economically and politically.

In Santana de Parnaíba, colonization occurred in discrete stages. In the first stage, Santana de Parnaíba was itself a frontier—poised between the wilderness to the west and the city of São Paulo to the east. As colonists came from São Paulo to the region and began to settle there in the late sixteenth century, a society emerged which blended Indian and Portuguese ways. Although it was not an egalitarian society, it was a fluid one, and social mobility was possible for those of Portuguese descent who successfully acquired land and Indian slaves from the wilderness. After Santana de Parnaíba became an established town in the early seventeenth century, it served as a jumping-off place for the frontier to the west. Throughout the seventeenth century, men from Parnaíba, but only occasionally women, set off into the frontier in search of their fortunes.

As the town grew and became a more complex community in the eighteenth century, it entered a second stage. Social classes began to emerge. A cash-crop commercial economy took root in the town, as did investments in commerce and mining. The influence of Indians waned. Slavery remained pervasive and unquestioned, but Africans replaced Indian slaves on the agricultural estates of the town. As in the first stage, those of the town who successfully exploited the frontier became or remained the wealthy and powerful in Santana de Parnaíba. The frontier continued to hold the key to social and economic success in the town.

In the third stage of this process, Santana de Parnaíba lost its ties to the wilderness and declined while towns farther west, many of which had been founded by men and women from Parnaíba, flourished. In this last stage, Parnaíba continued to remain a stratified community, with few rich slave-owning planters and an increasing number of small slaveless farmers. Eventually, the town faded into obscurity and became dependent on the growing city of São Paulo. This third stage began in the early years of the nineteenth century in the central parish of the town, somewhat later in the outlying rural parishes, and continued through the nineteenth century as the coffee frontier boomed farther west. Today, Santana de Parnaíba has entered a fourth stage as the region increasingly becomes part of greater São Paulo. The population has grown as city workers have sought inexpensive housing. Wealthy families have built expensive vacation homes there, too. By the next century, Santana de Parnaíba may well be another suburb of the city of São Paulo.

In each of these stages of development, the relationship between families and the frontier played a major role in shaping the lives of their individual members and structuring the contours of community life. Attitudes about how to survive that families consciously and unconsciously adopted affected how they perceived the frontier, raised their sons and daughters, divided their property, and farmed their lands. Many of these attitudes were formed during the first stage of colonization when families adapted and experimented in order to survive. One such attitude was the belief that the wilderness held the riches that individuals and families needed to survive in the town. This attitude had developed during the earliest stage of colonization and continued to characterize life in the later stages because of the proximity of the frontier.

The history of the frontier in Brazil holds much in common with the history of the frontier in North America. Indeed, the most influential work on the role of the frontier in American history describes some of the same features of the Brazilian frontier. In 1893, Frederick Jackson Turner's remarkable paper, "The Significance of the Frontier in American History," argued that America was different from Europe because of the frontier, the meeting point between wilderness inhabited by Indians and an expanding European population.[1] The existence of the frontier, and its continued colonization by wave after wave of colonists, was what in Turner's eyes made America unique. While in their first settlements along the Atlantic coast colonists did re-create much of their European culture, as they moved west they had to adapt to the wilderness and be transformed by it in order eventually to master it. Turner writes, "Moving westward, the frontier became more and more American. . . . Thus the advance of the frontier has meant a steady growth of independence on American lines. And to study this advance . . . is to study the really American part of our history."[2] For Turner, the "really American" part of American history was the growth of individualism and democracy on the frontier. These values created the basis for an American nationalism. Turner's thesis has been developed and critiqued by later historians, but his work remains provocative because of the questions he posed and the issues he raised.[3]

Brazilian historians such as Sérgio Buarque de Holanda also perceived the frontier to have been a critical factor in Brazilian development.[4] Like North America, Brazil began with a handful of coastal settlements that faced the Atlantic while behind them extended a vast, and to them unknown, wilderness. Brazil has expanded west, devouring the lands of Indians and creating a new, distinctly Brazilian culture. Brazilian development has depended on the cheap lands and resources of the frontier. But there is a big difference. The frontier in Brazil has rarely bred democracy or individualism. While many historians of North America now question whether the frontier in the United States really fostered democracy or individualism, the contrast with Brazil is nevertheless striking.[5] In northeastern Brazil, huge cattle ranches effectively colonized the frontier and concentrated immense tracts of lands into the hands of a few. In the south, sugar and coffee planters sought virgin forests to fell and transform into large agricultural estates worked by slaves. Relatively few parts of the Brazilian frontier were colonized by the yeoman farmers so eulogized by Turner—the hard-working entrepreneurial families who carved their homesteads out of the wilderness by the sweat of their own brows. While small farmers did move into the frontier in Brazil, they rarely legally owned the lands they claimed. As a result, when large agribusinesses arrived, they pushed out the small farmer, who either moved west, became a sharecropper, or migrated to the city.

As I will illustrate, the frontier provided the resources that allowed a small elite to form and to become wealthy and powerful in a town such as Santana de Parnaíba. Because of the way this elite perceived the frontier and made it an integral part of their family lives, succeeding generations of elite families were launched into the frontier, where they too found the resources to make themselves wealthy and powerful in their respective local communities. Other social groups did not benefit equally from the resources of the frontier and did not successfully incorporate strategies for developing the frontier into their family lives. Small farmers subsisted off the frontier but did not use it to make themselves wealthy, while slaves did not have the opportunity to acquire its resources. Thus, the way the frontier has been developed in Brazil is one of the roots of inequality in Brazilian society and continues to be to this day.

A second source of inequality in Brazilian society springs from family life. Historians of Latin America are increasingly aware that the family, particularly the elite family, has been one of the most powerful forces in colonial society. Though the region's economic and political institutions were planted in the colonies by Spain and Portugal, the families of the Creole (native-born) elites managed to infiltrate these institutions and to use them to their advantage. In the process, they deeply affected the character of colonial society itself.

After the discovery and conquest of Latin America, the colonies offered many opportunities to individual Spaniards and Portuguese who found the means to come to the New World. As these individuals settled and eventually formed families, they increasingly chafed at the many restrictions placed on them by Spain and Portugal. In particular, Spain regulated the colonies excessively, always with the intent of squeezing as much revenue from them as possible. These regulations continually hampered the aspirations of early conquerors and settlers. Such an environment meant that families that did succeed economically—through investments in agriculture or mining, for example—had to be exceedingly crafty to maintain their power and influence.

Historians of colonial Mexico and Peru have documented the exceptionally complex strategies that elite families pursued to preserve their status and influence. Studies by David Brading, Doris Ladd, and Richard Lindley (among others) for Mexico and Susan Ramírez, Fred Bronner, and Robert Keith for Peru illustrate how an elite formed in the sixteenth and seventeenth centuries and how, through their families, they maintained their power and influence.[6] They did so by carefully marrying their daughters, by grooming their sons for careers in the church or government or as managers of agricultural estates, by maintaining an extended kin network, by establishing fictive kinship ties to other influential families, and by planning for the transmission of property through inheritance. These strategies made the landowning elite rich and powerful and made it difficult for other social groups to achieve upward social mobility. Spain's colonial caste system, based on purity of blood (*limpieza de sangre*), further strangled the aspirations of the poor mestizos, blacks, and Indians.

In Brazil, a colonial society less rigid than Spanish America, a similar process occurred. In the sugar-growing region of the northeast, a powerful landowning elite emerged in the late sixteenth and early seventeenth centuries. This elite relied on family strategies to maintain itself economically and to guarantee its political power. By marrying their daughters to wealthy merchants, landowners bought themselves new capital. Marriages to powerful royal officials gave them influence. Family life in colonial Brazil, as in Spanish America, was critical to the formation and perpetuation of the elite.[7]

The behavior of elite families in Parnaíba similarly affected the evolution of a socially stratified town. Because wealthy families owned valuable resources of land and labor, how these families acquired property, held it in their families, and distributed it to their heirs affected not just their own families but the community as a whole. The dominance of elite families in local institutions—the town council, militia, and church—likewise contributed to social inequality. Such institutions reflected the interests of the elite, not those of the whole population, and thus served to reinforce the power of wealthy families.

As a few families successfully concentrated resources into their own hands and influenced local institutions to their advantage, they helped to create and reinforce social classes. The social world of Parnaíba was stratified in many different ways. Wealth, race, family ties, age, sex, and marital status all influenced how the townspeople perceived themselves and each other. Yet, increasingly in the seventeenth and eighteenth centuries, three social classes evolved in Parnaíba: planters, peasants, and slaves. Planters owned land and slaves and produced commercial crops, such as sugar, for sale. Peasants owned no slaves and primarily produced food crops for their own use and for local markets. Slaves had few resources beyond what they received from their masters. The majority of slaves did not own anything, not even their own labor. Each class had a unique relationship to the principal resources needed for survival in the town—land and labor. Each class had fundamentally different family lives. Each class interacted with the frontier in distinct ways.

Any typology invariably oversimplifies the social world experienced by individuals. In Parnaíba, a family with one slave was hardly much better off than a family without any slaves. Similarly, a freed slave who continued to serve her former master probably did not experience a radical life change from what she had known as a slave. Yet in terms of how families perceived themselves, it did matter to a former slave that freedom had been purchased, awarded, or promised. To a poor family with one slave, the possession of that slave accorded a status in the community that families without slaves did not have. Thus, while the boundaries between social classes might seem crude, they do serve to define the ranks of Parnaíba's society. In that society, the lives of planters (who owned slaves) differed fundamentally from the lives of peasants (who did not), and the lives of slaves similarly diverged from those of peasants and planters.

Historians of colonial Brazil disagree over what terminology to use to characterize the social structure of the colony.[8] Some argue that the colonial world was a society of castes; others, that it was a society of classes. Still others prefer the concept of estates. The proponents of the term "estate" borrow it from old regime France, which was divided into three estates: those who prayed (clergy), those who fought (nobility), and those who worked (peasants, artisans, the bourgeoisie). The term "caste" derives from studies of India wherein individuals were born into a caste and remained in it all their lives. I use the term "class" because it best describes the historical reality I find expressed in the sources. "Estate" does not rightly characterize a society that had no titled nobility, a weak clergy, and a large number of slaves. "Caste" implies a rigid society with no social mobility, yet the extensive ties to the frontier provided the residents of Parnaíba with such avenues. Even slaves could obtain their freedom. In contrast, "class" suggests a society in which large groups of people are differentiated by their relationship to material resources. Planters possessed land and labor; slaves did not. Peasants owned more resources than slaves, but fewer than planters. These simple facts increasingly differentiated the lives of individuals in the seventeenth and eighteenth centuries. Thus, I conceptualize Santana de Parnaíba as a class society composed of planters, peasants, and slaves.

Family life varied by class. Families of the planter elite lived in large hierarchical households where the interests of many had to be subdued and conflicts avoided. The importance of property in maintaining their status meant that family customs explicitly regulated events such as marriage and inheritance. These customs worked to keep women from wanting independent lives or from marrying the men of their choice. Other customs worked to minimize conflicts between brothers. Similarly, the paternalistic and benevolent ways in which these families treated their slaves and other servants served the very important function of smoothing over the inequalities that existed in such households.

For the peasantry, family life revolved around the cultivation of small plots of land by family members. They had to cooperate with each other and share in the work that provided the sustenance for all. The vast majority of these families lived in small nuclear households composed of parents and their children. Mothers and fathers taught their children how to work in the fields and in the house from a young age. These families valued cooperation between men and women, brothers and sisters, and families and neighbors.

Slave family life differed substantially from that of planters or peasants. Slavery afforded little room to create autonomous family lives. The economic fortunes of masters and the attitudes of masters toward slave families determined many aspects of slave family life. Other factors, such as the demographic characteristics of the slave population or the size of the estates on which slaves lived, also influenced the chances that slaves would marry and form families. Slave families tended to be less stable than those of planters and peasants because of constant change, occasioned not just by marriage, birth, or death but by transfer of ownership. Thus, of the three social classes of Parnaíba, slaves had the least control over their family lives.

Not only did family life vary by class but each class interacted with the frontier in different ways. Families of planters saw their survival in terms of acquiring property from the wilderness frontier and preserving it for future generations. This property could be land, Indian slaves, or gold. Moreover, when these families divided their property each generation, they expected some of their children to migrate west. Thus, they favored some heirs at the expense of others by allowing the favored heirs to inherit the bulk of the family resources and the social position of the parents in Parnaíba, knowing that other children would make their fortunes in the frontier. Heirs who remained in Parnaíba but were not favored paid a price: downward social mobility. They became small planters with few resources. Such customs of family life among the planter elite promoted the development of the frontier, maintained large agricultural estates in

Parnaíba, and created a growing substratum of the planter class composed of poor planters.

The peasantry also relied on the frontier for their survival. Primarily, they desired land to provide for themselves and their children. But because they often lacked the ability to protect their lands over time, they moved on with the frontier. These peasant farmers became the first wave of frontier settlement, often battling with Indian tribes for virgin forest to clear and plant. Those peasant families who were able to retain their lands in Parnaíba turned their attention to the developing city of São Paulo, which they furnished with their food surpluses and in which they worked as mule drivers and laborers. Many of the young men and women from peasant families migrated to the town center to become artisans or servants, and to the city of São Paulo.

Although some slaves did escape to the frontier where they formed runaway slave communities (*quilombos*), and many others were taken to the frontier to cultivate new sugar and coffee estates, the majority of slaves did not see the frontier as a place they might use to their advantage. Beyond running away to the frontier, slaves devised no strategies to exploit it. Their strategies for the survival of their families and kin networks developed in Parnaíba and its immediate environs, where they formed a black community. Slaves sought privileges from their masters which might make their lives more bearable. This might take the form of the right to plant a garden, the right to save for purchasing their freedom, or the right to marry a free person or a slave from a neighboring estate. Slaves formed religious brotherhoods with other slaves and free blacks; these associations created the basis for a black community in Parnaíba. Slaves thus devised their family lives in a very different context than the slave-owning planters or the slaveless peasants.

To summarize, frontier family life in this region of colonial Brazil developed in several contexts. First, family life varied for each social class. Second, families perceived the frontier in diverse ways and used it accordingly. Third, the frontier had a dissimilar impact on the families of each social class. Families of planters, for example, used the frontier to their advantage; slaves generally did not.

Through their varying strategies for survival, families participated in and reinforced the formation of social classes in Parnaíba. The resulting structure of power and authority reproduced itself in this community over many generations. The social structure of the community was neither preordained nor imposed from afar. Rather, it evolved as colonists in this region of the Portuguese empire made choices about how to live in and interact with the empire, choices that would shape the community inherited by their children and by their children's children.

Notes

1. Frederick Jackson Turner, *The Frontier in American History* (Tucson: University of Arizona Press, 1986).
2. Ibid., 4.
3. Ray Allen Billington and Martin Ridge, *Westward Expansion: A History of the American Frontier*, 5th ed. (New York: Macmillan Co., 1982). See also Billington, ed., *The Frontier Thesis: Valid Interpretation of American History?* (New York: Krieger Pub. Co., 1977), for representative positions on the debate for and against the Turner thesis.
4. Sérgio Buarque de Holanda, *Caminhos e fronteiras* (Rio de Janeiro: Livraria José Olympio Editôra, 1957) and *Monções*, 2d ed. (São Paulo: Editôra Alfa-Omega, 1976).
5. See Billington, *The Frontier Thesis*, as well as Harry N. Schieber, "Turner's Legacy and the Search for a Reorientation of Western History: A Review Essay," *New Mexico Historical Review* 44 (1969): 231–248; Jackson K. Putnam, "The Turner Thesis and Westward Movement: A Reappraisal," *Western Historical Quarterly* 7 (1976): 379–404, and Martin Ridge, "Frederick Jackson Turner, Ray Allen Billington, and American Frontier History," *Western Historical Quarterly* 19 (1988): 5–20, for three reviews in different decades of this literature and controversy. In "Turner, the Boltonians, and the Borderlands," *American Historical Review* 91 (1986): 66–81, David Weber argues that the Turner thesis has never been very influential in the study of Mexico's northern frontier or the U.S.-Mexico borderlands because of Turner's (and his students') failure to address ethnicity on the frontier.
6. David A. Brading, *Miners and Merchants in Bourbon Mexico 1763–1810* (Cambridge: Cambridge University Press, 1971); Doris M. Ladd, *The Mexican Nobility at Independence, 1780–1820* (Austin: University of Texas Press, 1976); Richard B. Lindley, *Haciendas and Economic Development: Guadalajara, Mexico, at Independence* (Austin: University of Texas Press, 1983); Susan E. Ramírez, *Provincial Patriarchs: The Economics of Power in Colonial Peru* (Albuquerque: University of New Mexico Press, 1985); Fred Bronner, "Peruvian Encomenderos in 1630: Elite Circulation and Consolidation," *Hispanic American Historical Review* 57 (1977): 633–659; Robert B. Keith, *Conquest and Agrarian Change* (Cambridge: Harvard University Press, 1976). Similar landowning élites evolved in frontier regions as well. See Charles H. Harris III, *A Mexican Family Empire: The Latifundio of the Sánchez Navarros, 1765–1867* (Austin: University of Texas Press, 1975); Robert J. Ferry, *The Colonial Elite of Early Caracas: Formation and Crisis, 1567–1767* (Berkeley, Los Angeles, Oxford: University of California Press, 1989); and Diana Balmori, Stuart F. Voss, and Miles Wortman, *Notable Family Networks in Latin America* (Chicago: University of Chicago Press, 1984). For an excellent review of the formation and consolidation of this elite, see Susan E. Ramírez, "Large Landowners," in *Cities and Society in Colonial Latin America*, ed. Louisa Hoberman and Susan Socolow (Albuquerque: University of New Mexico Press, 1986), 19–45.
7. Stuart B. Schwartz, *Sovereignty and Society in Colonial Brazil: The High Court of Bahia and Its Judges, 1609–1751* (Berkeley, Los Angeles, London: University of California Press, 1973); Schwartz, *Sugar Plantations in the Formation of Brazilian Society: Bahia, 1550–1835* (Cambridge: Cambridge University Press, 1985); Rae Jean Dell Flory and David Grant Smith, "Bahian Merchants

and Planters in the Seventeenth and Early Eighteenth Centuries," *Hispanic American Historical Review* 58 (1978): 571–594.

8. See Sedi Hirano, *Pre-capitalismo e capitalismo* (São Paulo: Editôra Hucitec, 1988), for a review of how the terms "estate," "class," and "caste" are used historically and in recent sociological and historical work on colonial Brazil.

IV

Frontier Peoples and National Identity

14 Hebe Clementi ◆ National Identity and the Frontier

Latin Americans have often asserted that, unlike in the North American West, frontier experiences in their countries did not provide the basis for national identity myths.* Here Hebe Clementi challenges this assumption by pointing out that like the pioneer of the United States, the Brazilian bandeirante *and the Argentine gaucho have come to embody the highest national virtues in the minds of their respective countrymen. In all three cases, she notes, the archetypes developed in colonial times long before political independence. Although they were pushed aside in the nineteenth century after the arrival of waves of immigrants, "the mythical appreciation of their passing and their achievements assumed gigantic proportions." Clementi believes that "in the widest sense, the frontier is for the whole continent the key to the various national histories," and her speculation that the gaucho might be seen as a symbol not just for Argentina but for the whole of Spanish America is sure to provoke passionate responses from Bolivian, Colombian, and Peruvian historians.*

Hebe Clementi is an Argentine historian who has written many books and articles on United States history as well as Western Hemisphere frontiers, most notably a four-volume work, La frontera en América *(1986–1988). She has been professor of American contemporary history at the*

From *American Studies International* 18 (Spring/Summer 1980): 36–44. Reprinted by permission.

*See, for example, Alistair Hennessy, who wrote that in Latin America "there was no frontier experience which could provide the basis for a nationalist myth. The frontier had either crushed those who had ventured to it, or in those cases where it had expanded successfully it had done so under the aegis of foreign capital.... This was not material from which national myths could be spun." *The Frontier in Latin American History* (Albuquerque: University of New Mexico Press, 1978), 21.

*Universidad Nacional de Buenos Aires, the Universidad de la Plata, and
the Instituto Superior Nacional del Profesorado.*

To approach the subject of national identity in American continental
history is to risk accusations of vagueness and unscientific method-
ologies. Moreover such an inquiry introduces what might be called myths.
The risk, which is present in all historical writing, is well worth taking in
the case of America where populations are composed of people from varied origins and where the occupation of the land is still incomplete.

The three cases treated here are to a certain extent already recognized as concentrated manifestations of the national identities of three
American countries: the pioneer of the United States, the *bandeirante* of
Brazil, and the *gaucho* of Argentina. The choice is based on two factors.
First, there is adequate documentary evidence for the study of those three
cases. Second, the connection of the three cases with the widening of
their respective frontiers shows these characters to be specific products
of their frontiers. With these two instruments it is possible to draw valid
conclusions by comparing in each case the historical development with
the subsequent archetype.

In the three cases considered, the archetypes developed in colonial
times, long before political independence. Only later, in the second
half of the nineteenth century, after the arrival of waves of immigrants,
were they pushed into the background. At the same time the mythical
appreciation of their passing and their achievements assumed gigantic
proportions.

The considerations that go with this analysis are intended to provide
a reliable insight into the roots of our American identity, on which the
national existence of each of these relatively new nations stands. It constitutes a kind of crystallization of the possibilities and attributes that
characterize American space, and serves as a milestone in the formation
of an American consciousness.

The North American Case: The Importance of the Pioneer

The figure of the pioneer is directly connected with the expansion of the
American frontier. Although the phenomenon was evident from the first
years of the English settlement in North America, it was only towards the
end of the last century, in 1893, that the historian Frederick Jackson Turner
did justice to its importance in an account that is now considered classic.
Subsequently, his thesis, that the frontier molded the historical trajectory
of the nation, giving it its best attributes, has been subjected to the most
acrimonious criticism because it was not universally valid, and because

the emphasis placed on the frontier led to the omission of other basic facts. However, many valid and indisputable points can be saved from his synthesis. Some of them are the following:

1. American history has taken its course under the predominant influence of the advance toward the West, owing to the existence of free land.
2. The characteristic property of American institutions is that they have been progressively adapted to the changes in an expanding society.
3. The American frontier is clearly different from a European one. It is not a fortified line on inhabited territory but a vaguely delineated and scarcely populated area.

The mobility of this frontier and its mixed population ensured the formation of a complex nation that under the influence of the environment was able to overcome regional particularism. Hence the most significant consequences of the process are:

a) The key element of the availability of land ensured the harmonious life and the economic potential of the colonies and the nation afterwards.
b) The frontier endowed the institutions with a flexible democratic idiosyncrasy, the egalitarian tendency of which had more to do with the open spaces than with European origins.
c) Democratic individualism was molded by the initiative and enterprising spirit of the frontiersman.

The concept of the frontier that Turner used in his work was that of insufficiently populated space, and on this basis he announced the end of the frontier, for there was—according to the latest information based on an official census—no territory left with "a density less than two persons per square mile." But, if this were the only criterion, the rest of the American continents except the urban concentrations would have had to be considered frontier area.

The American continents at the beginning of European settlement were empty space (if we exclude the Indian from consideration), and their occupation took place in different ways. The only one that was completely settled, even by Turner's standards, was the North American one, which is the reason why its course appears as the yardstick and prototype of territorial occupation. The main protagonist, the archetype in this epic

enterprise, was the pioneer. He was the incarnation of all the highest virtues: work, the spirit of initiative, and fidelity to the values fixed by the
religious community. Thus, the hunter, the lumberjack, the laborer, the
Indian fighter, the herdsman, belonged to the category of pioneers, as did
the successive waves of immigrants that were a constant phenomenon in
colonial North America. And in the South the pioneer category also included, although more vaguely, the rude Southern planter who opened up
new territory, cut down woods and forests and followed the rivers up-
stream with his gangs of Negro slaves.

By extension numerous individual protagonists came to be included
in the conceptual definition of the pioneer with its emphasis on individual
effort and success achieved against seemingly insuperable odds. The glorification of Andrew Jackson as the soldier-pioneer-Indian fighter-
conqueror of Spanish or Mexican territory to the South, is an example.
The same spirit is found in the concept of "manifest destiny" that stimulated the feverish confidence of the forty-niner and his expansive designs.
At a later period there were the railroad builders with the financial entrepreneurs and unscrupulous robber barons. Even the notorious Walker, the
last of the Caribbean pirates, was glorified by the public as a pioneer of
the eventual expansion of the Southern *golden-ring*.

It might be concluded that the concept of the pioneer that accompa-
nies the history of the advancing frontier from the first colony in the East
through all the successive steps of territorial expansion is all-inclusive
and hence becomes acceptable enough once it has been collated with historical reality. But its validity is not unlimited. It leaves out of sight the
process of the formation of cities. It does not allow any view at all of the
fate of those who failed in the effort to obtain a property as the fruit of
their pioneer labors. And in the last analysis, it does not afford any perception of the drama of history.

The resurgence of the Jeffersonian spirit after the Civil War expresses
this conflict between a supposed agrarian goodness and urban and financial corruption, although it is well enough known now that the conflict
between small property and other capitalist forms that were developing
and complicating society in this period was not very well understood at
the time. The resounding reputation of the frontier continued in the center of attention as the successful, harmonious, conciliating and inspiring
key to great undertakings. And it is not by chance that President John F.
Kennedy referred to the frontier when he adumbrated an Alliance for
Progress to link the national frontier with those of the other nations of the
American continent.

The evolution of the pioneer as protagonist in the occupation of the
North American space parallels history and in spite of innumerable limi-

tations and corrections between reality and the conceptual formulation, justifies his position as forger of the North American nationality.

The Brazilian Case: The Importance of the *Bandeirante*

At least three origins are given for the term *bandeirante: bandeira*—the flag followed by the banders; *bandeira*—a band of men under the captaincy of a chief; and *bandeira*—a raiding party separated from the main body of troops. (It is, moreover, a Portuguese medieval military unit of 36 men.) The established fact is that the first of these bands for which there is documentary evidence was organized by Governor Francisco de Souza in São Paulo: it was a *luso-tupi* formation and its organization was later perfected to oppose the invasion of the Dutch, who were beaten back by the unaided efforts of the locals themselves. The activity of catching Indians to be sold to the northeastern sugar plantations seems to have been concentrated at the time in the hands of the settlers of São Paulo de Piratininga, a modest defensive settlement to safeguard the possession of the land and the lives of the inhabitants of the *paulista* highland.

All through the sixteenth century the settlers carried out attacks on the valleys of Paraiba, Tiete, Moji Guacu, and Parapanema, which were inhabited by Indians; but the great century of the *bandeira* was the seventeenth. Society recognized the possession of Indian slaves as a sign of wealth and power, although it had been forbidden by the crown. Only the Jesuits, until they were expelled from São Paulo in 1640, opposed locally the appropriation of human beings. The decline of northeastern sugar production led to interruptions in the hunting of Indians but accentuated the role of the bands as seekers of gold and other metals northeastward. In this activity they managed to increase the Brazilian territory at the expense of Spanish possessions, as was ratified in the Treaty of San Ildefonso of 1777. The fact is, that due to this constant progressive movement, the *bandeira* should be credited with a number of incontestable virtues:

1. They expanded the Brazilian territory originally limited by the terms of the Treaty of Tordesillas.
2. They contributed to the exploration of the interior of South America.
3. They ensured the European settlement of the interior both by exploring the space and by the massive eradication of the indigenous population.
4. They favored the racial mixture between Indians and whites and contributed to the Americanization of the population.

5. They created new sources of income for the Brazilian population by fostering mining and cattle raising in the interior and stimulated the movement of the population.
6. They led to the exportation of minerals to Portugal, which from there passed into English hands and accelerated the English industrial revolution.

With the exception of the United States of North America, Brazil is the only country in America which has studied and reflected upon its spatial development. In this it has largely followed the lead of the country in the North. From this point of view the *bandeirante* was the germ of modern Brazil for his action and evolution ensured the territorial expansion the country has so far accomplished. The same idea might also inspire future expansion, such as a possible penetration on the African coast, based on an argument that the Africans are "bloodbrothers." An example is *The March to the West*, a book by Cassiano Ricardo written in 1942 and inspired even to the title by the North American example.

Following are the main points of Ricardo's conclusions: First, the *bandeira*, which originated in the republic of Piratininga, eventually formed the nucleus of Brazilian society through their conquest of the physical territory. Second, they were mobile groups, galloping over the serton, or the Brazilian wilderness, looking for emeralds and gold. Only occasionally did they interrupt this principal occupation to hunt and capture Indians for the slave markets, and then only in response to requests made by the planters. Third, the *bandeira* were instrumental in bridging the two cultures of Spanish and Indian. Fourth, their incredible mobility facilitated the establishment of settlements on the frontier. Fifth, the groups were anonymous, and therefore democratic. Their inclusion of slaves enhanced their cultural value. And sixth, their lack of education led to a better integration with the Indians than was possible for the Latin-educated Jesuit fathers.

Evidently, Ricardo omitted patent truths of Brazilian history. The hunting of the Indian as the principal incentive of the *bandeira*, the destruction in slavery of Indian culture, the negro slavery that persisted until the end of the nineteenth century, all cast a different light on our interpretation of the *bandeira*. On the other hand, there is a notable correspondence with historical truth. The effort to insert the problem of territory dynamically into the whole of Brazilian history, and the affirmation that "every road opened by the *bandeirante* was a cord that moored Brazil to itself", permit free view of the horizons of successive Brazilian frontiers.

In South America the case of Brazilian expansion is unique and conspicuous, especially when compared with the space that had been theoretically assigned to it by European diplomacy. At present the new vigor that is stimulating its interior frontiers by means of transcontinental roads, dams, and ports, is converting into reality the expansive design of lieutenant-colonel Mario Travassos, who conceived the territorial space of Brazil in a total geopolitical project in his *Continental Project of Brazil*, published in 1935.

In conclusion, the *bandeirante* was undoubtedly courageous, individualistic, independent, active. He was also cruel and rapacious. His thirst for plunder was insatiable. Eventually the introduction of coffee planting proved so profitable as to revolutionize the economic life of the region, and therewith gave a new orientation to the activity of the population. But the spirit of the *bandeirante* influenced the transformation of the empire into a republic. The myth will continue to nourish an ever dynamic and aggressive present.

The Argentine Case: The Importance of the *Gaucho*

When one thinks of Argentina, images might arise of the Spanish conquerors, the Indians of the *pampa*, the immigrants, whose descendants actually constitute the greatest part of the present-day population of Argentina. But, more often than any of these, it is the *gaucho* who is glorified as the archetype of the Argentine national character. From the beginning of Argentine history, the *gaucho*—the inhabitant of the mesopotamic regions and the humid *pampa*—has been the most noted by travelers and foreign visitors. This has been true from Concolorcorvo and Azara in the eighteenth century to the English of the first period of independence. The *gaucho* has acquired the traits of a generic stereotype.

The popular stereotype of the *gaucho* is that he was an excellent horseman who moved from place to place, always living in the open fields and making his living from the cattle-raising economy. *Gauchos*, the stereotype holds, were true creoles, or native sons of the land. Sometimes they had Negro or Indian blood. They never owned land or material possessions, save for knives. The one point on which the stereotype is ambiguous is the moral character of the *gaucho*. Some have judged him to have been discreet and modest, hospitable, patient, ingenious. Others hold that he was cruel, unreliable, lazy, quarrelsome and cowardly.

The fact that *gauchos* did not own land was not unique to Argentina, since similar situations existed in other areas of Spanish colonization. And, in spite of the mobility accorded him by his horse, the *gaucho* had little choice but to do the bidding of the landowner who engaged laborers for the tasks of the cattle-raising business. Otherwise he would have become an outcast in the cattle-raising society to which he belonged. If he revolted and elected to become an outcast, the risk of being arrested was great. If caught, he was likely to be sent to the frontier to fight the Indians. His only other alternative was to enter an Indian village and become a fugitive from justice. The story of this situation, related in the *Martín Fierro* (a literary creation that is considered a national epic), is repeated with less emotion and equal realism in countless historical documents.

The golden age of the *gaucho* is supposed by historians to coincide with the southward expansion of the frontier of Buenos Aires and with the optimum employment capacity of the salted meat export industry linked with cattle raising (1820–1850). The changes in the meat industry, the end of slavery, the influence of wool production, led inexorably to the elimination of the *gaucho* as the best mobile labor force. Caught between his uncompromising love of freedom, and the law that forced him to defend against the Indians the very society that was eroding that freedom, the *gaucho* gradually disappeared from the scene. When, at the end of the century, the new economic scheme based on the export of meat and agricultural products was consolidated with financial support from abroad, the *gaucho* was eliminated. Similarly, the Indian frontier disappeared as the nation consolidated its internal and international frontiers.

In conclusion it may be said that the *gaucho* constituted for Argentina the same kind of national archetype as did the pioneer and the *bandeirante* in the United States and Brazil respectively. The *gaucho* was the product of special frontier conditions. He was endowed with moral characteristics rather than practical qualifications, and possessed an intrepidity that was devoted to the defense of honor rather than to any definite and practical collective undertaking.

At the same time it is true that there were troops of *gaucho* cavalry in the national armies, where their combativity and devotion to the cause of liberty deserved high praise. But, in any case, the principal engagement of the *gaucho* was in his daily labor as a centaur, united with his horse. The state evidently left him little choice: give up being a *gaucho*, or end his days on the frontier fighting Indians or living like them or as a fugitive from justice.

The parallels between the story of the *gaucho* and the general movement of Argentine history further affirm his candidacy as a national archetype. This is true even though, strictly speaking, he only inhabited the eastern sector of the country. The fact that the efforts to consolidate a state in Rio Grande in Southern Brazil failed, confirms the historical importance of the archetype.

Thus, the historical facts agree with the popular myth that these three do embody certain archetypical traits of their respective national characters. Each helps to define his nation's character through his participation in the appropriation of empty land, and through his contact with the frontier.

The case of the *gaucho* might on closer consideration be seen as a symbol for the whole Spanish American area, where the frontier, understood as land free to be occupied, was already scarce in the sixteenth century. But we consider the Argentine space only, which was from the first moment a frontier away from Lima, the vice-regal center of colonial interest. As a door connecting the country with the Atlantic Ocean, this region always enjoyed a special autonomy and a vigor. That was put in evidence when it was converted into the Vice-Royalty of the River Plate, including Alto Peru (Bolivia today), the Cuyo region, and the broad continental region of Patagonia, which till then was limited to the coasts and the inter-oceanic passage.

After independence, Bolivia and Uruguay separated as a consequence of historical and geographical limitations. Later came the struggle for unification and centralization which finally consolidated Argentina around the port of Buenos Aires City, the original historical nucleus.

The occupation of the two extensive frontier spaces, the Gran Chaco to the North and Patagonia to the South, followed naturally. The southward expansion was directed into the *pampa* area—which had been the first scene of action of the *gaucho*—and was for historical and economic reasons the first to be annexed by the Argentine government. Both private business and the national army were called upon to assist in the expansion. Many *gauchos* undoubtedly took part, perhaps in military uniform and incorporated into the military organization. But the hope that the territory would flourish was not fulfilled, nor was there an internal market of sufficient importance to create a self-sufficient region. The first results of these expansions were speculation and the concentration of land ownership. Once the struggle with the Indian was concluded, the *gaucho*, displaced by immigrant workers or great landowners, disappeared as a protagonist of the expansion. His historical destiny remained thus half finished, just as these territories of the Argentine frontier are themselves still only half incorporated into the national territory. They remain underpopulated and their resources continue to be largely unexploited.

With all the variations that are possible in the three cases, the incidence of the frontier or the occupation of the space has been the motive power. In the widest sense, the frontier is for the whole continent the key to the various national histories.

In Gran Chaco, the presence of considerable numbers of natives and their possible utilization as a labor force, the exploitation of *quebracho*, and the difficulties of the geography and the terrain have delayed the complete occupation of this region up to now.

When the process of occupation has reached a stage where it becomes a part of the national scheme, the protagonist changes into a sort of dynamic and inspiring myth while he disappears as a physical reality. His historical existence, which had been conditioned by time and place, then becomes atemporal and archetypal.

Bibliography

Berkhofer, Robert, Jr. "Space, Time, Culture and the New Frontier." *Agricultural History* 28, 1 (1964): 21–30.

Hanke, Lewis, ed. *Do the Americas Have a Common History? A Critique of the Bolton Theory.* New York: Alfred A. Knopf, Borzoi Books, 1964.

Hennessy, Alistair. *The Frontier in Latin American History.* Albuquerque: University of New Mexico Press, 1978.

Hernandez, José. *Martín Fierro.* Albany: SUNY Press, 1967.

Hofstadter, Richard. *The Progressive Historians.* New York: Alfred A. Knopf, 1969.

Ireland, Gordo. *Conflictos de limites y de posesiones en Sud-America.* Buenos Aires: Circulo Militar, Biblioteca del Oficial, v. 284, 1942.

Ricardo, Cassiano. *Marcha para Oeste (A influencia da "bandeiro" na formacao social e politica do Brasil).* 2 vols. Rio de Janeiro: Livraria Jose Olympo Editora, 1959.

Travassos, Mario. *Projecao continental do Brasil.* São Paulo: 1935.

Turner, Frederick Jackson. *The Significance of the Frontier in American History.* New York: Frederick Ungar Publishing, 1963.

———. *The Frontier in American History.* New York: Henry Holt & Co., 1958.

Wyman, Walter D., and Kroeber, Clifton B., eds. *The Frontier in Perspective.* Madison: University of Wisconsin Press, 1965.

15 Richard W. Slatta ◆ The Gaucho in Argentina's Quest for National Identity

Whatever his importance historically, Argentina's quintessential frontiers-man, the gaucho, took on increasing significance after his era had ended. Probing Argentine literature and the popular press, Richard Slatta explains how, beginning in the 1890s, some Argentine intellectuals, writers, and politicians converted the gaucho into the single most important symbol of national identity. The process of romanticizing these rustic cow-boys, and of transforming provincials into representatives of the nation, was laden with irony, as Slatta makes clear. And if a reimagined gaucho served as a useful figure for unifying a fragmented nation, a symbolic gaucho could also be employed by demagogues and authoritarians to advance their own ambitions.

Professor of history at North Carolina State University, Slatta earned his Ph.D. at the University of Texas at Austin. In 1992 the University of Nebraska Press published a paperback edition of his prize-winning book Gauchos and the Vanishing Frontier *(Lincoln: University of Nebraska Press, 1983). A more recent work,* Cowboys of the Americas *(New Haven: Yale University Press, 1990), is a fascinating comparative history of Argentine gauchos, Chilean* huasos, *Venezuelan* llaneros, *Mexican vaqueros, and North American cowboys.*

The formation of national identity is a complex, never-ending process. Most developed nations have evolved a comfortable self-image based on a core of characteristics they believe typify their citizenry. Argentina, recently stricken with yet another disaster, the humiliating loss in the Falklands war, continues to search for such a consensus to its national identity. This essay elucidates the growth of Argentine cultural nationalism. The literati promoted the gaucho as the foremost symbol of their nation's essential character, and thereby revised Argentine history. To many intellectuals, the gaucho of the littoral became the symbol for all native-born Argentines (*criollos*), including those of the interior.

The intelligentsia's quest to define *argentinidad* or "Argentinity" has frequently focussed upon the gaucho, the itinerant horseman and ranch worker of the pampas. For nearly two centuries, gauchos rode the plains of the Río de la Plata, killing wild cattle for food, catching and taming *pingos*, or mounts, herding wild and later domesticated livestock on large *estancias*, and battling as conscripted militiamen in myriad civil and

Abridged from the *Canadian Review of Studies in Nationalism* 12, no. 1 (Spring 1985): 99–122. Reprinted by permission.

foreign conflicts. A powerful landowning elite operated through subservient governments to exploit the gaucho's labour, to impress him into military service to defend its interests, and ultimately to eliminate him when he became obsolescent on a modernizing pampa. Ironically, the persecuted, proscriptive nineteenth-century gaucho became the twentieth century's national hero, as the ruling élite sought a unifying symbol to counter the impact of the immigrant masses.

The individualistic, independent gauchos attracted the animosity of Europeanizing liberal élite leaders by frequently serving as fierce cavalrymen for opposition caudillos of the interior provinces. Bent upon modernizing the nation, nineteenth-century liberals, such as Bernardino Rivadavia, Juan Bautista Alberdi, Domingo F. Sarmiento, and Bartolomé Mitre, advocated massive immigration, free trade, political centralization, and public education. Alberdi noted that "to civilize by means of population it is necessary to have civilized populations; to educate our America in liberty and industry it is necessary to populate it with people from Europe."[1] Six years later, Alberdi repeated his fervent support for European immigration: "South America can cure its economic malaise only by increasing its population through immigration from rich and productive European areas. With this outlook and with this result in mind, the fundamental institutions of the Spanish colonial period, which still linger in our midst, must be eradicated."[2] To nineteenth-century liberals the gaucho masses epitomized Argentina's negative heritage.

Sarmiento shared the liberal élite's world view, which reduced Argentina's central problem to the social conflict between urban European civiliation centred in Buenos Aires and rural "barbarism" epitomized by federalist caudillos of the interior, and the gauchos who supported them. This dualistic vision of Argentine society persisted in intellectual circles into the twentieth century.[3] They perceived the gaucho as a symbol of the anarchy and backwardness that Argentina struggled to overcome. Asserting that the gaucho was unable to adapt to modern civilization, many leaders doomed him to marginality and extinction. Legal and political persecution placed gauchos outside the law. The modernizing juggernaut eliminated the horsemen as a distinctive social group by the 1870s and 1880s.

Even as the gaucho disappeared, his mythical counterpart was being created by the governing élite as a symbol of stability in a nation buffeted by rapid, conflictive social change. Reacting to successive modernization crises with concern bordering on xenophobia, élite writers and politicians resurrected a reformed gaucho as their symbol for *argentinidad*—as the paladin of national virtue to counter the erosion of Argentine culture and values. This transformation from social outcast to symbol of Argentine national character forms a significant chapter in the nation's quest for a unifying, positive self-image.

The concern of Argentines over nationality and their reassessment of the gaucho's character and history heightened during the 1880s through the First World War, the decades of massive European immigration. Italians formed the largest proportion of immigrants until 1906, when the Spaniards surged ahead. The proportion of immigrants from other nations, such as Russia, Poland, and Syria, whose peoples many Argentines considered undesirable, also rose after 1906. Buenos Aires, the nation's largest, richest, and most populous province, absorbed many foreigners, as its immigrant population rose to 28% of the total population in 1914 and 31% by 1921.[4] Foreigners integrated themselves into virtually every aspect of national life, and even invaded some traditionally native domains. Many Argentines and foreigners considered the immigrant masses as saviours importing superior racial and cultural attributes to uplift the nation and welcomed the extinction of the gaucho class, considered to be lazy, lawless, and unsuited to modern civilization. Jorge MacKitchie, British manager of the "500" ranch in Buenos Aires province, revealed a widely shared attitude towards natives in a letter written to his employer in mid-1911. He found one native employee to be "like the average argentine very empty-headed and dont know much"(*sic*!).[5]

Alarmed by the cultural and political disruptions triggered by the immigrant masses, turn-of-the-century Argentine nationalists began revising the conventional wisdom that disparaged native abilities and potential. Frightened by foreign-born labour radicals, social violence, and the infusion of alien influences in language and literature, and disappointed with the failure of massive immigration to propel the country to great nation status, Argentina's national leadership reappraised the relative worth of natives and foreigners. The gaucho's odyssey from pariah to paragon had begun.[6]

Nationalist writers built upon gaucho-inspired literary images that extended well back into the nineteenth century. Gauchesque poetry traditionally utilized the rustic pampa dialect to communicate political messages and satire directed against competing factions in strife-ridden Argentina. Bartolomé Hidalgo (1788–1822), the Uruguayan father of gauchesque poetry, moved the genre from the realm of oral, anonymous verse to literary medium with his *Diálogos patrióticos* (Patriotic Dialogues) published in 1820. Following Hidalgo's inspiration, Juan Gaulberto Godoy (1793–1864) and Hilario Ascusubi (1807–1875) penned numerous political polemical poems. José Hernández (1834–1886) combined socio-political criticism with poetry in the first part of his Argentine epic, *Martín Fierro*, published late in 1872. Hernández rounded out the most prominent of the gauchesque works with the *Return of Martín Fierro* in 1879.[7]

The gaucho made his prose appearance later, and did not become prominent until Santiago Estrada (1841–1891) published *El hogar en la pampa* (Home on the Pampa) in 1866. It remained for Eduardo Gutiérrez (1851–1889) to develop fully the gaucho novel, with the protagonist as an honourable figure victimized by a repressive government and forced to live a fugitive nomadic existence. Gutiérrez wrote *Juan Moreira* (1879–1880), a novel suggested by a historical personage who, like Martín Fierro, typified the persecuted social bandit and outcast. Many other late-nineteenth and early-twentieth-century gauchesque and criollo novels elaborated on native themes.[8]

Building upon these literary foundations, turn-of-the-century nationalists and traditionalists projected the gaucho of folkloric literature to a position of national cultural prominence. Writers identified with the influential and prolific "Generation of 'Eighty" penned novels and wrote essays which demonstrated the ruling oligarchy's strong cultural and political nationalism. The cultural penetration of the immigrant masses troubled many Argentine intellectuals. Ernesto Quesada (1858–1934) deplored the corrupting influences of Italian immigration upon the Spanish language in *El problema del idioma nacional* (The Problem of the National Language) (1900) and *El "criollismo" en la literatura argentina* ("Creolism" in Argentine Literature) (1902). Carlos María Ocantos (1860–1949) lamented the fundamental linguistic and cultural changes being wrought by immigrants, in a 1911 novel titled *El peligro* (The Danger), and he worried about the future of Argentine national character in view of the massive alteration and erosion.[9] The ruling élite feared political radicalization and the loss of its monopoly over national policy.

The upper-class writers of the Generation of 'Eighty utilized racial arguments and biological determinism to justify Argentina's sharp class divisions. Italians and Jews became particular targets for xenophobic abuse and racial slander, and a mythical gaucho gradually emerged as a heroic, pure, Spanish counterpoint to the inferior, threatening, foreign-born hordes. The nexus of xenophobia and *criollismo* (exalting native virtues) emerged in the naturalistic novels of Eugenio Cambaceres (1843–1888) and Julián Martel (pseudonym for José María Miró [1867–1896]). The latter's novel *La Bolsa* (Stock Exchange) (1891), focussing on the Argentine stock exchange, is overtly anti-Semitic. Miró's protagonist, Dr. Glow, worries that "now we do not even know what we are—French or Spanish, Italians, or English."[10]

By 1912, many Argentines agreed with Enrique de Cires that foreigners, far from providing the key to future Argentine greatness, instead brought crime, mendicancy, cultural degeneration, and social and labour unrest. The foreign-born masses were allegedly unserviceable, unpatriotic, people with no concept of work, vagrants, and criminals. These characteristics had been widely applied to the gaucho during the previous century. Cires maintained that vagrants and the unemployable immigrants had arrived in far greater numbers than the European farmers Argentina wanted and needed to populate the vast, underutilized pampa.[11] Ironically, the gaucho, who had violently resisted élite domination in the nineteenth century, now became the élite's symbolic weapon for socio-political control in the early twentieth.

It remained for three nationalists from the interior provinces—Ricardo Rojas, Leopoldo Lugones, and Manuel Gálvez—to establish the regional gaucho as a national symbol. Ricardo Rojas (1882–1957) identified the creole of the interior, whom he confused with the gaucho of the littoral, as the true Argentine. His liberal nationalism, unlike the authoritarian integral nationalist strain, posited the gaucho as the representative of Spanish individualism. Twentieth-century liberal nationalism adapted the thought of Sarmiento and Mitre to the modern world, by stressing constitutional, representative democracy, free trade and cooperation with Europe, and civilian rule. "I am an American," wrote Rojas, "Buenos Aires is strange to me, therefore Buenos Aires is not America." "The genuine American" allegedly resided in the countryside, not in the cities, according to the nationalist from Santiago del Estero. "We believe . . . that what is collectively Argentine and genuinely 'ours' are found in the gaucho as the human prototype of our nationality."[12]

Rojas pressed for a concerted educational effort to "Argentinize" the immigrant masses; indeed, he popularized the term "*argentinidad*." In a 1909 report to the Ministry of Education (*La restauración nacionalista* [The Nationalist Restoration]), he urged the adoption of patriotic, nationalistic education. Others echoed his sentiments and joined the drive to revitalize nationality through education. Dr. José María Ramos Mejía (1842–1914), the nativist head of the National Council of Education, Carlos Octavo Bunge (1875–1918), and Enrique de Vedia also urged reform measures to promote *argentinidad*. . . .[13]

Leopoldo Lugones (1874–1938), a nationalist writer from the interior who moved from the political left to the far right, placed the gaucho at the centre of the nation's quest for self-understanding. In 1913 he delivered a series of interpretive lectures at the Odeon Theatre to the cultural-intellectual élite of Buenos Aires on the Hernández poem *Martín*

Fierro. These lectures, published in 1916 as *El payador* (The Balladeer), climaxed the élite's apotheosis of the gaucho. "The gaucho was the hero and the civilizer of the pampa," according to Lugones, "the prototype of the present-day Argentine."[14]

Manuel Gálvez (1882–1963), an integral nationalist, considered the native creole the preserver and bearer of traditional Hispanic/Catholic spiritual and moral values essential for the survival of the nation. A creole élite guiding a creole populace would ensure cultural and moral continuity with the Spanish past in the face of immigrant-inspired materialism, immorality, and skepticism. In 1913, Gálvez posed the dichotomy between "historic" nationalism which he favoured and "progressive" nationalism which he feared. The former "laments the loss of our old moral and material physiognomy; it wants to curtail immigration . . . and it seeks to restore the fervent nationalism of the past. The second tendency is cosmopolitan and liberal; it dislikes our romantic past and perhaps our Spanish origin; it desires progress at any price and totally ignores that the country has its own unique soul."[15] Like Lugones, Gálvez pitted the gaucho, the bearer of Hispanic virtue, against the *gringo*, the instrument of corrosive modernity and materialism.

While Lugones delivered his seminal lectures in 1913, *Nosotros* (We), a popular *porteño* literary magazine, polled leading writers and thinkers on whether *Martín Fierro* qualified as an epic literary masterpiece. The positive responses confirmed the gaucho's rising stock among the Argentine cultural élite. For generations, cultured *porteños* had belittled the gaucho and the Hernandez poem, but the crucible of the early 1900s' social conflict stimulated a wide-ranging reappraisal. Responding to the poll, Rojas and Lugones termed the poem the basic work of Argentine national literature, and Lugones reaffirmed the gaucho's central historical and patriotic role as liberating warrior in the battle for independence.[16] Martiniano Leguizamón (1858–1935), a traditionalist writer from Entre Ríos province, concurred. He pronounced the work to be "our national poem" that "condenses the noblest aspirations, the deepest and most generous ideals" of the Argentine people. He traced the power of the poem to its ability to reveal the "most recondite intimacies" of the gaucho and hence of the Argentine people.[17]

Despite the rising prestige accorded to *Martín Fierro* and the gaucho, many intellectuals continued voicing reservations about their importance in Argentine culture and history. In a May 1916 lecture, Carlos María Urien maintained that "the gaucho represents nothing" in Argentina unless it is barbarism and anarchy—a restatement of Sarmiento's view. Writing on national literature in 1924, Arturo Costa Alvarez affirmed that "the genuine Argentine has never been, is not, and will never be the Indian and the gaucho." The gaucho, according to the Hispanophile literary circle, lived as a "parasite," consuming without producing, and thus could represent neither the nation's spirit nor its character.[18] The gaucho's critics and partisans resurrected many of the arguments and positions developed during the nineteenth century, and the debate over the gaucho's character and significance persisted. . . .

Resurgent integral nationalism, which swept Argentina during the 1930s, found its political expression in a series of military-backed conservative regimes that ruled the nation. Integral nationalists emerged as the political power-brokers under General José F. Uriburu in 1931. They maintained a corporatist ideology grounded in economic nationalism, nativism, autocracy and military rule—a strong state allied with the Catholic Church to ensure a society of "hierarchy and order." Leopoldo Lugones had expressed the desire for such a regime in 1919: "It is scarcely necessary to point out that because of their scientific and administrative training, their spirit of sacrifice, their disciplined lives, and their devotion to honor, military officers constitute the best conceivable governing body."[19] Other nationalists of the right included Gálvez, Rodolfo and Julio Irazusta, Ernesto Palacio, Ramón Doll, César Pico, Juan E. Carulla, and Carlos Ibarguren. Many joined Lugones to admire [Benito] Mussolini, and to urge the creation of a neo-fascist state in Argentina.[20] They rejected the forms and ideology of political liberalism, which they regarded as an invitation to Protestantism, Free Masonry, secularism, individualism, and moral relativism.

This political revival of the right that ousted aging President Hipólito Yrigoyen in 1930, was parallelled by a growing popular cultural nationalism. Many Argentines agreed with Repetto that the gaucho deserved a national monument to commemorate his contributions to the country's development. As early as 1915, Dr. Benjamín D. Martínez had urged the construction of a monument to the gaucho. He reaffirmed support for the project in 1924 in the pages of *Nativa* magazine.[21] Neighbouring Uruguay, where gauchos had also played a significant economic and military role, preempted Argentina in December 1927 by inaugurating a monument to the gaucho in Montevideo, whereupon the Argentine Minister of Public Instruction wired a congratulatory message to his Uruguayan counterpart. He commended gauchos as "the race that gave all for the formation of the free nations of America." *La Prensa*, a major *porteño* daily and long-time voice of the conservative élite, criticized the minister's glorification of the gaucho, who, in its editor's view, was rebellious and loath to work.[22] Despite intermittent efforts over the years, particularly during the late 1940s, no gaucho monument was erected in the port city. In 1973, Carlos Alberto Allende, a skilled Argentine sculptor, completed

a slightly larger than life bronze statue of a mounted gaucho, outside the
city of Tandil in southern Buenos Aires province. The project had begun
with popular contributions, and reached completion with a major dona-
tion by the military government under General Alejandro Lanusse.[23]

Although they did not succeed in erecting a monument to the gaucho,
partisans did establish a "Day of Tradition" in 1939. A traditionalist literary circle, *Agrupación Bases* (Basics Group), formulated the plan at a
late 1937 meeting in La Plata, the capital of Buenos Aires province. They
suggested that 10 November, the birthday of José Hernández, be declared
the Day of Tradition; in August 1939, the provincial legislature promulgated such a decree. It resolved to promote patriotism, and to honour the
nation's creole and gaucho roots. Henceforth, on 10 November, public
schools would conduct classes on native art, science and music, and
especially on *Martín Fierro*, the "immortal poem of Hernández," the
official radio station would broadcast exclusively autochthonous music,
and at the creole park "Ricardo Güiraldes," in the Museum of Luján, and
at other appropriate sites, the provincial government would organize celebrations of a regional character. . . .[24]

Throughout the 1930s, traditionalist authors dangled positive images
of the gaucho before the reading public. In addition to folklore journals
such as *Nativa*, newspapers played a significant role in promoting knowledge and appreciation of the gaucho among a mass audience. . . .

Another measure of growing mass traditionalist sentiment during the
1930s was in the popularity and proliferation of folklore museums. Felix
Bunge bequeathed his lovely Buenos Aires residence on Avenida del
Libertador to the municipality, specifying that it be used as a museum
with an Argentine cultural theme. In 1937, the city opened the Museo de
Motivos Populares Argentinos "José Hernández," thus honouring the
author of the gaucho epic poem. . . .

In October 1938, the province of Buenos Aires opened a traditionalist centre in San Antonio de Areco. The project included a "creole park"
of some 38 hectares, complete with livestock, and a gauchesque museum
housed in a traditional pampean ranch house, both named in honour of
Güiraldes, who had lived and was buried in the town. . . .

Skirmishes between the gaucho's critics and defenders peaked during the 1940s, when Argentine nationalism also reached its zenith. The
rocky road of national politics, particularly the unsettling "infamous decade" of the 1930s and Juan Perón's rise in the 1940s, disillusioned many
intellectuals. The fatalism, pessimism, and frustration of many thinkers
emerged in their writings, but perhaps none demonstrated the power and
erratic brilliance of Ezequiel Martínez Estrada (1895–1964). Like Lugones
and Güiraldes, Martínez Estrada focussed on the pampa and the gaucho

in seeking to unravel the anomalous skein of Argentine historical development. Like other disillusioned intellectuals, he suffered alienation and pessimism in contemplating the nation's stagnation and failure to fulfill its destiny. For Martínez Estrada, the dispossessed gaucho personified the travail of the past century which had left Argentina a legacy of dehumanization, distrust, violence, fragmentation, and "patriotic delusions of grandeur." The destructive forces that had doomed and exterminated the gaucho persisted as constant reminders in national life, thus condemning the country to continued frustration, stagnation, and alienation.[25]

Martínez Estrada elucidated his gloomy, brooding fatalism in myriad essays and two major books—*X-Ray of the Pampa* (1933) and the two-volume *Death and Transfiguration of Martín Fierro* (1948). He accused the nation's nineteenth-century liberal élite with distorting the country's trajectory with unrealistic, foreign-inspired panaceas: "Rivadavia, Sarmiento, Mitre, Rawson, Avellaneda, Pellegrini, and a few others created myths in that they introduced, as Argentina dogmas, foreign idols that did not address the national faith."[26] The liberal élite, in his view, exerted intense political and legal pressure, but could not excise all vestiges of "barbarism," nor implant fully European civilization. In short, they could not destroy the gaucho ethos. "The creators of fictions were the promoters of civilization, in opposition to the agents of barbarity, who were closer to the repudiated reality. . . . French and English were spoken, and dress coats were worn; but the gaucho lurked under the pressed shirt." For Martínez Estrada, the gaucho represented the permanent central core of Argentine history and character—one that could not be eliminated completely by legal oppression nor the wishful thinking of the Europhile élite. . . .[27]

General Pedro Ramírez's administration institutionalized some elements of creole nationalism in 1943. Late in that year the government created the "National Institute of Tradition" to promote the study of native culture. In October 1943 the Senate of Buenos Aires province proposed that the Day of Tradition be made a national holiday. The senators also resurrected the long-frustrated project for a monument honouring the gaucho. In May 1947, they authorized the expenditure of 300,000 pesos to erect a monument in the provincial capital of La Plata. The provincial Chamber of Deputies supported the project but wished to spend only half that sum. Political wrangling between the two houses persisted for a year, and once again frustrated the project.[28]

Peronism drew support from urban workers, and included populist techniques of mass mobilization. At the same time, as Kalman H. Silvert has noted, it also marked a rightist reaction to "rapid social and political change in an environment of internal political schism and international

war, uncertainty, and ideological dispute." The regime condoned a
resurgent anti-Semitism, until [Juan] Perón withdrew official support in
1945. The gaucho emerged as the symbol of Argentine independence in
the face of what integral nationalists viewed as British and North American imperialist opposition to Perón. Some Peronists compared their
leader favourably with Juan Manuel de Rosas, the nineteenth-century
caudillo who had risen to power with gaucho militia and popular support,
and had stood firm against European intervention until his overthrow in
1852.[29]

The Peron government announced its support for creole virtues and
values. Peron urged the propagation of native culture and themes, and
promised public support for such ventures. Government-supported literary magazines, such as *Argentina* and *Sexto Continente*, both founded in
1949, fostered national themes and talent. Nationalist writers, including
Gálvez, Raul Scalabrini Ortiz, Hugh Wast, and Guillermo House, published essays in the Peronist journals. The first Five Year Plan clarified
the nexus between traditionalist sentiments and Perón's "revolutionary"
goals for the "New Order." Argentina's "new man" was to have his spirit
shaped "through an eminently traditionalist conception," and by adapting
"old spiritual essences and creole virtues" to modern conditions. The plan
reaffirmed the Ramírez military government's goals in 1943 to promote
the study of native culture.[30]

Peron took the traditionalist/gaucho model and values and moved them
into the twentieth century by enshrining the "urban gaucho," the
descamisado or shirtless urban labourer, as the new representative of the
dispossessed masses. Evita Perón observed that the *descamisado* "appears
on the Argentine political scene as a reincarnation of the gaucho." The
porteño élite, which had despised the gaucho in the nineteenth century,
referred to the shirtless workers as *cabecitas negras*, "little blackheads,"
because many were mestizo migrants from the interior provinces. Under
Perón, the shirtless ones temporarily became the new paragons of nationalism, but his fall in 1955 marked the rejection of that model and the
renewed suppression of urban labourers.[31] Violent political conflict and
economic crisis became constant irritants in Argentine national life.

The intellectuals' urgency to define the Argentine national character,
and the continued frustration of that need has permeated twentieth-
century Argentine thought and letters. Many intellectuals, in their struggle
for self-definition, did not focus upon the gaucho, but agonized as deeply
as the gauchophiles and gauchophobes. Eduardo Mallea, Carlos Alberto
Erro, H. A. Murena, Raul Scalabrini Ortiz, and others, grappled with the
conundrum of Argentine national identity without manipulating or invok-
ing the image of the gaucho. As Scalabrini Ortiz phrased it, "our greatest

anguish comes from not knowing who we are. . . . We speak in Spanish, we act in English, our tastes are French. . . ."[32]

Argentines were not unique in their difficult quest for national identity, in using the rural masses as symbols of national virtue, nor in mistaking a regional subculture for the whole nation. However, Argentina suffered a further debilitating paradox that has complicated its search for national identity. Because Argentina appeared to be approaching great nation status and prosperity in the early twentieth century, the frustrations and painful introspection generated by that failure cut all the more deeply.

Argentina remains a nation with an identity crisis. The arguments presented early in the search for self-understanding remain: universalism versus particularism, cosmopolitanism versus localism, city versus country, and gaucho versus *gringo*. Seemingly irreconcilable dualities suffuse Argentine society and politics. One of the clearest and most destructive is the clash between Peronists and anti-Peronists, and the ensuing fragmentation and anomie. In 1969, Argentina's leading writer, Jorge Luis Borges, voiced a frustration experienced by many of his countrymen in his search for *argentinidad*: "With each day that passes our country becomes more provincial. More provincial and more conceited, as if it had its eyes shut. It would not surprise me were the teaching of Latin to be replaced by that of Guaraní," an Indian language spoken in Paraguay and southern Brazil.[33] Borges and other Argentine cosmopolitans viewed the gaucho and other autochthonous elements of the nation's culture as pieces in a mosaic, but not as the essence of the Argentine character. Yet the power and appeal of the mythical gaucho persist. When Argentina hosted the World Cup soccer tournament in 1978, the popular mascot chosen to symbolize the event was "Mundialito," a little gaucho boy with a soccer ball. A modernized gaucho represented the Argentine people to the rest of the world.

The quest for *argentinidad* will continue until the numerous dilemmas, dichotomies, and dualities that have shattered and divided the Argentine nation are reconciled. Economic hyper-inflation, political repression, militarism, and cultural censorship and sterility do not facilitate this task. With his idiosyncratic insight, Borges offered another cogent observation concerning the Argentine identity crisis: "Through the years, a man peoples a space with images or provinces, kingdoms, mountains, bays, ships, islands, fishes, rooms, tools, stars, horses, and people. Shortly before his death, he discovers that the patient labyrinth of lines traces the image of his own face."[34] Argentina's odyssey in search of a satisfactory national image will persist until the country resolves the problems and contradictions that touched off the quest early in the twentieth century. Such a resolution would attenuate the nation's need to search for its essence, terminate decades of frustration, and possibly leave Argentines content with selfhood.

Notes

1. See Alberdi, *Bases y puntos de partida para la organización política de la República Argentina* (Bases and Points of Departure for the Political Organization of the Argentine Republic) (Buenos Aires: Plus Ultra, 1974), quoted in William Rex Crawford, *A Century of Latin-American Thought* (Cambridge, MA: Harvard University Press, 1944), pp. 21 and 24; José Luis Romero, *A History of Argentine Political Thought*, trans. Thomas F. McGann (Stanford: Stanford University Press, 1963), pp. 160 and 163; Arthur P. Whitaker, *Nationalism in Latin America*, reprint edition (Westport, CT: Greenwood Press, 1976), pp. 30–37.

2. Quoted in Frederick B. Pike, "The Problem of Identity and National Destiny in Peru and Argentina," in Pike, ed., *Latin American History: Select Problems* (New York: Harcourt, Brace and World, 1969), p. 205.

3. See Sarmiento, *Life in the Argentine Republic in the Days of the Tyrants: or Civilization and Barbarism*, trans. Mrs. Horace Mann, reprint edition (New York: Hafner, 1971), pp. 1–55; Pike, "Problem of Identity," pp. 184–185.

4. Argentine Republic, Dirección de Estadistica de la Nación, *La población y el movimiento demográfico de la República Argentina en el período 1910–1925* (The Population and Demographic Movement of Argentina during 1910–1925) (Buenos Aires: Kraft, 1926), p. 72.

5. Jorge MacKitchie to William Walker, letter of 11 August 1911, uncatalogued ranch papers of William Walker, Instituto Torcuato DiTella (Buenos Aires); Antonio Jorge Pérez Amuchástegui, *Mentalidades argentinas (1860–1930)* (Argentine Mentalities), second edition (Buenos Aires: Eudeba, 1970), p. 220; Carl Solberg, *Immigration and Nationalism: Argentina and Chile, 1890–1914* (Austin: University of Texas Press, 1970), pp. 13 and 157.

6. Solberg, *Immigration and Nationalism*, pp. 134–157; Martin S. Stabb, *In Quest of Identity: Patterns in the Spanish American Essay of Ideas, 1890–1960* (Chapel Hill: University of North Carolina Press, 1967), pp. 146–181.

7. Horacio J. Becco, Félix Weinberg, Rodolfo A. Borello, and Adolfo Prieto, *Trayectoria de la poesía gauchesca* (The Trajectory of Gauchesque Poetry) (Buenos Aires: Plus Ultra, 1977), pp. 37–80; Edward Larocque Tinker, *The Horsemen of the Americas and the Literature They Inspired*, second revised edition (Austin: University of Texas Press, 1967), pp. 33–51.

8. Federico Tobal, "Los libros populares de Eduardo Gutiérrez: el gaucho y el árabe," *La Nación* (16 February and 2 March 1886); Myron I. Lichtblau, "Formation of the Gaucho Novel in Argentina," *Hispania*, 41, No. 3 (September, 1958), 294–299; Lichtblau, *The Argentine Novel in the Nineteenth Century* (New York: Hispanic Institute in the United States, 1959), pp. 121–129; Enrique Williams Alzaga, *La pampa en la novela argentina* (The Pampa in the Argentine Novel) (Buenos Aires: Estrada, 1955), pp. 135–137.

9. Solberg, *Immigration and Nationalism*, pp. 139–140; Ernesto Quesada, "El criollismo en la literature argentina," *Estudios*, 1, No. 3 (1902), 301–302 and 306.

10. Julián Martel, *La Bolsa* (Buenos Aires: Estrada, 1946), pp. 76–77; Zulma E. Pagliari de Moreno, "Argentina, 1880–1890: filosolía, letras, ciencias, artes"

(Argentina, 1880–1890: Philosophy, Letters, Sciences, Arts), *Universidad*, 73 (October, 1967), 157–163; Gladys S. Onega, *La inmigración en la literatura argentina, 1880–1910* (Immigration in Argentine Literature) (Buenos Aires: Galerna, 1969), p. 89. On anti-Semitism, see Robert Weisbrot, *The Jews of Argentina from the Inquisition to Perón* (Philadelphia: Jewish Publication Society of America, 1979), pp. 214–222.

11. Enrique de Cires, "La inmigración en Buenos Aires" (Immigration in Buenos Aires), *Revista Argentina de Ciencias Políticas*, 2 (September, 1912), 737 and 741.

12. Antonio Pages Larraya, "Ricardo Rojas y la formación de la conciencia nacional" (Ricardo Rojas and the Formation of National Consciousness), *Revista de la Universidad Nacional de Córdoba*, 2nd series, 6, No. 3 (July, 1965), 802; Ricardo Rojas, *Los Gauchescos* (The Gauchesques) (Buenos Aires: Losada, 1948), pp. 549 and 630–631; Pike, "Problems of Identity," p. 186.

13. Rojas popularized the term *"argentinidad"* in a 1916 work by that title. On his liberal cultural nationalism, see Earl T. Glaubert, "Ricardo Rojas and the Emergence of Argentine Cultural Nationalism," *Hispanic American Historical Review*, 43, No. 1 (February, 1963), 1–13; Solberg, *Immigration and Nationalism*, pp. 144–146; Rojas, *La restauración nacionalista*, second edition (Buenos Aires: La Facultad, 1922), pp. 172–183, 339, and 343; Stabb, *In Quest of Identity*, pp. 147–148.

14. Leopoldo Lugones, *El payador*, fourth edition (Buenos Aires: Huemul, 1972), pp. 49 and 66.

15. Gálvez, quoted in Pike, "Problem of Identity," p. 208; see also pp. 185–186; and Crawford, *Latin-American Thought*, pp. 160–164.

16. *Nosotros*, 10, No. 49 (May, 1913) 232–233; 10, No. 50 (June, 1913) 425.

17. *Ibid.*, 10, No. 50 (June, 1913), 427–429. "Traditionalists" stressed native, regionalist, and folkloric themes, and concentrated upon cultural matters, whereas the politically concerned "nationalists" propounded policy solutions to national problems.

18. Carlos María Urien, "Monumento al gaucho" (The Gaucho Monument) (Buenos Aires: José Tragant, 1916), 8–9 (pamphlet); Arturo Costa Alvarez, "Nuestro preceptismo literario: indianismo, americanismo, gauchoismo, criollismo, nacionalismo" (Our Literary Precepts: Indianism, Americanism, Gauchism, Criollism, Nationalism), *Humanidades*, 9 (1924), 112 and 159.

19. Pike, "Problem of Identity," p. 211; Marvin Goldwert, *Democracy, Militarism, and Nationalism in Argentina, 1930–1966: An Interpretation* (Austin: University of Texas Press, 1972), p. xviii; Navarro Gerassi, *Nacionalistas*, pp. 16 and 170–171.

20. Romero, *Political Thought*, pp. 228, 239, and 242–243; Glaubert, "Rojas," pp. 5–6; Marysa Navarro Gerassi, *Los Nacionalistas* (Buenos Aires: Jorge Alvarez, 1968), pp. 170–171.

21. *Nativa*, 1, No. 3 (28 March 1924), 115–116.

22. *La Prensa* (Buenos Aires) (9 January 1928); *Nativa*, 5, No. 50 (29 February 1928).

23. Interview with Carlos Alberto Allende, Tandil, Buenos Aires province, 19 April 1978.

24. Honorable Senado de Buenos Aires, *Día de la Tradición y monumento al gaucho: Antecedentes legislativos* (La Plata: Taller de Impresiones Oficiales, 1948), pp. 15–16.

25. Peter G. Earle, *Prophet in the Wilderness: The Works of Ezequiel Martínez Estrada* (Austin: University of Texas Press, 1971), pp. 16, 57, 79, 137, and 139. See also James Maharg, *A Call to Authenticity: The Essays of Ezequiel Martínez Estrada* (University, Miss.: Romance Monographs, 1977).

26. Ezequiel Martínez Estrada, *X-Ray of the Pampa*, trans. Alain Swietlicki (Austin: University of Texas Press, 1971), p. 376.

27. Martínez Estrada, *X-Ray*, p. 392; Earle, *Prophet*, pp. 78–105.

28. *La Razón* (21 December 1943); Honorable Senado de Buenos Aires, *Día de la Tradición*, pp. 41–42 and 59–88.

29. Kalman H. Silvert, "Peronism in Argentina: A Rightist Reaction to the Social Problem of Latin America," in Frederick B. Pike, ed., *Latin American History: Select Problems* (New York: Harcourt, Brace and World, 1969), p. 342; George I. Blanksten, *Perón's Argentina* (Chicago: University of Chicago Press, 1953), pp. 224–228; Glaubert, "Rojas," pp. 10–13, on Peronists and *rosistas*, see Clifton B. Kroeber, *Rosas y la revisión de la historia argentina*, trans. J. L. Muñoz Azpiri (Buenos Aires: Fondo Editor Argentino, 1964), pp. 43–45; Roberto Etchepareborda, *Rosas: Controvertida historiografía* (Buenos Aires: Pleamar, 1972); Navarro Gerassi, *Nacionalistas*, pp. 131–145.

30. Honorable Senado de Buenos Aires, *Día de la Tradición*, pp. 92–94; Martin S. Stabb, "Argentine Letters and the Peronato: An Overview," *Journal of Inter-American Studies and World Affairs*, 13, No. 3 (July, 1971), 435–436; Navarro Gerassi, *Nacionalistas*, pp. 195–213.

31. Blanksten, *Perón's Argentina*, pp. 271–272; quote on p. 318.

32. Mark Falcoff, "Raul Scalabrini Ortiz: The Making of an Argentine Nationalist," *Hispanic American Historical Review*, 52, No. 1 (February 1972), 80; Eduardo Mallea, *Historia de una pasión argentina* (Buenos Aires: Espasa-Calpe, 1937); Earle, *Prophet*, p. 16; Stabb, *In Quest of Identity*, pp. 146–181.

33. Quoted in John Sturrock, *Paper Tigers: The Ideal Fictions of Jorge Luis Borges* (Oxford: Clarendon Press, 1977), p. 15.

34. Jorge Luis Borges, *A Personal Anthology*, ed. Anthony Kerrigan (New York: Grove Press, 1967), p. 203.

16 Clodomir Vianna Moog ◆
Bandeirantes and Pioneers

In his important book, Bandeirantes e pioneiros *(1954), a work that is more a meditation than an empirically based historical study, Brazilian writer Clodomir Vianna Moog begins by asking why the United States, younger and smaller than Brazil, has become the preeminent country in the world while Brazil lags far behind. He finds an essential part of the answer in the different ways each country advanced its frontier—as he makes clear in this brief selection from his book.**

Vianna Moog found striking contrasts between conquerers and colonizers of North America—the "pioneers"—and their Brazilian counterparts—the bandeirantes. *Vianna Moog argues that his generalizations about the differences between Brazil and the United States apply equally well to Spanish America and the United States. His study, he says, could justifiably bear the title "Conquistadors and Colonizers."*

One of Brazil's leading writers, a lawyer, and a public official, Clodomir Vianna Moog was born in 1906 in São Leopoldo in the state of Rio Grande do Sul. He represented his country on agencies of the United Nations and the Organization of American States and served as ambassador to Mexico. Of his many books, Bandeirantes e pioneiros *is the best-known title in English.*

For a long time this question has been in the air, awaiting a comprehensive answer: How was it possible for the United States, a country younger than Brazil and smaller in its continuous continental area, to achieve the almost miraculous progress that it has, and come down to our own time in the forefront of nations, an amazing present-day reality—in many ways the most amazing and stupendous reality of all times—whereas Brazil, whose history antedates that of the United States by more than a century, still appears, even in the light of the most optimistic interpretations and prophecies, only as the uncertain land of the future?

How has all this been possible? What happened to bring it about? What facts can have so determined the course of the two histories as to produce so great a contrast? . . .

From the outset, between the history of Brazil and that of the United States, everything or nearly everything is contrast; and the initial

From *Bandeirantes and Pioneers* (1964), trans. L. I. Barrett, 5, 91–97. © 1954 by George Braziller, Inc. Reprinted by permission.

*For other viewpoints, see Richard B. Morse, ed., *The Bandeirantes: The Historical Role of the Brazilian Pathfinders* (New York: Knopf, 1965), especially the essay "Westward March," by Cassiano Ricardo (pp. 191–211).

contrasts, through their repercussions on the religious, economic, social, moral, political, psychological, and cultural planes, were to end by conditioning all the others.

2

There is of course a fundamental difference of motives in the settlement of the two countries: an initially spiritual, practical, and constructive spirit in the development of North America, and a predatory, extractive and almost only secondarily religious spirit in the development of Brazil.

The first settlers of the English colonies of America, principally the Puritans of the *Mayflower*, did not come to the New World only or predominantly in search of gold and silver mines and easy riches. They came, instead, driven by persecution in their country of origin, in search of lands where they could worship their God, read and interpret their Bible, work, help one another, and celebrate the ritual of their cult in their own way. As they embarked, bringing with them all their possessions, their wives and children, they turned their backs on Europe to found on this side of the Atlantic a new fatherland, the theocratic fatherland of the Calvinists. They did not think of returning; for them there was only one way of being pleasing to God: to read the Bible and to labor, to labor and prosper, to prosper and to accumulate wealth. They were colonizers, not conquerors. Later, it is true, there were those who broke away to the West in search of gold and easy fortune, but when this happened, the *sense*, the *rhythm* of North American history was already established and definitively established—constructive, moral, practical.

In Brazil, unfortunately, precisely the contrary occurred in nearly everything. The Portuguese who came first to take possession of the lands of Santa Cruz were all faithful vassals of the King of Portugal. If, on the one hand, they desired to enlarge the dominion of Christianity, "the Faith and the Empire," their eyes were already over-dilated with greed. They were initially conquistadors, not colonizers, as they would later be *bandeirantes* and not pioneers. Like the King, like the whole Court, after the discovery of the route to the Indies they wanted spoils and riches. And no one took ship with any notion of never more returning to the Lusitanian fatherland. And no one brought with him the purpose of getting rich through constant devotion to work. They were leaving behind their land, their friends, their families, their normal occupations, in the hope of El Dorado. They talked a great deal about honor and glory, about the Faith and the Empire, but they did not fool the old man at the Restêlo, in Camoens' poem:

What new disasters dost thou now prepare
Against these kingdoms and against their seed?
What peril and what death for them to bear,
Under some mighty name, has thou decreed?
What mines of gold now dost thou promise fair?
What kingdoms?—promise lightly made indeed!
What fame dost thou propose? What legend glorious?
What palm? What triumph? And what war victorious?[1]

In the Portuguese world they did not fool Camoens; in the Spanish
world they did not fool Lope de Vega:

On pretext of religion
They go seeking silver and gold
Of the hidden treasure.[2]

If there were doubts about the purpose or motive of the great sea
voyages that followed the opening of the route to the Indies, the letter of
Pero Vaz de Caminha was there to dissipate them. The chronicler really
leaves no room for doubt about the gold fever, the hunger for gold, that
overpowered Portugal hard on the heels of the discoveries and almost
simultaneously with them. In no less than four passages in the letter does
he dwell at length on the obsession of finding gold.

When, for example, one of the Indians sees some rosary beads and
makes signs for them to be given him, gleefully playing with them then,
putting them first around his neck, then rolling them round his arm while
pointing to the land and then to the beads and to the commander's collar,
they all got the impression that the Indian was trying to indicate that he
would give gold for the beads. Immediately, however, Caminha goes on
to the conclusion with this delightful, precise comment: "We took it so
because we wanted it to be so."[3]

See the nature of the interrogations to which the Portuguese subject
the natives: "Then the Captain went up along the river which runs down
to the beach. There an old man waited, carrying a native canoe paddle in
his hand. He talked, while the Captain was with him, in the presence of us
all, without anyone's ever understanding him—or he us, all the things we
asked about gold, for we wished to find out whether there was any in the
land."[4]

And the preoccupation with the Faith, had it disappeared already?
Not yet. It was still very much alive, to judge by the description of the
first Mass held in Brazil, that famous first Mass celebrated on Easter
Sunday by Frei Henrique de Coimbra:

He had an awning set up in the island, and inside it a very proper altar.
And there with all of us he caused Mass to be said, which was said by

Frei Henrique in chanting voice and aided in the same voice by the other priests and religious who were there. The Mass, in my opinion, was heard by all with great pleasure and devoutness. . . .

While we were at Mass and at sermon, there were about as many people as we on the beach, more or less the same number as yesterday, with their bows and arrows, taking their ease. And looking at us, they sat down. And, once Mass was over, we sitting at sermon, many of them got up, blew a kind of horn and began to leap and dance a bit.[5]

It was the time in which the land was still called Santa Cruz, or Vera Cruz, as it had been officially christened. In fact, however, the Catholic faith for a long time had been yielding to the mercantilistic spirit of the time, and within a little while the name of Vera Cruz would be "changed for that of the wealth which was then supposed to be the principal one," to the profound displeasure of João de Barros, who in the purity of his Christian faith could not bear that "through diabolic arts" the name of "Santa Cruz, so pious and devout" should be turned into "that of a wood for dyeing cloth."[6]

But before the intensive exploitation of the wood for dyeing cloth began, as no gold, "nor silver, nor any metal or iron" were found in the land, Brazil was a disappointment for the conquerors. No gold? No silver? Then it held no interest.

It was useless for Pero Vaz de Caminha to praise the land, pointing to agriculture as a possible recourse. No one wanted to hear about the lands of Santa Cruz. And had it not been for the incursions of the French on the coasts of Brazil, putting the Portuguese conquest in check, the Court would not have thought of initiating the settlement. For a quarter of a century Portugal was to do nothing more, as far as producing a civilization in the recently discovered land was concerned, than send a few caravels, two or three annually, unloading on the littoral the mails and the dregs of society, to take back to Portugal cargoes of brazilwood and enslaved Indians, by way of staple exports, together with parrots and monkeys, under the heading of novelties.

As for the rest, when it could do so without creating political complications with Spain over the Tordesillas Line, the Court would dispatch royal letters and more royal letters, or secret instructions, urging the colonists to press on into the backlands in quest of the coveted metal.

Such expeditions, when not ordered by the government and paid for out of royal funds, were encouraged, protected, and organized by the local authorities. Radiating out from Piratininga, from Bahia, from Recife, they were to become a national phenomenon, not merely regional, often to the detriment of those forms of more or less useful, more or less stable, more or less constructive work which were developing on the coast around the mills for the production of sugar, a merchandise more and more highly valued and in demand in the European markets.

So, while the pioneer conquers the land inch by inch, planting towns and cities, the *bandeiras*, as Capistrano de Abreu emphasizes,

> contributed rather to depopulating than to peopling our land, taking Indians away from the places where they lived, causing their deaths in great numbers, either in attacks on villages and settlements or with ill treatment inflicted during the journeys, or, when these were over, by fatal and constant epidemics here and elsewhere as soon as the forest-dwellers come into contact with the civilized men. Moreover, the *bandeirantes* went and returned, they never settled down in the territories they crossed.[7]

While for the Portuguese who came to conquer Brazil—a Renaissance Portuguese, a crusader, more the crusader of the predatory phase of assaults on Moorish castles than a truly Catholic crusader—regular work gradually ceased to be a blessing, for the Puritan Anglo-Saxon, there was only one way to be pleasing to God: to labor and to pile up riches; always to work, never to stop.[8]

While the Portuguese immigrant, in his thirst for gold, comes utterly unprovided with economic virtues, public spirit, and the will to political self-determination, the Anglo-Saxon colonists in their famous *Mayflower Compact*—having sworn before God to constitute themselves into a civil and political body for their own preservation, promising each other to devise and decree laws, acts, and ordinances that would best promote the common good, and to revise those laws from time to time when deemed suitable to the interest of the Colony, to which all owed submission and obedience—already presage the future American independence, both political and economic, in the form in which it was put into effect.[9] More than this: they already presage, with their Puritanism, the advent of capitalism.

3

It will be said that not all the settlers of Brazil were conquistadors and adventurers; nor were all the settlers of the Anglo-Saxon colonies of America victims of religious persecution or born handlers of money, ready to profit by opportunity.

Indeed, that is true, and to attribute to the Portuguese, as to the Spaniards, only greed for gold, forgetting the eagerness for glory and for evangelism that they sometimes possessed, and to attribute to the English only noble religious motives underlying the desire for profit, would be to oversimplify the problem. Not only to oversimplify the problem but to omit, on the one hand, the thousands of farmers, artisans, merchants, and artists who in time established themselves on the Brazilian littoral, while the adventurers plunged into the backlands in search of wealth, and on the other hand, to forget that the colonies of Virginia, New York, and the Carolinas were established principally by men who, going there in quest of riches, shared the official religion of England.

In spite of the tendency to polarization, there was no exclusive and single historical process at work on either side. As the American historian Charles C. Griffin has observed in a notable study undertaken for the Pan-American Institute of Geography and History, not even in New England itself, the main goal of the Calvinists' Puritan immigration, do we find a society founded exclusively for religious ends, for even the Pilgrim Fathers of Plymouth, who bulk so large in the national history of the United States as saintly men imbued only with the desire for freedom of worship, were also seekers after easy profit, and English colonists blinded by eagerness for gold were never lacking. Many died in the first years of the Virginia colony, obsessed with the golden dream, and did not cease hunting for mines until the tobacco cultivated by Negroes began to offer them a surer road to fortune. "The difference which has been stressed so much is due, more than to anything else," concludes Griffin, "to the fact that in Mexico, Peru, and New Granada precious metals existed, while in Virginia and New England such metals were not to be found."[10]

All this is certainly irrefutable. It happens, nevertheless, that in the history of Anglo-Saxon America, whether for geographic or for psychological motives, or for a combination of the two, the spirit of colonization prevailed over that of conquest, while in Latin America precisely the reverse occurred: it was not the pioneer who prevailed over the *bandeirante*, but the *bandeirante* over the pioneer. It is true that the English also were greatly deluded by dreams of riches and power, for the myth of the Seven Cities of Cibola or of other great sources of gold and precious stones in the center of the continent must have lasted long. But, as the historian James Truslow Adams observes, the Anglo-Saxon adventurers, after some frustrated attempts at predatory exploration, turned to fishing, to cultivating tobacco, and to hard daily toil to get their sustenance from the land or from the sea. "Empire builders though they were, they seemed to think and move in inches, tilling their farms or plantations in serried rows as they advanced. No mines of Potosí, disappointingly but fortunately, turned their minds from the steady work of daily toil, nor did it occur to them to go on wild expeditions merely to trace the course of rivers a thousand miles from where their shops needed tending or their fields tilling."[11]

Notes

1. Luis de Camoens, *The Lusiads*, trans. Leonard Bacon (The Hispanic Society of America, New York, 1950), IV, 97. By permission of the Hispanic Society of America.

2. Lope de Vega, *El Nuevo Mundo de Cristóbal Colón*, Act I, sc. 2 in Don Eugenio de Ochoa, *Tesoro del teatro español* (Livr. Europea de Bandry, Paris, 1838), 594.

3. In Jaime Cortesao, *A Carta de Pero Vaz de Caminha* (Ed. Livros de Portugal, Rio de Janeiro, 1943), 207.

4. *Ibid.*, 220.

5. *Ibid.*, 213–214.

6. Roberto Simonsen, *História Econômica do Brasil* (Cia. Editora Nacional, São Paulo, 1937), I, 51.

7. J. Capistrano de Abreu, *Caminhos Antigos e Povoamento do Brasil* (Sociedade Capistrano de Abreu, Rio de Janeiro, 1930), 65.

8. This circumstance is probably of much greater importance than the *quality* of the immigrants. The countries colonized by the immigration of convicted criminals who have every intention of rehabilitating themselves (as was the case with the early settlers of Australia) derive more benefit from such immigration than those others settled by immigration of *hidalgos* of the purest lineage intent only on "making America."

9. That is how John Adams can say of the American Revolution that it was effected before the war actually began: "The Revolution was in the minds and hearts of the People." See Catherine Drinker Bowen, *John Adams and the American Revolution* (Little, Brown and Company, Boston, 1950).

10. Charles C. Griffin, "Unidad y variedad en la historia americana," in *Ensayos sobre la história del Nuevo Mundo* (Imprenta Universitaria, México, 1946), 108.

11. James Truslow Adams, *The Epic of America* (Little, Brown and Company, Boston, 1947), 30.

V

Contemporary Frontiers

17 James Sewastynowicz ◆ "Two-Step" Migration and Upward Mobility on the Frontier: The Safety Valve Effect in Pejibaye, Costa Rica

Although many scholars have concluded that frontiers did not serve as places of opportunity for the poor, James Sewastynowicz criticizes them for overstating their case. In Costa Rica, Sewastynowicz has discovered, those who arrived during the earliest stages of a region's development or arrived with modest amounts of capital did improve their economic standing. And with good timing, by arriving at the beginning of the development of a frontier region, the poor could begin to acquire capital in stages.

In the essay reprinted here Sewastynowicz proposes a modification of the "safety valve" theory first elaborated by Frederick Jackson Turner and vigorously debated ever since. Using data generated by participant observation, questionnaires, and personal interviews, he demonstrates that in Pejibaye, upward mobility was geared to " 'two-step' migration involving serial movement between at least two distinct frontiers." Citing previous studies in Brazil and Colombia that show the same pattern of success, he concludes that while lack of capital may preclude upward mobility on a single frontier, "when the perspective is broadened to consider multiple frontier movements, capital constraints lose their determinative value. Thus, although it may not be a place of unlimited opportunity, the frontier does seem to provide favorable conditions for economic self-betterment for those who migrate there."

James Sewastynowicz received a Ph.D. in anthropology from Ohio State University and is a professor in the Department of Geography and Anthropology at Jacksonville State University in Jacksonville, Alabama.

Abridged and adapted from *Economic Development and Culture Change* 34, no. 4 (July 1986): 731–53. © 1986 by the University of Chicago. Reprinted by permission of the author and the University of Chicago.

He has conducted field research in Honduras and Mexico as well as Costa Rica and has presented papers at numerous professional meetings. At present he is studying frontier dynamics in Brazilian Amazonia.

Introduction

A large part of the history of the United States is dominated by the westward expansion of its people across the North American wilderness. This same phenomenon of frontier settlement is currently taking place in many parts of Latin America, where vast areas of virgin rain forest are only now being colonized by modern pioneers. In many basic respects, these two regions contrast sharply. But, together with many other parts of the world, they share a recent tradition of frontier expansion, a tradition that many believe has been instrumental in shaping the evolution of contemporary social patterns. It is small wonder, then, that for nearly a century the frontier has constituted a major focus of research by historians, geographers, and sociologists alike.

In Latin America, recognition of the potential key role of the frontier in the past and future development of the region is demonstrated by the plethora of recent studies dealing with both planned and spontaneous colonization.[1] Although exploring a broad range of issues, many show a single, overriding concern: to assess the potential of the frontier for absorbing excess and discontented elements of the rural population, thereby raising the living standards of the impoverished masses and simultaneously alleviating the social and economic bases of revolt.

In its broadest formulation, this concern is with the degree to which a "safety valve" model accurately portrays the outcome of the colonization process. This model is derived through analogy with the corresponding mechanism of a steam boiler. It assumes that, by siphoning excess population from densely settled rural areas, the frontier permits the gradual release of otherwise explosive social and economic pressures.[2] In detail, the safety valve interpretation has both societal and individual aspects: on the one hand, population losses in long-settled regions and incorporation of the new resources of the frontier have consequences for society as a whole; on the other hand, migration to the frontier provides the individual colonist a means of achieving upward socioeconomic mobility.[3]

It is not surprising that scholarly opinion about the validity of so all-encompassing a theory has vacillated widely, ranging from outright acceptance to outright rejection of its basic tenets. During the early part of this century, when the "frontier thesis" of Frederick Jackson Turner was at its peak of popularity, the safety valve doctrine enjoyed virtually unquestioned support within the academic community. The frontier was generally viewed as "a gate of escape from the bondage of the past," as a place of unlimited opportunity where even the most disadvantaged might find rapid reward.[4] This unbridled optimism was soon quashed, however. In the storm of revisionist criticism unleashed against Turner's theories after his death in 1932, the safety valve doctrine was among the first to be swept away. Its death was pronounced, though somewhat prematurely, when Shannon delivered his famous "postmortem" over the remains of the theory.[5]

It was not long, however, before the pendulum began to swing in the opposite direction. A countermovement began, one aimed at restoring to the doctrine some measure of its former luster. This countermovement took four basic forms: (1) an economic approach using the principles of wage theory to argue that even small population losses would have vast repercussions on the labor situation in long-settled regions;[6] (2) a "resources" safety valve approach arguing that the sequential exploitation of frontier resources would raise wages in nonfrontier areas;[7] (3) an "indirect" safety valve approach pointing out that, if nothing else, the nineteenth-century U.S. frontier had prevented the exacerbation of existing social tensions by deflecting both eastern farmers and European immigrants from eastern urban areas;[8] and (4) a "psychological" safety valve approach emphasizing that, even if the safety valve did not work as normally supposed, members of the lower class *believed that it did* and therefore rejected mass radicalization as a solution to their problems.[9]

Yet if some measure of respectability has been restored to the societal aspect of the frontier safety valve, the same cannot be said about the perceived effects of frontier migration on the individual colonist. The consensus of contemporary opinion on this point is much the same as when Shannon denounced the doctrine 37 years ago: the frontier by no means provides the abundant opportunities that Turner and his followers so naively claimed for it. Rather, it is generally conceded that opportunities for upward mobility on any frontier are restricted to the small segment of the population already having substantial capital resources. In other words, it may well be that speculators and cattle barons reap enormous profits during the course of settlement, but seldom, if ever, do homesteaders.

Recent research in Latin America has bolstered confidence in the essential soundness of this position. Several studies have demonstrated that the major determinant of later socioeconomic mobility is indeed the amount of capital in hand on arrival.[10] Yet it is precisely because they lack capital and other resources that the majority of colonists are willing to endure the rigors of the frontier in the first place! For the destitute *peones* (wage laborers) and *campesinos* (peasants) who constitute the bulk of the colonization stream, prospects for upward mobility appear dim if not altogether nonexistent. In this light, it is hardly surprising that the majority of frontier theorists would agree wholeheartedly with Sandner's observation that "many colonists have seen their former standard of living worsened. They changed it in the hope that, after a few years of hard struggle, they would be able to obtain economic relief and enjoy comfort. They look backwards and discover that they have lost in the exchange."[11]

The failure of the poor colonist to improve his lot by migration to the frontier is a typical conclusion of current research. Like Shannon's earlier rebuttal of the safety valve on the U.S. frontier, most contemporary studies of frontier settlement in Latin America deny that intelligence, fortitude, and a modicum of luck can bring a person success. Perhaps the most succinct summary of the majority view was made by Margolis, who asserts, "I will question the frequent claim that the frontier provides unlimited opportunities for even the poorest stratum of society. . . . Thus, I seriously question Turner's famous thesis . . . that frontier areas afford the lower class opportunities not available elsewhere."[12]

It is, of course, easy to refute the notion that the frontier is a place of *unlimited* opportunity. However, in so doing, current theorists may well have overshifted in the opposite direction. In other words, while Turner may have been too optimistic in his assessment of frontier opportunities, current conceptions of frontier social mobility may be equally mistaken in their pessimism. This paper explores that possibility. It proposes that, although not unlimited in scope, new opportunities do arise on the frontier. It also proposes that these opportunities may sometimes be of sufficient weight to provide "a solid foundation to the rags-to-riches saga."[13]

These proposals shall be examined by reevaluating the results of several past studies in the light of new evidence from the recent frontier of Pejibaye, Costa Rica. This new evidence strongly suggests that opportunities for upward mobility were (1) available to even the most impoverished segments of Costa Rican society and (2) successfully utilized by a fair proportion of lower-class individuals who actually migrated to the frontier.

Subsequent analysis will contend that widespread upward mobility on the frontier of Pejibaye was no anomaly attributable solely to unique social or environmental circumstances. On the contrary, a specific behavioral pattern common to upwardly mobile migrants explains their later success. This pattern and its implications are described here as "two-step" migration involving serial movement between at least two distinct frontiers. As the model developed in this paper will demonstrate, movement of this type has the effect of negating the constraints imposed by initial lack of capital—constraints that would otherwise bar the lower class from a share in the rewards of the frontier. This suggests that the possibility, if not always the reality, or the rags-to-riches climb is an integral feature of the expanding frontier of Costa Rica.

It will also be contended that the data of several previous studies—many of which conclude that frontier social mobility is extremely limited—in fact suggest that this particular pattern of success on the frontier is found in countries other than Costa Rica, including the United States, Brazil, and possible Colombia. Based on these data, it is proposed that the pattern of two-step migration may be a generic feature of expanding frontiers the world over, as may substantial upward mobility on these frontiers. . . .

The Community

Pejibaye is one of eight districts of the canton of Pérez Zeledón, province of San José. Situated in the southwestern portion of Costa Rica, it covers an area of 210 square kilometers. Pejibaye is a predominantly rural, agricultural zone, and the majority of the district's nearly 8,000 inhabitants, independently farming their own land, form an essentially *campesino* stratum of the population.[14] Local farms specialize in the cultivation of maize, beans, and coffee, whereas many of the larger holdings are devoted to cattle grazing.[15]

The chief town and administrative center of the district is also named Pejibaye. With 400 inhabitants, it is the largest village in southern Pérez Zeledón. It is also a commercial hub of sorts, with an economic hinterland encompassing several adjacent districts. The town's business life is dominated by the several general stores, grain warehouses, dance halls, restaurants, and rooming houses located along its streets and by the numerous carpenters, tailors, and transporters who live there. There is also a coffee *beneficio* (processing plant) located just outside the town limits.

Because of its population density and agricultural importance, the national government of Costa Rica has taken an active interest in Pejibaye. This interest is concretely expressed in the form of numerous primary schools and a secondary school, branch offices of the National Production Council and the National Bank of Costa Rica, a medical dispensary, a post office, a police agency, community development and agricultural extension agents, and several roads and bridges.

But as prosperous as Pejibaye currently may be, scarcely 40 years ago it did not even exist. Settlement of the region commenced in 1942, the year in which three lone colonists first entered the rain forest that then covered the entire district.[16] During the next decade, several other pioneers joined them on this remote frontier outpost. Still, by the end of this initial phase of development in 1951, there were only about 25 families living in the vicinity of the present town of Pejibaye, and a few others lived elsewhere in the district.

The year 1952, however, ushered in an era of rapid social and economic development. In that year, the town of Pejibaye was founded and an airstrip was built on its outskirts. The pace of in-migration accelerated rapidly, resulting in the production of greater harvests and the emergence of a florescent commercial life. By the end of this second phase of its development in 1965, the population of Pejibaye stood at approximately 5,000 inhabitants.

A convenient bench mark for the beginning of the postfrontier history of Pejibaye is the legal creation of the district in 1966. In fact, the local frontier actually had been on the wane for perhaps a decade. Recent developments in Pejibaye include the intensification of social and economic disparities among its inhabitants and an ever more pervasive government presence in the district. These events need not be detailed further, since the frontier years at Pejibaye are the primary subject here.

Upward Mobility in Frontier Pejibaye

Information supplied by members of the 218 households in the research sample allowed the identification and analysis of 168 cases of in-migration in which the then head (or heads) of household currently resides in Pejibaye. Before arrival, 72% had been employed in agriculture, while the remainder had been government employees, merchants, and skilled or unskilled laborers. For the most part, this remaining 28% arrived in the late days of colonization and did not play a prominent role on the frontier.

During informal discussion, informants were asked to evaluate the success of their migration to Pejibaye. Their responses are revealing. Almost without exception, informants believed themselves better off in Pejibaye than they had been in their former residences.[17] Two basic reasons were given for this opinion: the ownership of more land or the holding of a better-paying job.[18] A typical remark was that in Pejibaye there is *mas vida* (more life).

However, these self-evaluations were not accepted entirely at face value. Objective confirmation was sought in the form of economic and occupational data supplied by the 121 informants who migrated to Pejibaye as farmers. These data attest to a strong positive relationship between upward mobility and migration to Pejibaye. Whereas prior to migration 77% of informants had been members of Costa Rica's lowest socioeconomic level, the *peón* class, only 36% remained in this category afterward. In the premigration group there was not a single individual who could remotely be considered wealthy. After migration, 16% ultimately managed to become either *hacendados* in possession of substantial landed estates, or prosperous merchants operating large-scale commercial businesses—or both. Today, such men are readily identified as *ricos* (rich men) by other members of the community.

Most upward mobility furthermore took place during the frontier phase of Pejibaye's history, that is, prior to 1966. Among migrants who arrived during 1942–65, 77% had formerly been *peones*, but only 27% remained at this level in 1977. Among migrants who arrived after 1965, however, the rate of upward mobility is considerably lower; the percentage of *peones* declines only slightly, from 76% before migration to 62% after migration.

Most of the real wealth accumulated in Pejibaye also belongs to men who arrived during the frontier epoch. Thus, while 20% of all 1942–65 migrants in the sample eventually achieved membership in the *hacendado* or merchant category, only one 1966–67 migrant, representing just 3% of those who arrived during this period, was able to achieve a comparable status. These figures would certainly seem to indicate that the opportunity for substantial wealth was largely, if not entirely, restricted to the frontier period of Pejibaye's history.

Underlying Factors

As the foregoing analysis suggests, there were indeed ample opportunities for upward mobility in frontier Pejibaye, and these were utilized by many of those who migrated there. These opportunities were of three major types: claiming or buying large tracts of land at low cost, specializing as retail merchants, or acting as middlemen in the grain business.

However, these opportunities were not equally available to all who migrated to Pejibaye. Free lands were quickly claimed by those who arrived during the first years of settlement; thereafter, prices rose steadily until land was beyond the means of the poorest of newcomers. On the other hand, once retail merchants and grain dealers had built their clienteles and acquired substantial capital reserves, they were in a position to effectively stifle most new competitors.

Upward mobility on the frontier of Pejibaye thus depended on two factors: time of arrival and initial capital. The earlier his arrival, the greater the opportunities available to the colonist; the more capital at his disposal, the greater his ability to take advantage of opportunities at any given time.

These factors are not unrelated. During the first decade of settlement, the basis for future prosperity in Pejibaye could be laid with a negligible capital outlay. Early colonists found fertile and virtually free lands. It was also relatively inexpensive to establish oneself as a merchant or grain dealer in the early 1950s, since competition was minimal and the initial investment relatively small.

As time passed, however, the price of success climbed sharply. Land values soared; established merchants and grain dealers built increasingly larger businesses against which ever-larger investments were needed to compete. The clear implication of these trends is that a man who arrived in Pejibaye with ¢1,000 in 1965 found himself in a much worse starting position than had the colonist who arrived 2 decades earlier with only one-tenth that amount.[19]

"Two-Step" Migration as a Strategy of Frontier Social Mobility

One vital question remains: If capital is so pervasive a factor in determining subsequent mobility on the frontier, how could the impoverished possibly have made the economic climb that so many did in Pejibaye? The answer is that the dual factors underlying postmigration success—capital and time of arrival—are nothing other than alternate expressions of the same formula and therefore to a large degree interchangeable. Lack of initial capital can be compensated for by early arrival on the frontier, whereas, conversely, late arrival can be compensated for by greater initial capital. In other words, it appears that by means of migration to the frontier, time can be "translated" into capital. If this principle is indeed valid, then by pursuing a course of serial migration from frontier to frontier, a man should be able to convert a store of time into a corresponding store of capital. Is this not a feasible strategy by which to rise from poverty to relative wealth?

Consider the hypothetical case of a man who arrived early in the settlement of Pejibaye, but with little or no capital. Like the majority of colonists, he lacked from the outset an essential ingredient determining later economic mobility. The most he was likely to achieve for having endured the hardships of frontier life was a modest success; although there are cases of *peones* becoming *hacendados* or merchants, these are relatively few, with contemporary positions of wealth by and large restricted to those who arrived with much greater capital at their disposal. But even though resources may be against such a man, time is on his side. After a decade or more, even the poorest of early colonists might find himself in a financial position equal or superior to that with which the more prosperous had arrived on the frontier. If he then left the "old" frontier and started

anew on another, by the conclusion of a second cycle of frontier development he might find himself a wealthy man.

This scenario is by no means farfetched. Rather, it is the logical outcome of two interrelated factors. The first and primary of these involves
what might be termed frontier "land inflation." In a region newly opened
to colonization, capital is a scarce resource, while land is initially almost
unlimited in supply. Over time, however, this situation reverses itself.
The net result: land prices rise sharply as continuing in-migration and
natural population growth put rising demand on what is rapidly becoming a scarce commodity.

This natural rise in frontier land values is reinforced, moreover, by a
second factor—the labor invested by the colonist over the course of several years' residence. The "time" that the colonist converts into capital
does not, in other words, consist entirely of idle time, but of time spent in
productive labor. By means of the simple technological devices at his
disposal, the colonist gradually clears the land of its forest cover and builds
fences, dwellings, wells, and other infrastructural components. Thus, he
converts a worthless property into an on-going agricultural enterprise,
increasing its value considerably in the process.

The combined effects of population pressure and the colonist's labor
investment are potentially quite spectacular. Dambaugh, for example,
documents how land prices near the frontier boomtown of Maringa in the
Paraiba Valley of Brazil rose 10,000% in 12 years.[20] In Pejibaye, a parallel trend took place as land prices rose 150-fold between 1945 and 1977.[21]
Such a developmental trajectory clearly presents a unique opportunity to
the early colonist, for it entails a substantial return on his initial investment. A settler who arrived in Pejibaye in 1945, for example, could have
purchased for only ¢100 a farm whose value would have risen to over
¢10,000 by 1965.[22]

An additional factor, moreover, enhances the advantage of early arrival on the frontier: because of sharply rising land values, latecomers are
effectively denied access to land and find themselves relegated to work
as *peones* on the farms of others. Where the stream of landless migrants
is heavy, as it was in Pejibaye, "land inflation" tends to create a cheap
and abundant supply of labor on which early colonists can draw to enhance their economic superiority.

Early in its settlement, then, the frontier typically presents ideal
opportunities for investment. However, to take advantage of these opportunities requires capital, and the meager finances of the average colonist
are normally insufficient for any but a modest economic climb. It is at
this juncture that the cumulative effect of the frontier migration process
comes into play: by migrating from one newly opened frontier to another

the poor colonist can build capital along the way, thereby paving the road to long-term economic improvement. In other words, it is only after migration to a second frontier that an initial small investment reaps truly large dividends. As already described, a man who arrived in Pejibaye with ¢100 in 1945 could have purchased a farm worth over ¢10,000 by 1965. Had he then reinvested this entire sum in land on a second frontier, by 1985 he would theoretically be in possession of assets valued at over ¢1,000,000.

The key to the rags-to-riches climb thus lies in embarking on a course of two-step interfrontier migration.[23]. . . For those individuals capable of carrying it out, this migratory strategy certainly proved quite effective in Pejibaye.[24] But what about elsewhere?

Two-Step Migration on Other American Frontiers

Were the pattern of two-step migration and its corollary, upward mobility on the frontier, a function entirely of factors specific to the environmental milieu of Pejibaye, they would be interesting but of doubtful theoretical value. However, a cursory review of the literature reveals several references strongly suggesting that two-step migration indeed may not be an uncommon frontier phenomenon. Elsewhere in Costa Rica, its importance can be inferred from the data presented by Sandner, who notes that, along all major frontiers in the country, first-wave colonists almost invariably sell their land to newcomers and move on to more distant frontiers.[25] Although this observation may not necessarily imply that these colonists were pursuing two-step strategies, that is the logical inference.

If two-step strategies were indeed followed, they may explain the high degree of upward mobility among colonists on the frontier of La Mansión de Nicoya, a region at the opposite end of the country from Pejibaye. Of 458 families surveyed in 1950, 63% had been *peones* before migration, and 35% had been *campesinos*. Following migration, only 5% of these same individuals remained *peones*, while 93% worked as *campesinos* on their own farms.[26] These figures are very similar to those described for Pejibaye and strengthen the evidence for a relationship between frontier migration and upward mobility in Costa Rica.

The two-step pattern can also be tentatively identified in Colombia. In her study of migration from the *municipio* of Fómeque to the Llanos Orientales frontier, Haney notes, "Rural-rural [frontier] migrant males from all ownership categories . . . except large owner, were more likely to be owners than tenants when compared to nonmigrants. Unfortunately, from our data we cannot ascertain the principal mode utilized to acquire this land."[27]

Ironically, in a passage apparently arguing that upward mobility is rare among lower-class settlers of the Llanos Orientales, Thome suggests what this mode of acquisition may have been: "Due to the almost insuperable hardships they face, colonos [colonists] often have to abandon their holdings, or sell them to a more prosperous neighbor, after only a few years of exploitation. They clear the land, but the benefits are reaped by those who can afford a long-term investment."[28]

As the principle of time-capital conversion presented in this paper suggests, in many cases the "successes" and the "failures" described by Thome may not be members of distinct social categories but rather the occupants of successive stages of a developmental cycle common to both. In other words, many of the Colombian settlers "who can afford a long-term investment" may be none other than two-step migrants who earlier in their lives had been poor colonists displaced from a previous frontier. On the other hand, with the added capital gained through sale of their farms, those colonists who "have to abandon their holdings" at present may well find themselves in a better position on arrival at another frontier.

But if the evidence from Colombia is inferential and therefore inconclusive, there can be little doubt of the significance of two-step migration along the nineteenth-century U.S. frontier:

> as other frontiersmen moved in . . . the pioneer farmer was infected with wanderlust. Sometimes he was driven onward by dislike of civilization and its ways, sometimes by the prospect of better lands ahead, but more often by the hope of gain. His cleared fields mounted steadily in value as population increased; if he was a squatter, he could sell his "improvements" at a profit; if he owned his farm he could dispose of his excess holdings, then the farm itself, for a handsome sum, while he moved on westward to begin the process anew.[29]

Nor can there be much question about the value of two-step migration along the Brazilian frontier:

> As a frontier community is settled, a significant portion of its land is purchased by former sharecroppers and renters who have earned money in older, more easterly areas of the state. Their small capital does not permit them to buy land in these former frontier regions, for by the time they have sufficient savings to invest in farms land values have skyrocketed, and they can afford to buy only the inexpensive lands of the frontier. As the frontier moves farther westward, leaving settled communities in its wake, former sharecroppers move along with it, buying small farms at its outer fringes. Upward mobility (as measured by the acquisition of land) does not occur in the same community where the sharecroppers worked to earn the purchase price of land. Invariably,

the transition from sharecropper to farmer takes place in two geographically distinct communities.[30]

Thus, it seems that two-step migration has been a common and viable strategy of upward mobility on at least three distinct frontiers and
possibly a fourth. If documented only in one country and on one frontier,
it might well be argued that this pattern is culturally or environmentally
specific. But when documented on the frontiers of three countries as
different as Costa Rica, the United States, and Brazil, it is more plausible
to suppose that two-step movement is a generic feature of expanding
frontiers regardless of temporal or cultural considerations.

Variables Influencing Utility

Although it has been demonstrated that two-step migration can operate
under a variety of conditions on diverse frontiers, it stands to reason that
certain conditions are more favorable than others. Among the variables
influencing the utility of two-step migration are (1) the distances separating successive frontiers, (2) the fertility of frontier soils, and (3) the degree of interference by governmental and corporate entities. Briefly, where
distances are longer, transportation costs are higher, eliminating the possibility of migration for the poorest and seriously depleting the scarce
capital reserves of many others. Where frontier soils are infertile, the
operation of "land inflation" is counteracted, leaving the colonist little
better off than he was prior to migration. Where governmental and corporate activity in controlling frontier lands and directing settlement is
greater, the lesser is the ability of individual colonists to profit from the
frontier; two-step migration, in other words, operates best in a "free-
market" setting.

In Costa Rica, conditions are optimal in allowing colonists the opportunities for two-step success: distances are short; frontier soils are relatively fertile; and governmental and corporate interference, with certain
exceptions, is minimal.[31] In both the United States and Amazonia, on the
other hand, greater distances separated or separate frontiers, necessitat-
ing higher transportation costs. Moreover, in much of Amazonia, infertile
soils counteract many of the beneficial effects of land inflation while the
ability of large business operations to monopolize huge tracts of land,
along with the wide scope of government-directed colonization, seriously
restricts the freedom to maneuver that migrants require in carrying out
two-step strategies. However, this by no means implies that the association between two-step migration and upward mobility is lacking altogether
on other frontiers, simply that it may not be as strong as it is in Costa
Rica.

Conclusions

During the past 50 years, portrayal of the frontier as a land of opportunity has been viewed with considerable skepticism. Several factors account for rejection of the safety valve interpretation. The more prominent among them include the excessive claims of its early proponents, coupled with their inability to explain adequately how and why upward mobility takes place on the frontier. Appealing largely to a social philosophy that was becoming increasingly obsolete during the 1930s, it was perhaps inevitable that the demise of the model should have been so abrupt and so complete.

The data presented in this paper, however, indicate that the earlier depiction of the frontier as safety valve was not entirely mistaken. In particular, identification of the two-step pattern of migration provides the model a firm theoretical basis and at the same time seriously undermines the chief objection of its opponents, namely, that lack of capital precludes upward mobility on the frontier. This dictum, it would appear, is valid only in a limited sense—when the research perspective is confined to movement to a single frontier. But when the perspective is broadened to consider multiple frontier movements, capital constraints lose their determinative value. Thus, while it may not be a place of *unlimited* opportunity, the frontier does seem to provide favorable conditions for economic self-betterment for those who migrate there.

This would appear to be the case not only in Costa Rica but on other frontiers as well. Nevertheless, it is unlikely that all frontiers perform safety valve functions with equal efficiency. Only further research in Amazonia and elsewhere will provide the data needed to specify more precisely the operation of two-step migration under variable circumstances. It is hoped that the ideas presented in this paper will stimulate such research, as well as encourage new approaches to the study of frontier life.

Notes

1. See, e.g., J. C. van Es, Eugene A. Wilkening, and João Bosco Guedes Pinto, "Rural Migrants in Central Brazil: A Study of Itumbiara, Goias," Research Paper no. 29 (Madison, Wis.: Land Tenure Center, 1968); Craig C. Dozier, *Land Development and Colonization in Latin America: Case Studies of Peru, Bolivia, Mexico* (New York: Frederick A. Praeger, Inc., 1969); James R. Taylor, "Agricultural Settlement and Development in Eastern Nicaragua," Research Paper no. 33 (Madison, Wis.: Land Tenure Center, 1969); Raymond E. Crist and Charles M. Nissly, *East from the Andes*, Social Sciences Monographs no. 1 (Gainesville: University of Florida Press, 1973); William C. Thiesenhusen, "Chile's Experiments in Agrarian Reform: Four Colonization Projects Revisited," *American Journal of Agricultural Economics* 56 (May 1974): 323–30; Nigel J. H. Smith,

Rainforest Corridors: The Transamazon Colonization Scheme (Berkeley and Los Angeles: University of California Press, 1982).

2. The safety valve theory was initially conceived as a means of explaining the relationship between frontier expansion and the social development of the United States during the nineteenth century. Discussions of its validity traditionally have been restricted to the U.S. frontier, and emphasis has been placed on its role in alleviating discontent among eastern factory workers. This paper, however, interprets the safety valve in somewhat broader terms. It accepts the proposition that frontier expansion may alleviate stress in rural areas, too, and asserts that frontier expansion may influence society in several additional ways.

3. Norman J. Simler, "The Safety Valve Doctrine Re-evaluated," *Agricultural History* 32 (October 1958): 250–57, esp. 256.

4. Frederick Jackson Turner, *The Frontier in American History* (New York: Henry Holt & Co., 1920), p. 38.

5. Fred A. Shannon, "A Post-Mortem on the Labor-Safety-Valve Theory," *Agricultural History* 19 (January 1945): 31–37.

6. Simler, pp. 250–57.

7. George G. S. Murphy and Arnold Zellner, "Sequential Growth, the Labor-Safety-Valve Doctrine, and the Development of American Unionism," *Journal of Economic History* 19 (September 1959): 402–21; Ellen von Nardroff, "The American Frontier as Safety Valve—the Life, Death, Reincarnation, and Justification of a Theory," *Agricultural History* 36 (July 1962): 139–40.

8. Simler, pp. 251–52; Ray Allen Billington, *Westward Expansion: A History of the American Frontier* (New York: Macmillan Publishing Co., 1967), p. 10.

9. Rush Welter, "The Frontier as Image of American Society, 1776–1860," *Pacific Northwest Quarterly* 52 (January 1961): 3–4; von Nardroff, p. 138; Billington, pp. 752–53.

10. Gerhard Sandner, *La colonización agrícola de Costa Rica*, 2 vols. (San José, Costa Rica: Instituto Geográfico de Costa Rica, 1962, 1964), 2:21; Maxine L. Margolis, *The Moving Frontier: Social and Economic Change in a Southern Brazilian Community*, Latin American Monographs, 2d series, no. 11 (Gainesville: University of Florida Press, 1973), p. 11.

11. Sandner, 2:21; author's translation from the Spanish.

12. Margolis, p. 11.

13. Murphy and Zellner, p. 418.

14. There is also a relatively small class of large landowners, or *hacendados*, as well as a numerically larger group of men with little or no land. Among the latter, those employed in the agricultural sector work as wage-laborers and/or lease land.

15. Pejibaye is one of the major food-producing regions in Costa Rica. With only 0.4% of the country's surface area, it harvests 5.6% of Costa Rica's bean crop and 2.9% of its maize.

16. It was only with the construction of the Interamerican Highway beginning in 1936 that large-scale settlement of the region surrounding Pejibaye became possible. Previously, this part of the country had been effectively isolated by the formidable peaks of the Cordillera de Talamanca.

17. The majority of migrants to Pejibaye originated either from the Valle Central in central Costa Rica or from towns in the vicinity of San Isidro, just to the north of the district.

18. The unit of land measure in Costa Rica is the *manzana*, equivalent to 0.7 ha. This unit will be used in this paper.

19. The unit of currency in Costa Rica is the colon (ϕ). In 1977, the official rate of exchange was ϕ8.6 = US$1.

20. Luella N. Dambaugh, *The Coffee Frontier in Brazil*, Latin American Monographs no. 7 (Gainesville: University of Florida Press, 1959), p. 26.

21. Of importance, this increase was in real monetary value since, until the early 1960s, the national rate of inflation in Costa Rica was near zero.

22. Moreover, in Costa Rica, land is customarily purchased in interest-free installments, with 10% of the sale price made as down payment, and another 10% paid annually until the debt is cancelled. Because of this practice, a settler would really have needed only ϕ10 in 1945 to purchase a farm worth ϕ10,000 by 1965; alternately, a ϕ100 down payment would actually have fetched a farm worth ϕ100,000 by 1965.

23. Theoretically, this process is capable of endless replication. However, the term "two-step" migration seems more appropriate than does "multistep" migration since the duration of the human life span places practical limits to the number of movements that can be achieved. Because an average of 10–20 years is needed on each frontier before "land inflation" takes full effect, movement is normally restricted to two frontiers. Among migrants to Pejibaye, none ever completed a third settlement of this type, although several purchased land on a third frontier while remaining in Pejibaye.

24. Apparently not all colonists were equally positioned to later effect two-step migratory strategies. Thus, successful two-step migrants were more likely than others to have (1) derived from families with a previous history of frontier settlement, a factor which provided them with the knowledge and experience needed for their successful transition to pioneer life; and (2) maintained and fully utilized kinship support networks which were critical both in providing them with information about newly opened frontiers as well as forming a social safety net which enabled them to take the risks necessary to ultimate success.

25. Sandner (n. 10 above), 1:151; 2:7–8.

26. Wilburg Jiménez Castro, *Migraciones internas en Costa Rica* (Washington, D.C.: Unión Panamericana, 1956), pp. 85–90.

27. Wava G. Haney, "Educational and Occupational Attainment of Migrants and Nonmigrants from a Colombian Highland Community" (Ph.D. diss., University of Wisconsin, 1972), p. 154.

28. Joseph R. Thome, "Title Problems in Rural Areas: A Colonization Example," in *Internal Colonialism and Structural Change in Colombia*, ed. A. Eugene Havens and William L. Flinn (New York: Praeger Publishers, 1970), p. 160.

29. Billington (n. 8 above), p. 6.

30. Margolis (n. 10 above), p. 11.

31. The most notable of these exceptions involves United Fruit Co. plantations on the east and west coasts of Costa Rica.

18 Joe Foweraker ◆ Violence on the Frontier

*In this selection from his 1981 study, British political scientist Joe
Foweraker explains the violent nature of Brazil frontiers, which deprive
peasants of opportunities to become landowners, much less Jeffersonian
democrats.* His cogent explanation of the internal causes of violence
appeared as part of a larger study, in which Foweraker attributed frontier violence to the world capitalist order. Countries like Brazil, he
argues, which are "dependent" in the world system, must adopt strong
measures to produce high rates of profit for foreign investors. They cannot afford the luxury of small, unprofitable peasant farms. In contrast to
the United States, which he defines as a liberal capitalist state, he regards Brazil and other dependent countries as authoritarian. "Violence,"
he asserts, "is one . . . characteristic of the authoritarian capitalist state"
(p. 214)—and clearly, in his view, of its frontiers.*

*Professor Foweraker is senior lecturer in Latin American politics at
the University of Essex in England. In addition to his work on Brazil, he
has published* Making Democracy in Spain: Grass-roots Struggle in the
South, 1955–1975 *(Cambridge: Cambridge University Press, 1989) and
is co-editor, with Ann L. Craig, of* Popular Movements and Political Change
in Mexico *(Boulder: Lynne Rienner, 1990).*

P easants come to the frontier in search of land to settle and so provide
for their subsistence. They and their families supply the labour to
clear the land, which they claim by their occupation of it. The journey to
the frontier may be long and hazardous and the work of clearing arduous.
But the peasants have heard the word of the 'common land,' the 'free
land,' the 'land of the nation' (Keller 1973), which they may take for
themselves. They press forward in the hope of land to have and to hold. It
is their activity on the ground which makes the frontier.

This initial occupation of the land combines abundant labour and land
in a spontaneous growth of subsistence agriculture which requires neither infrastructure nor a market. The peasants clear a space in forest or
scrub for cultivating the traditional staples (maize, manioc, rice, beans,
plantains) or raising a few pigs. Farming is extensive, by slash and burn

From *The Struggle for Land: A Political Economy of the Pioneer Frontier in
Brazil from 1930 to the Present Day*, 13–19. © 1981 by Cambridge University
Press. Reprinted by permission of Cambridge University Press.

*For developments since 1980, see Marianne Schmink and Charles Howard
Wood, *Contested Frontiers in Amazonia* (New York: Columbia University Press,
1992).

techniques, with little or no animal traction, and the hoe the only instrument of cultivation. Soon more peasants, perhaps relatives or friends, arrive and claim adjacent plots or buy or receive some of the land already claimed. As occupation intensifies so production increases and the peasants begin not only to produce for subsistence but to negotiate a surplus. Small 'centres' (*centros*) or 'villages' (*povoados*) grow up in such areas for marketing crops and providing basic services. These services include the sale of necessities and luxuries (kerosene, salt, hardware, alcohol, tobacco) and the many bars, hotels and brothels so typical of the frontier town. In short, it seems that occupation of the land will lead to settlement.

But the peasants' hold on the land is precarious and they may not enjoy possession of it for long. This precarity is partly intrinsic to the process of occupation itself, which sees a progressive reduction in the size of peasant plots as its intensity increases. This tendency for the small-holdings to become smaller may combine with a rapid decline in the fertility of the soil to cause crop yields to fall sharply after very few years. The weeds which were destroyed by the fire return and the land no longer 'gives'. This is the easily recognisable malaise of minifundio, which may force the peasant to move forward to the next frontier. But, just as minifundio can only be understood in the context of the near monopoly of land-holding in the Brazilian countryside in general, so the precarity of the pioneer peasants' hold on the land is only comprehensible in terms of the *reproduction* of that monopoly on the frontier.

Peasants claim the land by their labour on it and occupation of it. Their claims are nearly always contested, however, by local land-holders, regional 'political chiefs', or more or less distant entrepreneurs. These large land-holders and big companies assert their 'rights' to the land against the 'claims' of the peasants, and attempt to appropriate the land which the peasants have occupied. Significantly the 'rights' of the economically and politically powerful will very likely not prevent the peasants' occupation of the land, but only facilitate their final eviction from it. In this way a prospective cattle-rancher, for instance, can profit from the peasant labour of clearing the land, by putting down pasture and raising cattle in place of people. In general, it is not only land which is appropriated but the value created by peasant labour in the process of occupation.

This pattern of appropriation is nothing new in the history of the frontier. . . , and it is perpetuated contemporarily on the 'new' frontiers. The roads built from Brasília to Belém and Brasília to Acre, not to mention the Transamazônica, provoked a rush for land among entrepreneurs from Bahia, Espirito Santo, and Goiás, and companies and consortia from São

Paulo, Rio Grande do Sul, Paraná, and even the United States of America. The peasants who laid claim to the land find that it is 'bosses' land', 'legal land' like that they left behind, and are forced to leave (or, more rarely, to do 'hired work'). But their pioneering activity was already a result of a monopoly of land elsewhere in the Brazilian countryside, which has today left an estimated six million peasants landless (*Estado de São Paulo* 1975). As land is their means of survival they cannot capitulate so easily in this unequal competition for land. They face the competition by clinging to the land, and the economic process of occupation becomes a political struggle torn by violence.

Academic analysis has not taken sufficient account of this violence. On the one hand, most discussions of violence in the countryside in general have referred to the extra-economic coercion exercised on the large landed estates (Andrade 1963), to the fighting and feuding between local political bosses (Pereira de Queiroz 1969) or to the era of the *cangaçeiros* [bandits from Paraíba and Pernambuco] (Faco 1965); on the other, the best known of the frontier studies have tended to ignore it. Monbeig's study of the coffee frontier traces the expansion of the large estates of the São Paulo entrepreneurs, and where he does encounter frontier settlement by small farmers it is in the highly atypical case of the north of Paraná, which saw the most ordered colonisation ever experienced in Brazil (Monbeig 1952). Jean Roche, in his meticulous studies of the settlement of Rio Grande do Sul and Espirito Santo by German migrants and small farmers (Roche 1959, 1968), favours an analysis of the pattern of economic development and pays scant attention to its political context. Indeed, far from being presented as violent, the frontier has often been viewed as a 'safety-valve' which releases the social tensions in the countryside at large by providing possibilities for movement and improvement and so reducing the prevailing incidence of violence. Finally, where violence on the frontier cannot be ignored it is not explained, but simply classified as criminal (Fontana 1960).

In this respect academic analysis has not advanced beyond the dominant ideological view of the frontier violence, but has rather accepted the ideological categories as a true representation of reality. The purpose of these categories, which themselves resemble the nice distinctions of academic analysis, is to divide the frontier peasants into different *types* of social actor, and then blame the violence on one 'criminal' type. In this way the class nature of the struggle for land is negated, and the violence 'explained' at the level of the 'conspiracy'.

The pioneer peasant is known as the *posseiro*, and the complex range of ideological categories, which vary in time and place, have tended to coalesce around a broad but basic distinction between two types of *posseiro*

(Foweraker 1974). On the one hand there is the *posseiro* who occupies the land not to cultivate it but to sell it. He is probably the first to the frontier and works to stake a claim (*posse*) which he can then sell to another peasant. This type is often referred to as the *desbravador de mato*, or 'forest-cutter', and in this interpretation does not remain long on the land, but shifts repeatedly from one claim to the next. The reality underlying the type embraces the many, mostly unrecorded, transactions where claims are indeed sold, not only for money, but for pigs, cows, revolvers, women, and other frontier currency. On the other hand, there is the *posseiro* who does not wish to sell the land but to farm it. He may arrive later to the frontier and buy a claim rather than stake one out for himself. He wants to work the land, has probably paid for it, and so will be reluctant to move.

The second type of *posseiro* is seen as more or less socially 'acceptable'. He works the land and produces. When joined by family and friends from his region of origin he will form frontier communities and begin to civilise the jungle. And, in fact, as many as twenty families migrate together and cluster in the communities of this 'domestic colonisation' (*colonização mansa*), which brings cohesion to frontier society. But the forest-cutter is viewed with more ambivalence. He leads a wild and predatory existence and becomes brutalised by the nature of his work. He is confused, sometimes in fact but more often in fancy, with the criminals who escape society's retribution by living at its edge—on the frontier. Therefore if he is not criminal himself he is infected by an atmosphere of revolt and has nothing but contempt for 'owners'; in his work, possession of the land is its only true title.

Once these types are clearly established it is relatively easy to 'explain' the violence in one of two ways. Firstly, and true to the idea of 'conspiracy', it is possible to represent the 'forest-cutter' as a criminal minority, which will even engage in a '*posse* industry' (perhaps directed by 'subversives'), and invade land already claimed by others, or land which is in dispute, and afterwards sell it again, or demand compensation for withdrawal. Secondly, after recognising that frontier 'farmers' are prepared to respect boundary lines between claims, a more general 'explanation' can focus attention on the 'internal' antagonisms between the two types of *posseiro* with their contrasting behaviour patterns and contrary economic interests. Not surprisingly, academic analysis has taken up the latter, and supposedly 'structural' approach. Velho, in his monograph on Marabá (Velho 1972) speaks of a climate of violence existing between 'more marginal elements' and the farmers; and Monteiro, writing of the migrants of the north of Paraná, finds attitudes either of total conformity or of extreme unrest and revolt (Monteiro 1961). So the typologies which distinguish frontier farmers of 'good faith', on the one hand, who wish to develop a stable pattern of settlement, and the 'marginal minority' on the other, who revolt against the imposition of such a pattern, allow the latter to carry the blame for conflicts over land.

The peasant view of the violence which appears in the popular lore of the frontier is very different. In broad terms peasant perceptions are mystified but reflect their lived experience of subjection and exploitation. The *posseiro* is not seen as actively shaping frontier society, but, on the contrary, as passively moulded by the environment (Westphalen 1968). Just as violence is done to nature, so violence is done to men, and the rules of human interaction match the harshness of the frontier. The peasants do not refer to the misery of a life of bare subsistence, with no vestige of comfort or security, but to the prevailing economic activity on the frontier, which is predatory. In this aggressive atmosphere man degenerates, he attacks nature in search of survival but in the end 'it is the man who is finished'. Moreover, these perceptions are compatible with more general 'explanations' of the poverty and disease of the frontier population as the results of certain characteristics of the 'race' or 'blood' which make the peasant incapable of improvement, and 'uncooperative'. There is no possibility of progress on the frontier because 'here in Brazil everyone wants to eat everyone else'.

Even at this level peasant perceptions are more successful in pinpointing the causes of violence than the dominant ideological categories, if only because personal vendettas and predation of the environment no doubt contribute to the violence. In particular, it is lumbering activity which is notorious in this respect; on every frontier literally hundreds of 'undercover' sawmills whine away during the process of occupation, trees even being cut under cover of darkness by peasants employed by the companies and armed with chainsaws (CODEPAR 1964). Lumber interests often provoke conflict and encourage invasion of land in order to put property rights in doubt (Shigueru 1972; Souza Melo 1976), so as to extract the trees more easily. Finally, however, explorations of this order must refer to the different fractions of capital ('extractive', 'commercial') which compete in the appropriation of the land, and of the frontier surplus. . . .

Moreover, frontier lore also points occasionally to certain regional groups as responsible for the violence (Keller 1973). Such groups may include southerners, *paulistas, mineiros, bahianos, capixabas, goiânos* [residents of the provinces of São Paulo, Minas Gerais, Bahía, Espirito Santo, and Goiás, respectively], depending on the period and place of the frontier. This peasant name-calling successfully identifies as a group not the peasants themselves, who may also have a predominantly regional origin, but the large landowners and entrepreneurs who threaten the peasants' possession of the land. In referring to those 'others' from 'over there', far from their world, the peasants conceive of the antagonism at the level of the secondary, cultural or regional, contradiction but, inevitably, throw into relief the primary class contradiction between themselves and the large owners as the cause of the violence. Their view may be provincial but it is shaped by struggle.

The peasant view goes a long way toward capturing what is common to these 'others', who may appear on the frontier in different guises—or may never appear themselves at all—and so make 'their' identification difficult. The 'others' may include local land-holders and politicians, individual entrepreneurs, and large economic enterprises associated with both national and international capital. They assert their 'rights' against the peasants' claims to land, although they may have no better title and far less right to the land than the peasants themselves (who, in law, may assert 'right of possession' by occupying and working the land). They accuse the peasant *posseiros* of invading land which is private property or of criminal practice of a *posse* industry, but among their number must be included the land-grabbers and land-speculators (*grileiros* in the vernacular) who attempt to validate their claims through fraudulent titles to land, which are corruptly issued, or through forged titles which are, of course, never issued at all. In short, while some of the title-holders arriving fresh to the frontier may be genuine applicants for land, many are simply speculators looking to amass large estates and cheat the peasants of the land. Such divergent motives, however, merge in the objective class interest in monopoly of land, which sets the peasants against these 'others'; they are 'others' in the essential sense of seeking profit from land, and not simply survival.

In their struggle for land the peasants confront not only the 'others' but also 'their' representatives both 'public' and 'private' (Ianni 1977). The public representatives are principally the cadres of the bureaucracy and legal apparatuses of the State, while the private representatives are the gunmen hired by the others to protect their land from invasion or to clear peasants from land which they claim. The primary antagonism on the frontier exists between the peasants and the 'others', but, as suggested above, this antagonism is mediated by the operation of law and bureaucracy, and the direct exercise of violence.

The bureaucratic cadres present on the frontier include the officers and employees and technical advisers of local state departments and extension services, and Federal State agencies, especially land and 'development' agencies. The law is manifest in police, lawyers and judges. It is relatively rare for the army itself to intervene on the frontier, except in cases of widespread unrest, but many of the administrators are in fact military men. The gunmen are the 'owners' bandits (*jagunços*); they are usually peasants who try to escape the burdens of class and poverty by joining the oppressors (individual rebelliousness is socially neutral— Hobsbawm 1959). Some may be condemned criminals (recruited from the state prisons, it is rumoured on the frontier); others come from outside Brazil. Private and public representatives may join forces as when gunmen and police operate together, or as when gunmen (*mata-páu*) are employed by the police. But even where they do not, the private practice of violence and intimidation, and the public mediation of the struggle are closely linked.

The peasants on the frontier experience violence not occasionally but persistently. It pervades their struggle for land both in their confrontation with civil society in the form of the 'others' and in their contacts with the State. Like all peasantries, they themselves have no representation at the level of the State, and it becomes clear through their contacts with the State that the range of legal and political apparatuses present on the frontier are finally arrayed against them. This is not to deny the conflicts and contradictions among these apparatuses, nor the limited victories won by the peasants in their struggle, both of which will become apparent in the subsequent analysis; it is merely to assert that (private) violence and State apparatuses complement each other in mediating the struggle for land, and hence the cycle of accumulation on the frontier.

References

Andrade, M. C. 1963. *A terra e o homem no nordeste*. Brasiliense, Rio de Janeiro.
CODEPAR (Companhia de Desenvolvimento do Paraná). 1964. *O Paraná e a Economia Madeireira*.
Estado de São Paulo. 1975. "Amazônia: dez anos de colonização," by Lucio Flavio Pinto et al. 3–11 November.
Faco, R. 1965. *Cangaçeiros e fanáticos: gênese e lutas*. Civilização Brasileira, Rio de Janeiro.
Fontana, A. 1960. "A colonização do oeste catarinense." *Anúario Brasileiro de Imigração e Colonização*, p. 37.
Foweraker, J. W. 1974. "Political conflict on the frontier." D.Phil., Oxford University.
Hobsbawm, E. J. 1959. *Primitive rebels*. University of Manchester Press.
Ianni, O. 1977. *A luta pela terra*. CEBRAP—Programa de População—Pesquisa Nacional sobre Reprodução Humana, São Paulo. March.
Keller, F. I. V. 1973. "O homen da frente de expansão: permanência, mundança e conflito." Divisão de Antropologia, Museu Nacional.
Monbeig, P. 1952. *Pionniers et planteurs de São Paulo*. Armand Colin, Paris.
———. 1957. "Evolucao de generos de vida rural tradicionals no sudoeste do Brasil." *Novos Estudos de Geografia Humana Brasileira*. DIFEL. São Paulo.

Monteiro, D. T. 1961. "Estrutura social e vida economica em uma área de pequena propriedade e de monocultura." *Revista brasileira de Estudos Políticos* No. 12. October.

Pereira de Queiroz, M. I. 1969. *O Mandonismo local na vida política brasileira.* Universidade de São Paulo.

Roche, J. 1959. *La Colonisation Allemande et le Rio Grande do Sul.* Université de Paris (Institut des Hautes Études). Paris.

———. 1968. *A colonização alemã no Espirito Santo.* DIFEL. São Paulo.

Velho, O. G. 1969. "O conceito do camponês e sua aplicação a análise do meio rural brasileiro." *América Latina* No. 1. January–March.

Westphalen, C. M.; Pinheiro Machado, B.; Balhama, A. P. 1968. *Nota prévia ao estudo da ocupação da terra no Paraná.* Boletim da Universidade Federal do Paraná, Conselho de Pesquisas Departamento da Historia No. 7.

19 Alcida R. Ramos ◆ Frontier Expansion and Indian Peoples in the Brazilian Amazon

The expansion of European frontiers has been at the expense of native peoples everywhere in the Western Hemisphere. In Brazil, for example, only 190,000 aborigines remain today of an estimated population of up to five million in the sixteenth century. Moreover, as Alcida R. Ramos shows in this essay, since World War II the devastation of native cultures has intensified in the Amazon region because of government-sponsored highway construction, colonization, and unrestrained exploitation by national and multinational agribusiness firms. Her description of the ineffectiveness of official institutions founded to defend the natives and the blatant subversion of protective legislation by government officials is a tragic reminder of the human costs of so-called development. Perhaps the only bright spot in this deplorable history has been the efforts of the Indians since 1970 to organize themselves after decades of neglect and misinformation. Ramos believes that the new Indian movement is a living demonstration of their resilience. She suggests that although the discrimination and oppression are certain to continue, the young Indian leaders are aware that with the support of civil society, they must interact and negotiate their claims with the government to ensure the survival of their cultures.

Ramos is a Brazilian anthropologist who has carried out extensive research with the Sanuma, a subgroup of the Yanomami Indians in north Brazil. She received her Ph.D. from the University of Wisconsin in Madison and currently teaches at the University of Brasília in Brazil.

Since the discovery of Brazil, contact between Indians and whites has been a repeated history of Indian decimation, flight, and withdrawal, until now when there is no refuge left. Hemming (1978) has written in great detail of the destruction and displacement of Indian groups from 1500 to the 1760s. Darcy Ribeiro (1970) provides a vivid account of the losses suffered by indigenous peoples in their tragic contact with whites into the twentieth century. From an estimated population of two to five million in the 1500s, the number of Indians in Brazil dropped to around 150,000 in the 1950s.

In this century alone, at least eighty-seven Indian groups have become extinct or nearly so. In 1900 about 46 percent of the estimated total

From *Frontier Expansion in Amazonia*, ed. Marianne Schmink and Charles H. Wood (Gainesville: University of Florida Press, 1984), 83–104. Reprinted by permission.

Indian population was isolated from white contact. Sixty years later, only half that percentage was still living in isolation (Ribeiro 1970:237). Today there are at most three or four uncontacted groups. These data convey some idea of the intensity and speed of encroachment on Indian populations. The total number of Indians in Brazil is now estimated to be just under 190,000, or less than 0.2 percent of the country's population (*Porantim*, April 1982:3–13). Their total territory has been reduced to less than 6 percent of the country's area.

From the sixteenth century to the present, Indian decimation and displacement in Brazil have resulted from continued attempts to attain economic development at the expense of the country's Indian inhabitants. Beginning on the coast during the sixteenth century, many Indians were enslaved, to work first in the extraction of *pau-brasil* and later on the sugar plantations of the Northeast. Much Indian territory was expropriated. Crowded into missionary "reductions," thousands of Indians died of imported Old World diseases. Most of the early aboriginal inhabitants of the Northeast have disappeared, and the remaining groups are a small remnant of their original populations (Ribeiro 1970:57, Carvalho 1982).

Cattle ranching has threatened Indian life in the Northeast and other regions. In the South, land-hungry cattle ranchers occupied enormous tracts of land and organized expeditions to kill off entire Indian communities. . . . Later, colonizing Europeans and coffee planters continued the massacres and usurpation of lands of surviving Indian groups in the South. In summary, the opening up of new frontiers has historically resulted in the decimation and, in many cases, the total extinction of Indian groups. Western diseases, slavery, and punitive expeditions have been the three main instruments which have wiped out Indian populations in Brazil (Ramos 1980a:222).

Economic activities and their attendant missionization are not new in Amazonia. The region has witnessed several surges in the extraction of products, including sarsaparilla, various essences, resins, rubber, guaraná, pepper, jute, and, more recently, cocoa. Since the sixteenth century these activities were carried out often at the cost of Indian lives and welfare, taking the heaviest toll on those groups who lived along the main rivers. By the end of the eighteenth century, such groups as the Omagua and the Tapajós were extinct, after having been culturally deprived by the force of missionary action (Meggers 1971). The rubber industry was responsible for much enslaving, uprooting, unrest, and death among Indian populations forcibly engaged in latex extraction.

Indians became a demographic minority not only in Brazil but also in Canada and in the United States. In these North American countries, Indian groups were relegated to land areas of negligible size compared to the territories they originally occupied. The struggle to maintain even those small holdings continues, not only in Brazil but also in most New World countries. While disease has been a major cause of decimation (Jennings 1975, Ribeiro 1970), economic forces and official policies and legislation vis-à-vis indigenous people have also played a part.

A massive intensification of economic activities has occurred in recent decades in Amazonia, with disastrous effects for the region's indigenous populations. In response to the threats posed by these numerous development projects, a pan-Indian movement began to emerge in Brazil in the 1970s. In the remainder of this paper, I will explore recent economic changes in Amazonia, evolving official policies vis-à-vis Indians in Brazil, and the responses of indigenous groups to these threats.

The Amazonian Frontier

The current intensified assault on Amazonia had its origin several decades ago. During and after World War II, the so-called *Marcha para o Oeste* called for the occupation of the hinterlands west of the coastal states and Minas Gerais. Ideological justifications stressed national sovereignty and the need for Brazilians to occupy these "empty spaces." The states of Goiás and Mato Grosso were the main targets of the Marcha, and Indian groups living in these areas were directly affected by the expansion of the national society. Led by the Villas Boas brothers and others, the Roncador-Xingu expedition in the late 1940s resulted in the creation of the Xingu Park, in which congregated more than a dozen Indian groups. During this period, peoples such as the Bororo and Tapirapé went through an acute phase of depopulation. The Sherente were plagued by conflicts with invading cattle ranchers. The Shavante were pacified in the 1940s. . . .

In the 1950s the construction of highways linked to the new capital of Brasília provoked another crisis for a number of small Indian groups. These Indian peoples underwent a sudden transition from isolation from *civilizados* to a dependence on the products of the national society: medicines, steel tools, clothing, salt, sugar, transistors, batteries, matches, alcohol. Prostitution, begging, and general social chaos replaced traditional ways of life. . . .

The military coup of 1964 did little to slow the demise of Indian populations. Instead, the locus of frontier expansion and investment shifted from the Center-West to Amazonia proper. The road construction program that began during President Médici's National Integration Plan (PIN) was followed by President [Ernestó] Geisel's Polamazonia program of mineral research and extraction, and the massive establishment of agribusiness and construction of hydroelectric dams. The same priorities have been followed by the current [João Batista] Figueiredo administration. The impact of road construction and of the implementation of large-scale development projects has been documented for numerous cases in the Amazon region.

Highways constructed under the PIN infringed on the territory of no less than ninety-six Indian groups (56 percent of the total number in Amazonia). Another sixty-five Indian groups are located within a hundred kilometers of one or another highway (Goodland and Irwin 1975:74). Road construction has had disastrous effects on formerly isolated Indian communities that were exposed to workers carrying measles, malaria, influenza, and other respiratory diseases. . . .

National and multinational firms, responding to government incentives for agribusiness in the Amazon region, also threaten native communities. In the mid-1970s it was reported that these Indians would suffer the direct consequences of deforestation and occupation of their lands: nine Apalaí villages and several Kayapó groups in the state of Pará; the Tembé/Urubu Kaapor Indian reserves in Maranhão; the northern groups of the Xingu Park, several Shavante reserves, the Tapirapé Indians and the Araguaia Indian Park in Mato Grosso (*Opinião* April 18, 1975; Davis 1977). . . .

Among the largest colonization enterprises in Amazonia is the Polonoroeste Project in the states of Mato Grosso and Rondônia. One of its main purposes is to rationalize the settlement process in the area in question, which experienced a population increase on the order of 11 percent per year between 1970 and 1980. By 1985 it is expected to have over 2 million people. For the future settlement of 30,000 families in the area, the Brazilian government will invest approximately $1.4 billion (35 percent of which is a loan from the World Bank) to construct and pave a vast road network, and to demarcate 3 million hectares of rural properties (*Jornal de Brasília*, May 28, 1981). The project also provides for extraction of minerals and forest products as well as for agribusiness operations.

There are about thirty Indian groups in the area with a total of around 8,000 people living in fifty-eight villages. While different groups vary in their degree of contact with the national society, the land rights of all groups are equally threatened (CEDI 1982). . . .

The mining operations programmed during the Geisel administration have also had disruptive effects on Indian groups. Those perhaps worst hit so far have been the Indians of the Aripuanã area in Rondônia and Mato Grosso, where large deposits of cassiterite and other minerals have been found. The Cinta Larga, Suruí, Arara, and other groups of the region have had the size of their territories drastically reduced, and their populations have declined considerably. The presence of minerals in their lands has subjected the Cita Larga to air bombings, food poisoning, and other acts of violence by adventurers in search of riches. These events were much publicized in 1963. And, again, Western diseases have contributed heavily to the near extinction of this group. . . .

The most recent threat to Indians in Amazonia is posed by the enormous Carajás Project in Pará and Maranhão. The project will directly affect nine Indian groups in Pará, Maranhão, and Northern Goiás, a total of 4,360 Indians living in 42 villages. With a total cost of $62 billion, this initiative is comprised of numerous subprojects that involve a mineral-metallurgical scheme and agricultural, cattle-ranching, and reforestation projects. Related infrastructural investments include the Tucuruí dam, construction of the railroad from Carajás (in southern Pará) to Itaqui (on the Atlantic coast), and a network of 2,000 kilometers of river routes on the Araguaia and Tocantins. Six great industrial poles are being prepared in Pará and Maranhão (*Porantim*, No. 43, September 1982:8–10).

The initial phase of the project began in 1973 with the construction of the Tucuruí dam. Although the Carajás project has been under way for at least ten years, authorities have failed to provide the necessary protective measures for Indian peoples. . . .

Many other cases could be cited of Indian peoples who have been victimized by the expansion of Brazilian national society into Amazonia. Their presence belies the centuries-old rhetoric calling for the occupation of the nation's *espaços vazios* ("empty spaces"). The persistence of Indian populations, despite severe threats to their existence, poses a continuing dilemma for those seeking to promote frontier activities. Official Indian policies have addressed this question over the past seventy years.

Official Indian Policy

Before 1910 there was no overall federal policy regarding Indian populations in Brazil. Land donations, expropriations, evictions, and deals of various kinds related to Indians were in the hands of the colonial officials and later of the provincial and state authorities. The creation of the SPI (Indian Protection Service) in 1910 marked the new era of state responsibility for the Indians. Since then the Brazilian state has assumed the role of intermediary between the rights of the Indian peoples and the interests of the national (and sometimes foreign) society.

Since the creation of the SPI, official efforts have been directed toward bringing hostile or isolated Indians into contact with the national society under the supervision of the protectionist agency. It was the SPI's founder, Marshal Candido Mariano da Silva Rondon, who established the practice known as pacification, more recently relabeled "attraction." Pacification or attraction teams approach Indians who either have no contact or are hostile to whites and lure them into accepting the presence of invaders. Steel tools, beads, cooking pots, combs, and other trinkets are used in the process. It sometimes takes many years before an Indian group finally gives in and lets itself be persuaded to accept the outsiders in a friendly way. But by that time the Indians have become accustomed to the free gifts provided. The all-too-common begging that follows pacification may result from this phase of courting (a term used by the *sertanistas*). Attraction teams produce what must seem to an Indian an inexhaustible supply of trade goods. The shock of realizing that they have to pay dearly for these goods comes too late to most Indians. Successful pacification is but the first step to forcing the Indians into an irreversible condition of dependence on the national society, one from which they are unlikely ever to escape.

With the creation of the Indian Protection Service, Brazilian Indians came to be legally considered minors under the wardship of the state. The civil code is explicit in declaring the Indians, along with individuals under eighteen years of age, to be relatively incapable. Indians could not be considered normal citizens due to their ethnic specificities and their unfamiliarity with the ways of the national society. In order to provide legally for the special status of the Indians vis-à-vis Brazilian citizens, the government adopted this solution of guardianship, which had been practiced in the New World since the eighteenth century (Bennett 1978:7). Although their condition as wards of the state leaves the Indians highly vulnerable to paternalistic attitudes and actions, it is nevertheless one way to guarantee their protection against exploitation.

The humanitarian and conscientious attitude that apparently guided the pioneer pacification teams has steadily deteriorated. In recent years there have been cases of Indians catching venereal diseases, tuberculosis, influenza, measles, and other illnesses from members of attraction teams. Increasing corruption and complicity with outside interests eventually led to the collapse of the SPI. In 1967 an investigative committee documented the corruption and criminal activities of many SPI employees. The lengthy report (5,115 pages) concluded that the SPI was no longer able to defend Indian rights. In 1968 a new agency replaced the SPI, the National Indian Foundation (FUNAI).

FUNAI not only inherited the basic problem that crippled its predecessor; it also generated problems of its own. Being a division of the Ministry of the Interior, FUNAI does not possess sufficient political and financial autonomy to assist the Indians when such aid runs contrary to interests of the government or of the private sector. Moreover, even within its narrow margin for operation as genuine protector and guardian of Indian interests, FUNAI is often ineffective. Unwarranted decisions taken by incompetent bureaucrats at all levels of its rigid hierarchy, and corruption by some of its officials, have led to some lamentable performances by FUNAI.

For two or three years after it was created, FUNAI was administered by people who, if not stern defenders of Indian rights, at least could not be considered enemies of the Indians. But from 1970 on, with few exceptions, FUNAI's presidents and high officials have taken actions that have definitely harmed Indian interests. General Bandeira de Mello, whose term coincided with Médici's highway program in Amazonia, is notorious for having issued a number of negative certificates to cattle ranchers in the Guaporé Valley. These certificates, the issuing of which is FUNAI's exclusive responsibility, affirm that since no Indians live in the area in question, the land is available for occupation. In fact, it is well known that the Guaporé Valley has been the homeland of many Nambiquara communities as well as those of other groups. Yet Bandeira de Mello defended the routing of highways through Indian areas as a means of bringing progress to the Indians.

In 1974 the presidency of FUNAI passed from General Bandeira de Mello to General Ismarth de Araújo Oliveira, a change that meant a three-year period of relative respite for the Indians. But before the end of Araújo's term, the Indians faced one of the greatest threats to their ethnic and territorial integrity, the attempt to emancipate them by presidential decree. This attempt will be explored in greater detail.

General Ismarth's presidency was followed by a short-lived hopeful period under Adhemar Ribeiro da Silva (former director of the National Highway Department) who, to everyone's surprise, showed himself inclined to defend the Indian cause. He resigned after seven months. His successor, Colonel João Nobre da Veiga, made Bandeira de Mello seem a mild figure by comparison. He issued outright anti-Indian statements, and his allegiance to economic groups interested in Indian resources was unconcealed. There were mass firings of competent anthropologists who had been hired during the terms of his two predecessors. Incompetent and ultrarightist military advisors were installed. Indian areas were closed to researchers, journalists, and other concerned people. All these actions contributed to a period of terror for Indians and for whites involved in Indian problems. The infamous criteria of Indianness, which will be discussed, were prepared during Nobre da Veiga's term of office.[1]

In 1981 Nobre da Veiga was replaced by Colonel Paulo Moreira Leal. As a member of the National Security Council, Leal had appeared to understand and sympathize with Indian problems. But within a year of his installation in office, Leal showed signs of moving in the opposite direction. Some positive results were achieved, such as the demarcation of the Tapirapé tribal territory. But Leal was under tremendous pressure from interest groups, especially in the turmoil of the preelection period.

The most outstanding victims of this pressure were the Hã-hã-hãe Pataxó in the state of Bahia. Powerful entrepreneurs had been leasing Pataxó lands since the 1920s, which had caused the Indians to be evicted from their own communities. In April of 1982, backed by FUNAI and the Federal Police, they returned to their homeland after having been dispersed in Bahia and Minas Gerais. There was quick, strong reaction from the cattle ranchers and cocoa growers in the area, with the undivided support of the governor, Antônio Carlos Magalhães of Bahia state. In the interest of the incumbent PDS [Partido Democrático Social], facing an electoral challenge, together they pressured the president of FUNAI to move the Indians to another place. Colonel Leal gave in and illegally proceeded to transfer fifty Pataxó families, promising them that they could return to their land in a few months (after the election on November 15, 1982).

Brazilian Indian policy has become more closely linked with questions of landownership and as such has become part of the national security issue. Land problems are now handled by the newly created Ministério Extraordinârio para Assuntos Fundiários (Extraordinary Ministry for Land Issues) under the responsibility of General Danillo Venturini, secretary of the National Security Council.[2]

The Indian Statute

In 1973, Law 6,001, the Indian Statute, was passed in Congress. Although not a single Indian was consulted about this legislation, the statute (and articles 4 and 198 of the 1967 Constitution) provides for the protection of Indian rights to land, to natural resources, to community life, and to their own culture and traditions. Some of its provisions, however, permit a margin for the government to remove Indians from their lands legally whenever national interests are at stake. Article 20 says that Indian groups can be removed to another area as an exceptional measure and by decree of the president of the Republic. Furthermore, according to Brazilian law, subsoil resources belong to the Union and not to those who own or occupy the land. This provision makes mining on Indian lands perfectly legal if done by means other than surface collecting. With these provisions in hand, the state has the necessary legal tools to remove Indian populations by simply declaring an Indian area to be a National Security Area. Nevertheless, as it stands, the Indian Statute still guarantees many

Indian rights, for example, the Indian populations' exclusive usufruct of the land they occupy (ownership rights belong to the Union) and to all its natural resources (excluding the subsoil).

Since the late 1970s, there have been several attempts by FUNAI, the Ministry of the Interior, and some politicians to find a way around the Indian Statute. The first attempt was the emancipation decree. In 1978, Minister of the Interior Rangel Reis prepared the draft of a decree that would have made it possible to impose emancipation on Indian groups and individuals. Willingly or not, the president of FUNAI, General Ismarth de Araújo, had to go along with his superior. As a result of the tremendous rash of protests within Brazil and from abroad against this initiative, the emancipation decree was shelved. . . .

The emancipation decree can be seen as an attempt on the part of the authorities to liberate Indian lands by terminating the wardship of the Indians. With emancipation, ownership of the land would be transferred from the Union to the Indians themselves in the form of individual titles. Because such measures have historical precedents elsewhere in the New World, we may surmise their probable outcome. The Indians would soon be relieved of their newly acquired property by the pressures put upon them by non-Indians. . . .

By declaring the Indians emancipated, the Brazilian government would become the accomplice of those whose economic interests result in the exploitation of Indian populations. The minister's rhetoric was reminiscent of the North American rationale for the Dawes Act: the intention of the government, the minister once said, was in the long run to allow the Indians to become politicians, generals, and even presidents of the Republic [*Jornal de Brasília*, October 19, 1978; *Time*, November 13, 1978). But the history of Indian-white contact and the present trend of Brazilian economy and politics suggest that the emancipation decree would have put the Indians in an impossible situation, unable to continue with their traditional ways of life yet ill-equipped to cope with white society. Predictably the emancipation plan was received with a blast of criticism from those who argue that development should not be achieved at the expense of the Indians.

Turning Indians suddenly into ordinary Brazilian citizens would have other consequences besides the loss of official protection of their lands. It would also mean a threat to their freedom to act according to their own traditions. Common practices such as polygamy, infanticide, nudity, the use of hallucinogens, some mortuary rites, and certain modes of social control would automatically fall under the sanctions contained in the national civil and penal codes and no doubt would be instantly outlawed from the moment an Indian individual or community became emancipated. The repercussions of such prohibitions would naturally be numerous and are not too difficult to imagine. Social disruption would quickly follow the initial phase of psychological disorientation and shock. . . .

Another attempt to weaken Indian protection policies was the so-called criteria for Indianness, a creation of Colonel Zanoni Hausen, a FUNAI advisor left over from Nobre da Veiga's era. In January 1981, Zanoni created a committee of three FUNAI employees to devise a list of more than sixty items which were meant to be indices of Indianness or of integration, among them whether the Indian is a bearer of a "primitive mentality," of a "mongolic birthmark," of relative lack of body hair; whether he shows "social marginalization"; whether his character identity is latent; and many other such senseless propositions. Zanoni also proposed the "blood criteria," which consisted of taking blood samples from Indians to check for the presence of elements such as the Diego Factor said to be most frequent among American Indians. The idea behind this exercise was to place Indian individuals and populations on a scale of zero to 100; those who showed less than 50 percent of the traits were considered non-Indians, therefore falling outside the sphere of FUNAI's protection. In response, outraged Indians, missionaries, anthropologists, lawyers, and journalists bombarded FUNAI in the press, in public gatherings, and in professional meetings with accusations of racism. The criteria were apparently dropped, but not before their application to some Indians in the Northeast and to the Guarani of Ocoí, who lived in the area to be flooded by the Itaipu dam. The remarkable thing about these criteria was their unabashed illegality. The Indian Law defines as Indian anyone of pre-Columbian origin who considers himself to be Indian and who is considered by others as such, regardless of specific physical traits, psychological disposition, or degree of contact. The Indian Statute also provides for the emancipation of Indians, when they are well versed in the national way of life and *at their own request*.

Besides these attempts from within FUNAI to find loopholes in the Indian Statute or to modify it outright, there have been occasional suggestions from individuals outside the organization to change the Indian Law. A case in point was Roraima Representative Hélio Campos, who makes no secret of his interest in the minerals buried in Yanomami territory. In the name of national security, Campos proposed that all Indians be removed from the 150-kilometer strip along the country's borders and sent to its interior. He cited the example of the United States Indian Removal, a historical event known as the Trail of Tears, which resulted in the death of four thousand Cherokee during their removal west of the Mississippi. His proposal would mean the displacement of nearly half of the Indian population in Brazil, who would be thrown into areas already riddled with land conflicts. Campos's main argument was that the Indians, being ignorant, are easy prey to foreign mineral smugglers who pose as missionaries, so the matter became one of national security. Because it was blatantly unconstitutional, the project was rejected after having been denounced in the press.

The purpose of these legal gambits—emancipation, criteria of Indianness, displacement of Indian populations—is integration of the Indians, that is, the elimination of their cultural specificities. The emancipation of Indian groups from the condition of wards of the state is not a new idea; it dates back at least to the creation of the SPI. Marshal Rondon was convinced that Indians would be happier if civilized. . . . Since then the matter of integration has been present in all legislation that concerns Indians, culminating with the Indian Statute.

Indian Response

In the early 1970s, under the sponsorship of the Indigenist Missionary Council (CIMI), a progressive branch of the Catholic Church, Indian leaders from various parts of the country began to get together to exchange experiences. By providing transportation and accommodations, CIMI gave the necessary spark for the beginnings of a pan-Indian movement in Brazil.

The increasing awareness on the part of the Indians of their rights and how to fight for them was given a strong boost in 1978 by the government's attempt to emancipate the Indians. In a statement addressed to the president of the Republic, leaders from thirteen different Indian groups took a firm position against the emancipation decree. Their awareness of its implications is clear in their statement:

> Just as public opinion has condemned this emancipation so we also, in the name of the Brazilian Indian Community, repudiate this emancipation. Let it be removed from your office and let our claims be taken into consideration. . . . The emancipation desired by the Minister will only bring detribalization to the Indian communities, and therefore the collective and individual destruction of their members. (CIMI 1978b:22–24).

In 1980 a group of Indians assembled in Campo Grande, Mato Grosso do Sul, created the first Brazilian Indian organization, UNI or UNIND (União das Nacões Indígenas). This was during Colonel Nobre da Veiga's term as president of FUNAI. Repression against the Indians took various forms. One was the withdrawal of scholarships from young Indians studying in Brasília and the express order that they return to their original areas. Some went back; some did not. International events such as the Russell

Tribunal and the Merida and Puyo meetings of the Interamerican Indigenist Institute no doubt contributed to curbing further repressive actions, although the distaste of the authorities for the existence of UNI was hardly concealed. There was, in fact, an attempt by General Golbery do Couto e Silva to introduce a provision in the Indian Statute that would outlaw UNI, with the justification that Indians under the wardship of the state cannot create an autonomous organization (*Porantim*, May 1981:4). This attempt has apparently been abandoned; but the authorities, including the various presidents of FUNAI, were unanimous in rejecting the concept of "Indian nations," viewed as a threat to national security. Brazil, they say, is a Union which admits of no nations in its midst.

To assist the Indians in their new organizational needs, and to keep open the channels for denunciation of breach of their rights and for claims for just treatment, a number of white support groups were formed in the late 1970s. Most states have at least one of these groups, which are represented in Brasília by a central executive secretariat. They have provided legal advice, have amassed funds for nationwide Indian meetings, and have published material on Indian problems.

Why did Brazilian Indians take so long to organize themselves? There are several reasons. The gigantic size of the country and the difficulties of transportation and communication between remote areas impede mobilization. Indian peoples are dispersed throughout nearly all states and territories. They are also fragmented into a myriad of small societies with different languages, customs, and degrees of contact with whites. Last, but not least, organization has been impeded by the nature of official actions regarding the wardship of Indian peoples. In total command of the affairs of Indian villages, the government, first through the SPI and later through FUNAI, has been an inadequate guardian both by omission and by its harmful actions. Lack of access to education as well as economic, administrative, and political obstacles to intercommunication are the norm. Keeping the Indians ignorant is one way of retaining control over them (Ramos 1982).

The Indians are now beginning to organize themselves after decades of neglect and misinformation. At last they are beginning to play an active role in their own history. The pattern of the Brazilian Indian movement is the reverse of other associations in South America. In Ecuador, for instance, organization has grown from the base upwards. The fact that in Brazil the Indian movement has only been able to emerge from the top results from the deprivations mentioned, which were imposed on the Indian populations of the country by the authoritarian nature of official policy and practice. The most active leaders of the movement are young Indians who have managed to overcome these deprivations.

Conclusion

It is neither a new nor a surprising revelation that frontier expansion is accomplished to the detriment of Indian populations. The process of extermination of Indian lives and of illegal expropriation of their lands has as long a history as Brazil itself. There has been a remarkable continuity of this trend throughout the centuries. If anything is new about these past decades, it is the scope, the speed, and the virulence of the impact that the national society is having on practically all Indian peoples in the country. While in the past a group under pressure would last some centuries before its final collapse, nowadays a few months of contact are sufficient to bring an Indian group to the brink of extinction. This is true in spite of the fact that for more than seventy years the Indians have been under official protection.

In terms of legislation, Brazil's provisions for its Indian populations have been considered by outside critics to be humane and advanced. The 39th International Labor Conference of 1956, for example, approved the Indian policy of Brazil and recommended that other countries adopt it (Ribeiro 1970:141). But is legislation alone enough to protect the Indians? More than half a century of experience shows that it is not. Indeed there are many cases where the Indians needed to be protected from their assigned protectors.[3] Such are the contradictions of the wardship system as it is put into actual practice.

It is common to hear people express the opinion that the Indians are doomed, that the inexorable march of progress leaves no room for atavisms such as Indian cultures. Will they survive? If we take the position that Indians are only those who live in the jungle, hunt with bow and arrow, go naked, and know nothing of white society, then the answer is no. Chances are that these characteristics will not survive in the present conditions of wholesale Western expansionism.

The creation of the criteria of Indianness was a manipulation of such a definition of the Indian. Yet ethnicity cannot be measured by culture traits alone, much less by blood types. Ethnicity involves a sentiment of belonging, an esprit de corps; it is an assertion of a *we* which is different from others. In this sense the Indians are here to stay. Their overall population is growing. They are Indians in the process of profound transformations in their way of life, in their world view, but nevertheless they are Indians. The nationwide meeting attended by 200 Indian leaders in June 1982 in Brasília was a living demonstration of this resilience. Using Portuguese as their lingua franca, these people spoke and listened, made decisions and plans, and insisted on their autonomy as a political body vis-à-vis all whites, including those who assisted them.

The Indian movement is aware that Indian policy is still firmly in the hands of the state, and its members have to come to terms with this reality. They need and use the support of civil society, but it is with the government that they must interact and negotiate their claims. It is thus impossible to understand Indian policy and the Indian movement without reference to the state, the same state that promotes the expansion of the internal frontiers.

Notes

1. During Nobre da Veiga's term news began to circulate about a FUNAI plan to transfer many of the agency's responsibilities either to the states or to FUNAI's regional delegacies. The consequences of this measure are potentially disastrous, as local governments are notoriously antagonistic to Indians. For example, in the early 1960s, while Leonel Brizola was the governor of Rio Grande do Sul, four Kaingang-Guarani reserves were extinguished in the name of a pseudo-agrarian reform. Decentralization would also mean the diffusion of responsibility and accountability of the federal government with regard to the making and implementation of official Indian policy.

2. Rumors have it that FUNAI will be moved from the Ministry of the Interior to the newly created Land Ministry. About the social and political implications of this militarily occupied ministry, see José de Souza Martins, "The State and the Militarization of the Agrarian Question in Brazil," in *Frontier Expansion in Amazonia*, ed. Marianne Schmink and Charles H. Wood (Gainesville: University of Florida Press, 1984); and idem, *A Militarização da Questão Agrária no Brasil* (Petrópolis: Vozes, 1984).

3. By way of illustration we might mention a few cases. For decades the Gaviões in the state of Pará had been exploited by FUNAI as the exclusive buyer of their Brazil nut production. FUNAI paid the Indians about 20 percent of the market price. In 1975, aided by an anthropologist, the Gaviões broke their dependence on FUNAI agents and began to market their own products at a profit.

Having been invited by the organizers of the 1980 Fourth Russell Tribunal, Mário Juruna, a Shavante leader, was denied permission to leave the country with the allegation that he was not emancipated. The Supreme Court ruled in Juruna's favor, against FUNAI, and he was able to go to Rotterdam and chair part of the meetings.

The Xokleng Indians in the state of Santa Catarina have requested a lawyer to assist them in suing FUNAI for damages from the construction of a dam and the felling of trees in their territory. FUNAI was forced to put a stop to the cutting and selling of the timber.

The case of the removal of the Pataxó is being taken to court by a number of Indian support groups on grounds of illegality, according to the provisions of the Indian Statute, on the part of FUNAI's president.

References Cited

Bennett, Gordon. 1978. *Aboriginal Rights in International Law*. London: Royal Anthropological Institute of Great Britain and Ireland/Survival International, Occasional Paper No. 37.

Bourne, Richard. 1978. *Assault on the Amazon*. London: Victor Gollanez.

Carelli, Vincent, and Milton Severiano. n.d. *Mào Branca Contra O Povo Cinza*. São Paulo: Brazil Debates.

Carvalho, Maria Rosário G. de. 1982. Indian Ethnic Identity in the Northeast of Brazil. Paper presented at the symposium "Territoriality, Indian Policy, and Ethnic Identity," 82nd Annual Meeting of the American Anthropological Association, Washington, D.C.

Centro Ecumênico de Documentação e Informação (CEDI). 1982. *Povos Indígenas no Brasil/1981*. Aconteceu. São Paulo: CEDI.

Comissão pela Criação do Parque Yanomami (CCPY). 1979. Yanomami Indian Park: Proposal and Justification. In *The Yanomami in Brazil 1979*. Copenhagen: ARC/IWGIA/SI Document 37, pp. 99–170.

Conselho Indigenista Missionário (CIMI). 1978a. Boletim No. 50, October.

———. 1978b. Boletim No. 52, December.

Davis, Shelton. 1977. *Victims of the Miracle*. New York: Cambridge University Press.

———. 1978. Emancipation: A Dawes Act for Brazilian Indians. Anthropology Resource Center Newsletter 2(4):I.

Eggan, Fred. 1978. Beyond the Bicentennial: The Future of the American Indian in the Perspective of the Past. *Journal of Anthropological Research* 34(2):161–80.

Goodland, Robert, J. A., and H. S. Irwin. 1975. *Amazing Jungle: Green Hell to Red Desert?* Amsterdam: Elsevier.

Heelas, Richard. 1978. An Historical Outline of the Panara (Kreen-Akarore) Tribe of Central Brazil. *Survival International Review* 3, 2(22):25–27.

Hemming, John. 1978. *Red Gold*. London: Macmillan.

Jennings, Francis. 1975. *The Invasion of America*. New York: W. W. Norton and Company.

Jornal de Brasília. 1978, October 19.

———. 1981, May 28.

Martins, José de Souza. 1984. *A Militarização da Questão Agrária no Brasil*. Petrópolis: Vozes.

Meggers, Betty. 1971. *Amazonia: Man and Culture in a Counterfeit Paradise*. Chicago: Aldine.

Melatti, Julio C. 1970. *Índios do Brasil*. Brasília: Coordenada Editora de Brasília, 1st ed.

Moura Pires, Maria Lígia. 1975. Guarani e Kaingang no Paraná. M.A. thesis, Universidade de Brasília.

Opinião. 1975, April 18.

———. 1981, May.

———. 1982, March.

———. 1982, April.

———. 1982, September.

Porantim. 1982, March, April, September.

Price, David. 1981. The Nambiquara. In *In the Path of the Polonoroeste: Endangered Peoples of Western Brazil*. Occasional Paper 6. Cambridge, MA: Cultural Survival Inc., pp. 23–27.

Ramos, Alcida R. 1979. Yanomami Indians in Northern Brazil Threatened by Highway. In *The Yanomami in Brazil 1979*. Copenhagen: ARC/IWGIA/SI Document 37, pp. 1–41.

―――. 1980a. Development, Integration and the Ethnic Integrity of Brazilian Indians. In *Land, People and Planning in Contemporary Amazonia*. F. Barbira-Scazzocchio, ed. Pp. 222–29. Cambridge: Centre of Latin American Studies, University of Cambridge.

―――. 1980b. *Hierarquia e Simbiose. Relações Intertribais no Brasil*. São Paulo: Hucitec.

―――. 1982. O Brasil No Movimento Indígena Latino-americano. Paper read at the Conference A Nova Consciência Indígena during the Semana do Índio, Museu Paraense Emílio Goeldi, Belém, Pará, April 19.

Reichel-Dolmatoff, Gerardo. 1972. El Misionero ante las Culturas Indígenas. *América Indígena* 32(4):1138–49.

Ribeiro, Darcy. 1970. *Os Índios e a Civilização*. Rio; Civilização Brasileira.

Sanders, Douglas. 1978. The Unique Constitutional Position of the Indian. IWGIA *Newsletter* 19. Copenhagen: IWGIA.

Taylor, Kenneth I. 1979. Development Against the Yanomami: The Case of Mining and Agriculture. In *The Yanomami in Brazil 1979*. Copenhagen: ARC/IWGIA/SI Document 37:43–98.

Time. 1978, November 13.

20 Emilio Willems ◆ Social Change
on the Latin American Frontier

Anthropologist Emilio Willems contends that Latin American frontiers did not engender most of the values or character traits that Turner ascribed to the American frontier, but he does find common patterns in what he calls "anonymous frontiers" of Latin America. By "anonymous frontiers" he means those places that did not flourish economically, and where newcomers had to adapt to local conditions, borrowing technology from Indians and altering their institutions and culture. He points to historical examples of Spaniards, Portuguese, and Germans moving into "anonymous frontiers." Then, drawing from field work that he began in Brazil in the 1930s, he argues provocatively that squatters, whose shantytowns surround all major Latin American cities, live in an urban version of an "anonymous frontier." As squatters, they invade the lands of hostile natives (the affluent city dwellers) and adapt to new conditions on the urban frontier as they try to exploit local resources and achieve upward mobility.

Willems, professor emeritus of anthropology and full-time researcher at Vanderbilt University, earned his Ph.D. in 1931 in Berlin. In an extraordinarily productive career spanning six decades he has written numerous books and articles on social change in Latin America. His Followers of the New Faith: Culture Change and the Rise of Protestantism *(Nashville: Vanderbilt University Press, 1967) is a ground-breaking study of twentieth-century Latin American Protestantism. His most recent book,* A Way of Life and Death: Three Centuries of Prussian-German Militarism: An Anthropological Approach *(Nashville: Vanderbilt University Press, 1986), deals with German history.*

A probe into the changes that frontier conditions presumably bring to an emerging society cannot really succeed without a careful redefinition of a term which has been known, at least in the United States, for its normative and emotional connotations. The attributes that, rightly or wrongly, have been ascribed to the North American frontier, have tended to gain acceptance as universal criteria by which frontier status has been bestowed upon or denied to other areas of the world. Few anthropologists, I believe, would go along with the idea that, to qualify as a frontier, social life on freshly occupied lands should necessarily generate indi-

Abridged from *The Frontier: Comparative Studies*, ed. David Harry Miller and Jerome O. Steffen, 259–73. © 1977 by the University of Oklahoma Press. Reprinted by permission.

vidualism, democracy, inventiveness, materialism, entrepreneurship, or whatever real or mythological traits are associated with North American frontier life. As an anthropologist I refuse to impose ethnocentric criteria on a process the component aspects of which are fairly uncomplicated and truly universal. By frontier I mean an area of highly variable size into which migrants have moved to exploit some of its known resources. The process of appropriating these resources is competitive and requires the establishment of a system of rules by which the new society proposes to live. The migrants of course attempt to transplant their own cultural traditions, but these do not always fit the situation and require changes. However, changes which may be agreeable to some are resisted by others. Antagonisms and conflict are aggravated if, as it happens most of the time, the cultural traditions of the migrants are at variance with each other. The frontier society is thus characterized by anomie and social disorganization, meaning that differing value systems and modes of behavior are pitted against each other. Once the resources are distributed and the emergent society has found a *modus vivendi*, the area begins to lose its frontier character.

I

There are cases of highly cohesive groups—mostly religious sects—that migrate to frontier areas as single bodies, whose internal solidarity would seem to preclude anomie. Although such groups may be able to avoid internal strife, they still have to face the (potentially antagonistic) competition of all those frontiersmen who do not share their persuasion and cannot be kept out of the general area. In fact, sectarian intransigence tends to become a divisive factor in the eventual development of community structures. The concept of the frontier does not imply that its resources have never been touched by human hands, or that it is totally uninhabited. The existence of a native population tends further to intensify the problems the migrants have to face. Needless to say, there are several ways of solving the problem of the "natives," and not all of these are mutually exclusive. The society emerging out of the frontier conditions may be relatively egalitarian or seigneurial, it may be composed of small holders or large estates, or of a mixture of both. It may be based on pastoral, agricultural, mineral, or other resources, but to qualify as frontier it does not have to be an economic "success." The frontier areas of Latin America that have come to the attention of social scientists have almost invariably been identified with some economically significant export crops, such as sugar, coffee, cotton, wheat, cacao, rubber, tobacco, beef, and so forth, or with the discovery of major mineral resources.

The conceptual restriction of the frontier to such characteristics seems totally unwarranted. I propose to study the "unsuccessful" frontier unsung by economists and historians. Oriented towards markets and international trade, the "successful" frontier has bestowed wealth on the upper classes, but it has proved quite unsuccessful in apportioning an adequate share of that wealth to the rural working class. The unsuccessful or anonymous frontier, on the other hand, is the frontier of the little man, who has not found wealth, but merely conditions of survival superior to those that prevailed in the area or country whence he came.

Frontier areas, particularly those linked to the development of mineral resources and commercial crops, have been known to generate their own forms of urbanization. While the distinction between rural and urban frontier seems neither new nor objectionable, my suggestion that the sprawling shantytowns surrounding numerous urban centers of Latin America be considered as a version of the urban frontier will probably come as a shock to many adherents of traditional frontier ideology.

It seems difficult indeed to think of squatter settlements except in terms of "social cancer," "incubators of rebels and gangsters," and "urbanistic monstrosities" (Leeds 1968: 41). One suspects judgments of this sort to come from middle- and upper-class people, but I venture to suggest that the indigenous peoples of North and South America judged the European frontier invading their homeland and appropriating or destroying its resources with the same abhorrence the established urban classes nowadays exhibit with regard to the proliferating squatter settlements.

II

No matter whether urban or rural, the anonymous frontier seems to have generated deeper and more comprehensive changes than economically successful frontier areas, at least in Latin America. More or less isolated in remote areas, the anonymous settler depended on his ability to use the resources of his immediate environment in order to stay alive. This might include the selective adoption of indigenous technology and custom, perhaps a complete amalgamation with local Indian groups, a rather common process manifest in the rapid emergence of a mestizo society with a hybrid culture. While on the anonymous frontier radical culture change was a question of survival, the wealth of the plantation and mining frontiers made it possible to maintain a European style of life by massive culture transfer from Portugal and Spain.

Paraguay in the sixteenth and early seventeenth century may be regarded as the prototype of the anonymous frontier. Originally, the few hundred Spaniards who moved into Paraguay were hardly different from any other group of conquistadores, but the complete failure to discover the expected mineral wealth forced the survivors of many fruitless expeditions to take up subsistence agriculture as a last resort. These three or four hundred Spaniards were a thousand miles away from the La Plata estuary, their numbers were not replenished by new settlers and, to complete isolation, trade restriction virtually closed the La Plata region to the rest of the world.

Under these conditions some kind of close association with the tractable Guaraní Indians became imperative. "Instead of attempting to force the Indians to become adapted to the Spanish system, the Spanish soldiers expediently adjusted themselves to native habits by bringing Indian women to Asunción as wives and concubines and living by the contributions in food and services which their Indian relatives and allies freely provided" (Service 1954: 30–31). It seems that most Spaniards lived in polygymous marriages, and already by the middle of the sixteenth century the number of mestizo children was estimated to be about six thousand (Service 1954: 34). Not surprisingly, native crops and agricultural techniques were added to European domestic plants and animals, and food preparation acquired a distinctive indigenous flavor. From their Indian mothers the mestizo children learned Guaraní rather than Spanish, and to this day Guaraní still is spoken by most Paraguayans (in addition to Spanish). The economy was based on barter rather than money exchange and, to the rare visitor, the Spanish settlers died out, the mestizo population proliferated and took over the frontier tradition by founding many new settlements in Paraguay.

The processes that changed Iberian, as well as the indigenous, culture occurred in many frontier areas of Latin America. In the Amazon and São Francisco river basins, in São Paulo, in northern Argentina, in large sections of Colombia, and in many parts of Central America, early frontier conditions led to large-scale miscegenation and cultural hybridization. In many of these areas indigenous groups almost ceased to exist as distinct biological and cultural entities, and so did the Portuguese and Spanish settlers. The more these were forced to rely on local resources and indigenous technology and custom, the profounder the changes their Iberian traditions underwent.

More often than not life in anonymous frontier areas involved the loss of significant elements of Iberian culture. Paradoxically, the disappearance of particular cultural elements proved adaptive in that the preservation of such elements would have jeopardized the viability of the frontier. The adaptive value of culture loss was even more forcefully demonstrated in certain frontier areas opened by European immigrants during the nineteenth century. Many early settlements established in the sub-tropical rain forests of Southern Brazil, mainly by German, Italian, and Polish immigrants, had to face two major problems: the extreme scarcity of capital and credit, combined with the remoteness of markets capable of absorbing agricultural surpluses. The new settler had to use farming techniques producing the highest yields within the shortest possible time, and at the lowest possible cost. As I have shown in my earlier studies of German immigration to southern Brazil, settlers who attempted to clear their jungle patches of the felled trees and tree roots, in order to use cultivation techniques brought over from Europe, often failed before the first year was over. They might have a nicely cleared field, but they had nothing to eat because the strategically crucial planting seasons were lost in preparatory tasks. However, those settlers that took over the indigenous slash-and-burn agriculture, and planted their first food crops among the partly carbonized tree trunks, survived the critical first year and stayed on. Since markets were distant and poor, there was no point in preserving or improving the intensive farming methods then prevailing in Europe. In other words, the adoption of primitive, indigenous agricultural methods, and indigenous crops, mainly maize and manioc, turned out to be adaptive in the frontier areas of Rio Grande do Sul and Santa Catarina (Willems 1946: 329ff). It is true that in time some of these settlements modernized as new groups of immigrants arrived, and urban markets expanded and became more accessible, but in many settlements, slash-and-burn agriculture associated with a predominance of native crops remained, and eventually outgrew their original usefulness.

Needless to say, in most earlier settlements established by European immigrants frugality became a way of life. Still in the nineteen thirties, I found the settlers of the Alto Itajaí Mirím frontier (Brusque, Santa Catarina) living in a barter economy and practicing indigenous agriculture. Their only tools were the hoe, the ax, the billhook, and the machete. Men, women, and children walked barefoot all year round, and their clothes were made of the cheapest available materials. They lived on a diet of corn bread, manioc, rice, black beans, jerked beef, and occasional salt pork.

While most people in Alto Itajaí Mirím were native-born of German descent, a few were immigrants, and one of these, a man from Pomerania, had discovered a way of linking local agricultural resources to the market economy. He had established a rendering plant to fatten hogs with low-priced corn bought from local settlers. In contrast to corn (or any other agricultural product) lard could be sold in the next town at a price which made the whole operation quite profitable, in spite of the fact that the lard had to be transported by pack train on a jungle trail, parts of which were flooded by heavy rainfalls most of the time. The settlers could demand cash for their corn, but since there was little opportunity to spend money, they preferred to exchange it for cloth, salt, kerosene, tools, or other articles from the local store.

Obviously the whole set-up involved a radical break with German peasant traditions. Technology, food habits, dress, and housing patterns had changed almost beyond recognition; instead of a peasant village there were widely scattered farmsteads, transportation was by ox cart or mule train, and the settlers' participation in the money economy was marginal at best. The Alto Itajaí Mirím area was not part of a broad pioneer "front" advancing slowly from east to west, but like so many Latin American frontiers, a small enclave which had been opened in the nineteen twenties by a landowner desirous of selling his holdings in small parcels.

The extent to which the anonymous frontier participates in the market economy varies considerably. In a recent study of black frontiersmen in the Pacific lowlands of Ecuador and Colombia, Norman E. Whitten, Jr., emphasizes strong temporary demands for resources partly controlled by the black settlers. Such short-lived "booms" account for the temporary role the frontiersmen play in the market, over and above the level of their traditional subsistence agriculture (Whitten 1974: 74ff).

III

The structure of the frontier society may be described as "loose," in contrast to the structures of the migrants' society of origin. This means, among other things, that a wider range of alternate ways of behavior is open to the individual frontiersman. He may, if he chooses to do so, engage in economic pursuits which will eventually move him or his children into a "higher" social class. Upward social mobility has, of course, been considered as the most desirable and also the most common change characterizing a frontier society, but it has been associated almost exclusively with the economically successful frontier. Even there, data about the social origin of the settlers tend to be vague. In my own study on social mobility I found that of 900 landowners in northern Paraná, Brazil, less than one-third acquired land shortly after arrival in the area. This simply means that most of them could not afford to make the requisite down payment on a small piece of land. At any rate, these settlers did not belong to the poorest stratum of migrants. Two-thirds of those who were landowners in 1967 had worked their way up from the level of rural laborers, tenant farmers, or sharecroppers. These agricultural activities were often combined with wage-earning jobs. But of course, northern Paraná has been one of the most successful frontiers of the twentieth century, and upward mobility has been so common that it is taken for granted by the local population (see also Margolis 1973: 214).

Unfortunately, the role of the frontier in the process of social mobility has often been underrated or misunderstood, particularly with regard to earlier frontiers.

First of all, one could argue, if there is a history of frontiers reaching back to the very Conquest, social mobility must have been rare or nonexistent, because the social structure of Spanish and Portuguese America remained essentially unchanged until the late nineteenth century. Actually, while social mobility was slow and difficult elsewhere, it was common in frontier areas. But it was also temporary, because, as frontier conditions began to fade, the social structure assumed the customary rigidity and eventually became indistinguishable from that of other traditional structures of Ibero-America. This process was particularly visible in the colonial cities, where the founding families initiated their social ascent by becoming recipients of land grants. If the new settlement proved viable, the first settlers, owning the choicest pieces of real estate, constituted the nucleus of a new upper class, although their family genealogy or past history rarely justified their status aspirations. Their social ascent was contingent on frontier conditions, but once the land had been allocated the new structure became as rigid as elsewhere in traditional urban society. Both in Spanish America and Brazil this process was common enough to constitute a cultural pattern (Morse 1965: 38).

IV

It has been said that in Latin America "genuine" frontier conditions have been rare because the latifundio monopolized all available land and deprived the mass of potential pioneer settlers of the social advantages of the North American frontier (Lambert 1963: 59). Actually, most Latin American frontiers generated social structures far more complex than the alleged dominance of the latifundio implies.

In the first place, pioneer migrants who succeeded in becoming owners of large estates in frontier areas, and thus members of the landholding upper class, were frequently of modest origin. A case in point is the coffee frontier in Brazil between 1800 and 1830. The beginnings were primitive indeed. The first settlers of the Vassouras region, for example, had to settle for "small-scale cultivation carried on by a few slaves, when coffee was slowly, hesitatingly adapted to the highland" (Stein 1957: 23). The main thing was to produce food crops and to become self-sufficient. Large estates and wealth appeared gradually after 1830. The great planters of Vassouras, many of whom were raised to the non-hereditary nobility of the Brazilian empire, were of "modest origin." They had been traders or small holders; some had made money in mining, and others were military men (Stein 1957: 120). In other words, social mobility was the rule rather than the exception. There was no prevalence of the large estate while Vassouras was frontier. Later, many small holdings were absorbed by the latifundios, but they never completely disappeared (Stein 1957: 225). . . .

VI

One of the most far-reaching changes in Latin America, and many other parts of the world, may be seen in the fact that the modern city has been competing with rural frontier areas as the "land of opportunity," attracting hundred thousands of migrants who cannot immediately be absorbed by the physical and social structure of any given city. Frequently, these migrants take possession of land that does not belong to them, and in doing so they merely follow a pattern as old as European colonization in America. Beginning in the sixteenth century countless Spanish and Portuguese settlers seized land without paying attention to the rights of the native population. The *composición*, a jural device to legalize ownership of such land for a fee, was instituted by the Spanish crown, and since then virtually all legal systems of Latin America include established procedures to convert squatters into lawful owners. This is, of course, the hope of the modern shantytown dweller: Based on known precedents he perceives a chance to become the legitimate owner of the piece of land where he builds his temporary shack.

As a rule, these migrants are not inexperienced peasants freshly arriving from some remote village. Those who settle in large metropolitan areas have often been exposed to similar experiences in provincial cities, and participated in more than one attempt to establish themselves in a shantytown (Mangin 1967: 68–69; Cardona Gutierrez 1968: 70). There is enough evidence to support the assumption that most squatters understand the risks involved in their undertakings, and many have had opportunity to acquire the political skills necessary to deal with such risks.

What are the resources the shantytown settler intends to exploit? The answer is simple: the land he settles on and the labor market of the nearby city. They are interconnected: without an advantageous location in the vicinity of the city, the chances of engaging in some gainful economic activity remain slim. And without some sort of income, however uncertain, the possibility of improving the dwellings, or the squatter settlement in general, is practically nonexistent.

The most serious problem the squatter has to cope with is the hostility of the "native" population, which more often than not seems determined to thwart the migrants' attempts to settle on vacant land. Unlike the settlers of the jungle frontier, the urban squatters face an immensely superior enemy which cannot be overpowered, driven off, or enslaved like the indigenous populations. The squatters must proceed with extreme caution to avoid open confrontation. It is always preferable to choose marginal land on steep hillsides or swampy terrain usually considered unfit for urban development. If, in addition, it is public domain or of uncertain or unknown ownership, the chances are that occupation by squatters will not immediately be challenged by urban authorities. Effective squatter strategy further demands that occupation be a concerted action of a large number of families who build their first shacks at once, to confront the city with a *fait accompli* (see Mangin 1967: 69). Such a strategy is not always successful, of course, but one of the impressive qualities of these frontiersmen is their persistence in the face of defeat. They try time and again, and not always for the same reason. A new settlement may survive the hazards of the social environment, but if it fails to live up to expectations, the most ambitious settlers join some more promising venture.

One of the most urgent requirements to be met by emerging shantytowns is social organization. Since urban institutional resources are not available to the settlers, they must find a *modus vivendi* by themselves. Virtually nothing is known about the earliest phases in the life of a new squatter settlement, but one may assume that a considerable amount of conflict is almost inevitable. Furthermore, to consolidate its existence, a new settlement must fight for almost everything other city dwellers take for granted. And this includes physical stability of the settlement, water, transportation, electricity, schools, police protection, hospitals, and so forth. Gradually, the almost amorphous mass of settlers acquires a structure, and becomes increasingly articulate. In the barrios of Caracas, for example, a junta is "elected" from among the first squatters, and one of the major tasks of the junta is to create an informal legal system concerning rights in land and housing. Since the majority of the squatters do not have legal title to the land they occupy, ownership of the house is separated from land ownership. Ownership then means the "rights to undisturbed possession" (Karst 1971: 562). It is an unwritten law that the owner has the right to sell his house, or to give it away, but if it remains vacant for several months, the junta may assign it to another family. Houses may be rented too, but the junta "prevents the landlord from evicting the tenant for nonpayment of rent" (Karst 1971: 565–566). Furthermore, the junta arbitrates conflicts between neighbors and in extreme cases may try to expel troublemakers.

The spontaneous emergence of such legal systems seems relevant because it illustrates the settler's ability for innovation. Although relatively few data are available about the legal systems of other urban frontiers, we may assume that no squatter settlement could possibly survive for any length of time without some such informal structure.

Essential for the permanence of any squatter settlement appear to be the perception of dissidence in the society at large and the development of strategies designed to take advantage of disagreements among the urban holders. So far very little attention has been paid to the fact that many shantytowns are allowed to survive, and to expand year after year, in spite of periodical outbursts of public indignation and political opposition, because they are inexhaustible sources of cheap labor. Numerous maids, gardeners, washerwomen, chauffeurs, janitors, porters, paper boys, and assorted repairmen serving most city districts come from nearby *favelas, barriadas, tugurios*, or whatever the local version of the squatter settlements may be.

Party politics, and the electoral system of most Latin American countries, also tend to further the permanence of the squatter settlements. What the settlers want is legal title to their house sites and all those improvements which would integrate the settlement into the urban service structure. Their expectations are reflected in the promises made by the party candidates running for municipal office. To make the most of the fierce competition among the different parties constitutes one of the major skills the settlers and their local leaders have to acquire. In one of the rare studies of political behavior in the *favelas* of Rio de Janeiro, it was found that, for the squatter, "universal suffrage is vital; it is an instrument of vindications and survival. It is through the ballot that he becomes clearly conscious of his needs and tests his representatives" (SAGMACS 1960: 35).

To the settler of the anonymous urban frontier, exploitation of the political resources of the city is as vital as his struggle for economic survival. There are two major avenues open to the squatters: They may choose between seeking jobs and starting some independent enterprise. Often enough both avenues are exploited by different members of the same family, including children. Neither wage earners nor independent operators can expect stability and continuing success in whatever field of endeavor is chosen, and wages and profits seldom cover more than the barest necessities. Whenever there is a small surplus it is probably invested in ameliorating or replacing the original shack with a more solid and larger structure. This is the advantage of the squatter settlement: it is highly adaptive under conditions of extreme economic instability. The settlers are not burdened with property taxes or any other kind of payment. No matter how long it takes, many families are capable of improving their housing conditions, and at the end of several years—usually from five to eight—they may own a modest brick house with a tile roof.

The risks and uncertainties the squatter of the urban frontier has to face are comparable to those confronting the rural frontiersman. Floods, droughts, pests, maladies of man and beast, lack of credit and markets constantly threaten the survival of the rural frontiersman as much as the urban squatter is imperiled by the spectre of coercive eviction, job instability, irregular income, low wages, and a host of problems associated with the lack of urban services. With luck and enormous effort both types of anonymous settlers may eventually rise to a level of relative stability. In the urban squatter settlement this point is reached when ownership of the lot is regulated, most original shanties have been replaced by permanent structures, and urban services have been made available to the population. Examples of this rather complex process exist in most major cities of Latin America.

Little is known about the social mobility in shantytowns. In the aforementioned study of several *favelas* of Rio de Janeiro, social mobility, upward as well as downward, was found to be "intense." Five "social strata" of settlers were described, the "highest consisting of people who had made it" and could afford to leave the *favela*. The members of the next lower stratum had improved their dwellings, and their way of life was somewhat above the level of mere survival. Next came the families who had to struggle hard to satisfy their most elementary necessities. The two lowest strata were barely distinguishable from each other, consisting of families living in the sort of squalor and social disorganization usually associated with life in shantytowns (SAGMACS 1960: 3). Similar levels of social mobility may be observed in most shantytowns, and some are quite visible, even to the casual visitor, in the way the houses differ from each other. However, it should be added that the dimensions of social change on the anonymous urban frontier go way beyond social mobility. Actually, they encompass all those processes by which the shantytown dweller acquires the outlook, attitudes, and skills that make it possible for him to survive in an extremely difficult urban environment.

Bibliography

Cardona Gutierrez, Ramiro, "Migración, Urbanización y Marginalidad," in Ramiro Cardona Gutierrez, ed. *Urbanización y Marginalidad*. Bogotá: Publicación de la Asociación Colombiana de Facultades de Medicina, 1968.

Karst, Kenneth L., "Rights in Land and Housing in an Informal Legal System: The Barrios of Caracas," *The American Journal of Comparative Law* 9 (3): 550–574, Summer 1971.

Lambert, Jacques, "Requirements for Rapid Economic and Social Development: The View of the Historian and Sociologist," in Egbert de Vries and José Medina Echavarria, eds., *Social Aspects of Economic Development in Latin America*, Vol. I. Paris: UNESCO, 1963.

Leeds, Anthony, "The Anthropology of Cities: Some Methodological Issues," in Elizabeth M. Eddy, ed. *Urban Anthropology. Research Perspectives and Strategies* (Southern Anthropological Society, Proceedings, No. 2). Athens: University of Georgia Press, 1968.

Mangin, William, "Latin American Squatter Settlements: A Problem and a Solution," *Latin American Research Review* 2 (3), 1967.

Margolis, Maxine L., *The Moving Frontier. Social and Economic Change in a Southern Brazilian Community*. Gainesville: University of Florida Press, 1973.

Monbeig, Pierre, *Pionniers et Planteurs de São Paulo*. Paris: Librairie Armand Colin, 1952.

Morse, Richard, "Recent Research on Latin American Urbanization: A Selective Survey with Commentary," *Latin American Research Review* 1 (Fall 1965).

SAGMACS, *Aspectos Humanos da Favela Carioca*. São Paulo: Estado de S. Paulo, Suplemento Especial 2, 1960.

Service, Elman R., *Spanish-Guarany Relations in Early Colonial Paraguay* (Anthropological Paper, No. 9, Museum of Anthropology, University of Michigan). Ann Arbor: University of Michigan Press, 1954.

Stein, Stanley, *Vassouras: A Brazilian Coffee County 1859–1900*. Cambridge: Harvard University Press, 1957.

Tinnermeyer, Ronald I., *New Land Settlements in the Eastern Lowlands of Colombia*. University of Wisconsin, unpublished Ph.D. Dissertation, 1964.

Whitten, Norman E., Jr., *Class, Kinship, and Power in an Ecuadorian Town*. Stanford: Stanford University Press, 1965.

————, *Black Frontiersmen: A South American Case*. New York: John Wiley and Sons, 1974.

Willems, Emilio, *A Aculturacão dos Alemáes no Brasil*. São Paulo: Companhia Editora Nacional, 1946.

Suggested Readings

Latin American Frontiers in Historical Literature

As the selections in this reader suggest, scholarly writing about Latin American frontiers is wide-ranging, multidisciplinary, and frequently cross-cultural. The only other attempt at a one-volume treatment of the subject is Alistair Hennessy, *The Frontier in Latin American History* (Albuquerque: University of New Mexico Press, 1978). Though somewhat disjointed in its attempt to embrace all of Latin American history under the rubric of "frontiers," it is still the best introduction. Hennessy's bibliography provides valuable guidance to the literature and can be supplemented by a more current historiographical essay by Richard W. Slatta, "Historical Frontier Imagery in the Americas," in *Latin American Frontiers, Borders and Hinterlands: Research Needs and Resources*, ed. Paula Covington (Albuquerque: SALAM, General Library, University of New Mexico, 1990), 5–25. Further guidance to sources in history and in the social sciences can be found in the notes accompanying the Introduction to the present volume. The list of books that follows is selective rather than comprehensive. We have chosen recent works in English that provide a starting point for those wishing to pursue frontier themes.

Richard Collier, *The River that God Forgot: The Story of the Amazon Rubber Boom* (London: Collins, 1968). A narrative history of the Amazon rubber boom geared to a general audience. Collier describes in detail the international scandal that erupted when the Peruvian Amazon Company was accused in 1910 of making a fortune in rubber at the cost of thirty thousand Indian lives in the Putumayo region of Peru and Colombia.

Raymond E. Crist and Charles M. Nissly, *East from the Andes: Pioneer Settlements in the South American Heartland* (Gainesville: University of Florida Press, 1973). Drawing on decades of personal research, two geographers survey human migration out of the Andes into the Amazon regions of Bolivia, Colombia, Ecuador, Peru, and Venezuela since World War II. Arguing that to understand immigration one must first become acquainted with the viewpoints of the people who leave the Andes, they discuss cultural, social, historical, and economic forces behind settlement, together with their relationship to the tropical landscapes.

Andre Gunder Frank, *Capitalism and Underdevelopment in Latin America: Historical Studies in Chile and Brazil* (Rev. ed., New York: Monthly Review Press, 1969). In this influential work in the development of "dependency theory," Frank elaborates the thesis of the "periphery" versus the "metropolis." Latin America's functional location on the "periphery" of the world system meant that the patterns of economic transformations there would differ from those that developed earlier in European and North American countries, which formed the "metropolis."

John Hemming, *Amazon Frontier: The Defeat of the Brazilian Indians* (Cambridge: Harvard University Press, 1987). In this massive but readable book Hemming recounts how the Brazilian conquest of the Amazon from the expulsion of the Jesuits in 1759 to the beginning of the twentieth century reduced the native population from approximately three and a half million to less than one million. He discusses missionaries and anthropologists and the efforts of the Indians to resist. Hemming shows how Europeans' basic misunderstanding of the tropical ecology destroyed their attempts at agriculture as well as their policies toward Indians.

Catherine LeGrand, *Frontier Expansion and Peasant Protest in Colombia, 1830–1936* (Albuquerque: University of New Mexico Press, 1986). LeGrand argues that frontier expansion occurred in two successive stages. First, peasant families moved into the wilderness and cleared and planted the land. After they had improved it, well-to-do entrepreneurs appeared, asserted property ownership, and reduced the peasants to tenant farmers. She also describes how the peasants fought to retain their rights and the impact that their struggle had on Colombian legislation.

Archibald R. Lewis and Thomas F. McGann, *The New World Looks at Its History* (Austin: University of Texas Press, 1966). A collection of papers presented at the Second International Congress of Historians of the United States and Mexico held in Austin, Texas, in 1958. Several essays concern aspects of the medieval Iberian frontier, Webb's "Great Frontier" thesis, and frontiers and ranching in the United States and Mexico.

James Lockhart and Stuart B. Schwartz, *Early Latin America: A History of Colonial Spanish America and Brazil* (Cambridge: Cambridge University Press, 1983). A general history of Latin America from conquest to independence. The authors regard Peru and Mexico as centers of settlement and the rest of the empire as peripheries, or fringe regions, "all parts of which were characterized by variants of the same kinds of change regardless of national and imperial borders." One of the most sophisticated attempts to adapt frontier concept to the Latin American historical context.

Richard M. Morse, ed., *The Bandeirantes: The Historical Role of the Brazilian Pathfinders* (New York: Knopf, 1967). A collection of readings, mainly by Brazilian scholars, that assesses the origins of the *bandeirante* movement, its development in the seventeenth and eighteenth centuries, and its significance from a historical perspective. Morse's introduction places the discussion within the framework of Turner's frontier thesis and suggests many possible avenues for new investigation.

Frederick B. Pike, *The United States and Latin America: Myths and Stereotypes of Civilization and Nature* (Austin: University of Texas Press, 1992). Pike shows how differing concepts of frontiers have contributed to the development of negative stereotypes held by North Americans and Latin Americans during the several centuries of mutual misunderstanding. His book probes the origins of these stereotypes and explores how they have influenced inter-American relations from the sixteenth to the end of the twentieth century.

Richard Price, ed., *Maroon Societies: Rebel Slave Communities in the Americas* (2d ed., Baltimore: Johns Hopkins University Press, 1979). Studies of Maroon societies that developed in Spanish America, Brazil, the Guianas, and the French and British Caribbean. The essays provide insight into the nature of these communities of escaped slaves, their problems of survival in difficult environments, and their alliances with other economic groups in order to maintain their freedom despite state efforts to return them to bondage.

Jane M. Rausch, *The Llanos Frontier in Colombian History, 1830–1930* (Albuquerque: University of New Mexico Press, 1993). A narrative history of the eastern tropical plains of Colombia. Using some Turnerian concepts, the author identifies the institutions and historical processes that characterized a frontier that failed to advance despite sporadic government efforts to encourage immigration.

Marianne Schmink and Charles Howard Wood, *Contested Frontiers in Amazonia* (New York: Columbia University Press, 1992). An anthropologist and a sociologist-demographer document and interpret the process of frontier change in Pará, Brazil. Part One surveys the history of Amazon colonization from the sixteenth century to the present, while Parts Two and Three focus specifically on southern Pará and the town of São Felix do Xingu between 1978 and 1989.

William F. Sharp, *Slavery on the Spanish Frontier: The Colombian Chocó, 1680–1810* (Norman: University of Oklahoma Press, 1976). A description and analysis of the economic and administrative system employed by Spaniards to exploit a mining frontier in the Pacific coast region of Chocó. Sharp concludes that the Spaniards created a "hollow" frontier weakly bound together by self-seeking miners, officials, and priests and that "individualism even among Indian slaves and freedmen was the prevailing philosophy."

Richard W. Slatta, *Cowboys of the Americas* (New Haven: Yale University Press, 1990). A general introduction to the rise and fall of cowboy types in the major Anglo-American and Spanish American ranching areas of the Western Hemisphere. Slatta compares and contrasts the social, economic, and cultural formation of American and Canadian cowboys, Mexican vaqueros, Argentine gauchos, Chilean *huasos*, and Venezuelan *llaneros* and considers their role in their respective national cultures and myths.

Richard W. Slatta, *Gauchos and the Vanishing Frontier* (2d ed., Lincoln: University of Nebraska Press, 1992). A socioeconomic history of the gauchos of Argentina analyzing the nineteenth-century forces that altered frontier society and brought about their decline. The author concludes with a look at the gaucho's cultural conversion from social outcast to national hero.

Walter Prescott Webb, *The Great Frontier* (1st ed., 1952; Austin: University of Texas Press, 1979). A provocative work that describes the Western Hemisphere as part of a much larger phenomenon called "The Great Frontier," which resulted from European expansion beginning in the fifteenth century. Webb's frontier has less to do with the development of national character, which was Turner's concern, and more to do with the rise of capitalism and its effect on Western European institutions.

David J. Weber, *New Spain's Far Northern Frontier: Essays on Spain in the American West, 1540–1821* (Albuquerque: University of New Mexico Press, 1979). Eighteen readable, interpretive essays that describe major institutions and developments in the Spanish borderlands of the United States. The collection includes Herbert Eugene Bolton's classic essay "The Mission as a Frontier Institution in the Spanish American Colonies," first published in 1916, and Marc Simmons's pioneering work on "Settlement Patterns and Village Plans," originally published in 1969.

David J. Weber, *The Spanish Frontier in North America* (New Haven: Yale University Press, 1992). A narrative history of the Spanish colonial period in North America, which discusses the first Spanish-Indian contacts and describes the establishment, expansion, and retraction of the Spanish frontier from Florida to California.

Walker D. Wyman and Clifton B. Kroeber, eds., *The Frontier in Perspective* (Madison: University of Wisconsin Press, 1965). Thirteen essays, unified by Turner's writing on the frontier, that examine not only the modifications of the idea as applied geographically but also its varied aspects in the eyes of historians, anthropologists, and specialists in languages and literatures. Includes essays on frontiers in Hispanic America, Russia, China, and the Mediterranean.

Frontiers in Latin American Fiction

Some of Latin America's most respected authors have chosen frontier themes for their novels and poems. Listed below are representative works that have been translated into English.

Amado, Jorge. *The Violent Land* (1943). Translated by Samuel Putnam. New York: Knopf, 1965. A chronicle of the "cacao rush" in southern Bahia as Colonel Horacio da Silveira battles with the Badaró brothers for control of a frontier land of fertile cacao-producing soil.

Carpentier, Alejo. *The Lost Steps* (1953). Translated by Harriet de Onis. Harmondsworth: Penguin, 1968. Cuban author contrasts life in modern cities with that in the Orinoco jungle in an early example of "magical realism."

Cunha, Euclydes da. *Rebellion in the Backlands* (1902). Translated by Samuel Putnam. Chicago: University of Chicago Press, 1944. Complex, epic account of four expeditions sent to the backlands of northern Bahia to capture Antonio Conselheiro, a religious mystic, whose supporters launch a heroic but doomed resistance.

Gallegos, Rómulo. *Doña Bárbara* (1929). Translated by Robert Malloy. New York: Peter Smith, 1948. Sarmiento's "civilization versus barbarism" theme in a Venezuelan setting. A classic novel of the Venezuelan llanos.

Güiraldes, Ricardo. *Don Segundo Sombra: Shadows on the Pampas* (1926). Translated by Harriet de Onis. New York: New American Library, 1966. Stylized depiction of the Argentine gaucho that heralds the end of his existence.

Hernandez, José. *The Gaucho Martín Fierro* (Part 1, 1872; Part 2, 1879). Translated by C. E. Ward. Albany: State University of New York Press, 1967. Lyrical poem of gaucho life that attacks the Europeanized government of Buenos Aires for destroying gaucho traditions.

Quiroga, Horacio. *South American Jungle Tales* (1918). Translated by Arthur Livingston. New York: Dodd-Mead, 1950. Eight vivid short stories describe how the jungles of Argentina and Uruguay overpower the human protagonists.

Rivera, José Eustacio. *The Vortex* (1924). Translated by Earle K. James. New York: Putnam, 1935. One of the original "green hell" novels, in which a Colombian couple flees to the Amazon, only to be destroyed there.

Souza, Márcio. *The Emperor of the Amazon* (1977). Translated by Thomas Cholchie. New York: Avon, 1980. Humorous but critical tale of the rubber boom in Manaus. The book's publication cost Souza his job with the Brazilian Ministry of Culture.

Vargas Llosa, Mario. *The Green House* (1965). Translated by Gregory Rabassa. New York: Avon, 1973. Complex novel contrasting life in the Peruvian jungle with that in the northern coastal city of Piura.

Suggested Films

Latin American frontier themes have inspired numerous feature films. Listed below are representative works available on 16mm film or video that can be rented or purchased in the United States.

Aguirre, the Wrath of God (German-made but filmed in Peru, color, 94 minutes, German dialogue with English subtitles, 1973). Directed by Werner Herzog. Distributor: 16mm film—New Yorker/VHS video—Facets. Fictional portrayal of the real-life exploits of Lope de Aguirre, a sixteenth-century Spanish conquistador. While searching for El Dorado in the Amazon jungle, Aguirre rebelled against Pizarro and went on a rampage of terror and destruction through northern South America. Herzog's film strays from the actual historical events, but the superb photography, authentic costumes, and presentation of Spanish-Indian relationships offer insight into the earliest Spanish American frontier.

Cangaçeiro (*The Bandit*) (Brazil, black and white, 92 minutes, Portuguese dialogue with English subtitles, 1954). Directed by Lima Barreto. Distributor: 16mm film—Films, Inc. One of the first of several Brazilian films that sought to glorify the *cangaçeiros*, or outlaws, of the Northeast as proto-social revolutionaries. Tells the story of the violent animosity that develops between a bandit leader and his lieutenant when the latter takes pity on a beautiful schoolteacher whom the bandits have abducted. Despite a conventional plot, the film is an excellent introduction to life on the northeast frontier.

Doña Bárbara (Mexico, black and white, 138 minutes, Spanish dialogue with English subtitles, 1943). Directed by Fernando de Fuentes. Distributor: 16mm film—TransWorld Films/VHS video—World Video. Legendary Mexican film star María Felix plays Doña Bárbara in this film version of Gallegos's novel. Dramatizes the struggle between civilization and barbarism on the Venezuelan llanos frontier as Santos Luzardo, a Caracas lawyer, returns to the plains and fights to regain possession of his ranch illegally seized by Doña Bárbara. Although now somewhat dated, the film faithfully portrays Gallegos's themes and characters.

Don Segundo Sombra (Argentina, color, 110 minutes, Spanish dialogue with English subtitles, 1969). Directed by Manuel Antín. Distributor: VHS video—World Video. Narrates the story of Fabio Caceres as he grows into adulthood and learns from his mentor, an old gaucho named Don Segundo Sombra, who teaches him moral and human values. Based on Ricardo Güiraldes's novel, it presents an ideal, almost mythical portrait of the Argentine gaucho.

Fitzcarraldo (German-made but filmed in Peru and Brazil, color, 157 minutes, German dialogue with English subtitles, 1982). Directed by Werner Herzog. Distributor: VHS video—Warner Home Video. Klaus Kinski stars as Fitzcarraldo, an opera-loving Irish adventurer who seeks his fortune in the Amazon jungle during the rubber boom at the end of the nineteenth century. Well acted with fine photography, including extraordinary footage of Fitzcarraldo's twelve-hundred-mile boat trip down the Amazon River from Iquitos to Manaus to hear Caruso sing.

The Green Wall (Peru, color, 110 minutes, Spanish dialogue with English subtitles, 1970). Directed by Armando Robles Godoy. Distributor: 16mm films—Film, Inc. Godoy's autobiographical story concerns a young family that decides to abandon life in Lima to build a home in the lush Peruvian jungle. Their idyllic life is suddenly threatened when the Land Reform Commission challenges their claim. While the father journeys to the city to fight for their home, the six-year-old son is bitten by a poisonous snake. His mother, alone and on foot, must race through the jungle to save his life. A well-made film that dramatizes the joys and perils of frontier life.

How Tasty Was My Little Frenchman (Brazil, color, 80 minutes, Portuguese and Tupi dialogue with English subtitles, 1971). Directed by Nelson Pereira dos Santos. Distributor: 16mm film—New Yorker. This Cinema Novo film tells the story of a Frenchman who is captured by Brazilian Indians in the sixteenth century and lives for more than a year as their slave. The contrast between his attitude and theirs vividly reveals the result of different cultures colliding on South American frontiers. Director dos Santos based his plot on the true adventures of Hans Staden, a German who sailed as a gunner on a Portuguese ship on two voyages to Brazil in 1548 and 1549. The sets and costumes are authentic, and the whole atmosphere derives from paintings and writings of the period.

The Mission (American-made but filmed in Argentina and Colombia, color, 126 minutes, English dialogue, 1986). Directed by Roland Joffé. Distributor: VHS video—Facets. Prize-winning epic film about the conflict between Spain, Portugal, and Jesuit missionaries when the Treaty of Madrid signed in 1750 required that seven Jesuit missions in formerly Spanish territory be turned over to the Portuguese. The film centers on the crises of conscience faced by two very different priests. By posing the question of whether the priests should take up arms against the crown to defend the natives, director Joffé draws a parallel between the eighteenth century and the late twentieth century, when many priests in Latin America have found themselves at odds with Rome.

The Mosquito Coast (American-made but filmed in Belize, color, 118 minutes, English dialogue, 1986). Directed by Peter Weir. Distributor: VHS video—Warner Home Video. Allie Fox, an American inventor, takes his family to settle in a section of the Honduran jungle known as the Mosquito Coast, in an effort to recover the pioneer spirit. Initially he is able to build a neo-Eden out of the jungle, but things go wrong when he alienates the Indians and some Spanish-speaking white men of mysterious origins. Well-photographed but painfully lethargic dramatization of Paul Theroux's adventure novel of the same name.

Quilombo (Brazil, color, 114 minutes, Portuguese dialogue with English subtitles, 1984). Directed by Carlos Diegues. Distributor: 16mm film—New Yorker/VHS video—New Yorker. Lavish musical recounting the story of the life and death of Palmares, the fugitive slave settlement, or *quilombo*, whose existence between 1605 and 1695 threatened Portuguese rule in Brazil. This is epic cinema with great heroes, terrible events, self-sacrifice, and victory of the spirit, but Diegues uses authentic costumes and recreates the seventeenth-century ambience. The result is a vivid portrayal of a unique type of frontier society.

Film and Video Distributors

Facets Multimedia, Inc.
1517 West Fullerton Avenue
Chicago, IL 60614
(312) 281-9075, (800) 331-6197

Films, Inc.
5547 North Ravenswood Avenue
Chicago, IL 60640-9979
(800) 323-4222, ext. 43

New Yorker Films
16 West 61st Street
New York, NY 10023
(212) 247-6110

TransWorld Films, Inc.
332 South Michigan Avenue
Chicago, IL 60604
(312) 427-4545

Warner Home Video, Inc.
4000 Warner Boulevard
Burbank, CA 91522
(818) 954-6000

World Video
P.O. Box 30469
Knoxville, TN 37930-0469
(615) 691-9827

About the Editors

DAVID J. WEBER, the Robert and Nancy Dedman Professor of History at Southern Methodist University, is the author of several books including *The Mexican Frontier, 1821–1846: The American Southwest under Mexico* (1982) and *The Spanish Frontier in North America* (1992). Trained in Latin American history at the University of New Mexico, he has taught at San Diego State University and at the Universidad de Costa Rica as a Fulbright Lecturer. A past president of the Western History Association, he is the only American historian elected to membership in both the Mexican Academy of History and the Society of American Historians.

JANE M. RAUSCH, a professor of history at the University of Massachusetts-Amherst, received her doctoral training in comparative tropical history at the University of Wisconsin-Madison. She is a specialist in Colombian history, and her previous publications include *A Tropical Plains Frontier: The Llanos of Colombia, 1531–1831* (1984) and *The Llanos Frontier in Colombian History, 1830–1930* (1993). A contributing editor to the *Handbook of Latin American Studies*, she maintains a lively interest in the use of film in classroom teaching.